The Genealogist's Internet

To the memory of
Douglas Godfrey Christian
1923–1974

The
Genealogist's
Internet

Peter Christian

the national archives

First edition published in 2001 by the Public Record Office (1 903365 16 3)

Second edition first published in 2003 by

The National Archives
Kew, Richmond
Surrey, TW9 4DU
UK

www.nationalarchives.gov.uk/

The National Archives was formed when the Public Record Office and Historical Manuscripts Commission combined in April 2003.

Reprinted 2003, 2004

ISBN 1 903365 46 5

Front cover, from top: the Reverend John Eliot, 1890 (TNA: PRO COPY 1/402; photographer Richard Michael Latham, Stroud); 1891 census return for West Newton, Norfolk (TNA: PRO RG 12/1564); baby in bath, 1884 (TNA: PRO COPY 1/370; photographer Henry Johnson, Wood Green); marriage of Alexander McCurry and Charlotte King, 1919 (author's photograph); Sergeant Frederick Marshall of the Queen's Royal (West Surrey) Regiment, c. 1915 (author's photograph); carte de visite, 1862; photographer unknown (reproduced courtesy of Robert Pols). While every effort has been made to trace the copyright holders, this has not always proved possible because of the antiquity of the images.

Back cover: photograph of the author, by Catherin Priest.

Typeset by Textype, Cambridge, Cambridgeshire
Printed in the UK by Antony Rowe, Chippenham, Wiltshire

Contents

Preface

One difficulty with any book on the internet and genealogy is deciding what knowledge to presuppose in the reader, particularly since both are in themselves such vast subjects.

For the internet, I have assumed a reader who is already connected and is familiar with e-mail and a web browser, but I have not assumed any further internet expertise. For that reason there is detailed discussion of search engines, mailing lists, newsgroups and web publishing in the later chapters. The queries and problems which are raised in on-line discussion forums suggest that even quite seasoned internet users often do not make the most of these resources.

I have not assumed expert knowledge of genealogy, but a genealogy tutorial is beyond the scope of this book. Internet resources for the novice genealogist are mentioned in Chapter 2 but if you are completely, or fairly, new to family history you'll need a good book on off-line genealogy (see p. 6 for recommendations).

Citing internet addresses

In this book URLs (Uniform Resource Locators) for internet resources have been placed between angled brackets. According to strict citation standards, every internet resource should begin with a specification of its type: the National Archives home page on the World Wide Web should be cited as <http://www.nationalarchives.gov.uk/> rather than simply as <www.nationalarchives.gov.uk>. However, since web browsers manage perfectly well without the 'http//:' I have allowed myself to omit these. Newsgroup names are discussed in Chapter 15: although they may look similar to web addresses, either the context or the word newsgroup in the text will identify them correctly.

Any hyphen within a URL is an essential part of the reference, not a piece of ad hoc hyphenation. Some of the longer URLs in this text have been broken over two lines for typographical reasons, but the URL should be read as an unbroken sequence of characters – there are *never* spaces or line breaks in internet addresses.

Addresses for web pages are *partially* case sensitive. Anything up to the first / is not case sensitive; anything after that usually *must* be in the correct case. URLs are mostly all lower case, but note that Genuki in particular uses upper case for county abbreviations (e.g. LAN in all the Lancashire pages) and often has the first letter after a / in upper case.

In general, titles of web sites have been indicated solely by initial capitals, while individual pages are between inverted commas. However, the distinction between a site and page is not always easy to make, and I wouldn't claim to have been thoroughly consistent in this respect.

Occasionally, a URL has been so long that I have given instructions on how to get to the page rather than give the full URL. Unfortunately, this tendency for long URLs seems to be increasing, as more and more sites deliver their pages from a database rather than giving them a permanent location. In such cases the direct link is usually available on the web site for this book at <www.spub.co.uk/tgi2/>, except where this would bypass a page the site-owner needs you to see first.

Disappearing resources

Internet resources are in a constant state of flux. Around 10% of all the web pages mentioned in the first edition of this book had moved within a year of publication, and a dozen had disappeared entirely. Of course, personal sites are particularly liable to vanish or move without warning. But official and commercial sites, too, are regularly being redesigned and reorganised, and the old pages do not always redirect you to the new location as good practice demands. With these sites, admittedly, you can be reasonably sure that the material is still there somewhere, and there's usually a site search facility to help. But it can be very hard to discover what has become of valuable resources made available by individuals. There is no reason to think that the material in this edition will be any more stable, I'm afraid.

For print, this is an impossible situation, and it is something all internet books have to live with. But one of the advantages of the Web is that links can be kept up to date, so on the web site for this book at <www.spub.co.uk/tgi2/>, there are links to all the resources mentioned in the text, and the aim to is to keep those links current.

One set of anticipated changes relate to the web site of the National Archives. This new body was formed in April 2003 from the Public Record Office and the Historical Manuscripts Commission. Initially, the National Archives site at <www.nationalarchives.gov.uk> is simply acting as a gateway for the existing PRO and HMC sites. But before long the material on the old sites will start to be reorganised and integrated.

What's new in this edition

The many sites that have moved or disappeared are one good reason for a new edition of this book. But there has also been an explosion in the amount of data available, both from official sources and from family history societies. Scotland is now well on the way to having all its pre-20th-century vital records on-line, while similar things are happening for England and Wales with the relaxation of rules on publishing GRO indexes, the increasing amount of census data, and the unveiling of the Federation of Family History Societies' on-line data service FamilyHistoryOnline.

Another significant development has been the launch of a number of large-scale projects, often Lottery-funded, that were initiated in 2000 and 2001 – for example, the Old Bailey Proceedings and the Digital Library of Historical Directories. These now offer large bodies of material that go beyond vital records and mean that a wider range of historical sources is available. This is of value particularly to the family historian who has already exploited registration and census records to the full.

The result of these developments is that this edition is substantially larger than the first, with individual chapters on each of the main types of on-line sources, and broader coverage of areas such as pedigree databases and photographs. All in all around 200 more web sites are mentioned or discussed.

Acknowledgements

It would be impossible here to thank all those who have, in the last few years, drawn my attention to particular resources mentioned in the text, or discussed the issues raised by particular uses of the internet for genealogy. However, among those whose work has regularly alerted me to new material, I must mention Jane Cavell's internet columns in *Family Tree Magazine* (see p. 263), Dick Eastman's on-line newsletter (p. 264), and John Fuller's regular announcements of new mailing lists (p. 187).

Reviewers and readers of the first edition have made a number of suggestions which have led to additions. David Hawgood offered helpful comments on the draft text of the previous edition, and I am indebted to Roland Clare for suggesting stylistic improvements to both editions.

Particular thanks are due to the Genuki volunteers and to Cyndi Howells for creating and maintaining web sites which not only saved me a lot of work, but which I have been able to direct readers to again and again for further resources.

The web site for this book is at <**www.spub.co.uk/tgi2/**>

1 Introduction

Genealogy and the internet

The steady growth in the number of people interested in family history may have its roots in greater leisure time, or it may be a reaction to social and geographical mobility. Recent television programmes on family history and using DNA to trace migration patterns must also have made a contribution. But above all it is closely related to the growth of the internet and the widening access to it. While the internet has not changed the fundamental principles of genealogical research, it has changed the way in which some of that research is done and made a huge difference in what the individual genealogist can do with ease.

Transcriptions of primary records, or at least indexes to them, are increasingly available on the internet. Even where records themselves are not on-line the ability to check the holdings of record offices and libraries off-line means that a visit can be better prepared and more productive. Those who have previously made little progress with their family tree for lack of time or mobility to visit archives can pursue their researches much more conveniently, with access to an increasing range of records from their desktop. Likewise, those who live on the other side of the world from the repositories where records of their ancestors' lives are stored can make progress without having to employ a researcher. On-line data is a boon, too, for those who have difficulty reading from microfilm or original records.

Archives have realised that the internet is also a remedy for some of their pressing concerns: lack of space on their premises, how to make their collections available while preserving them from damage, and the pressure from government to provide wider access. In addition, there is the obvious commercial potential: on-line record transcriptions can attract distant and, particularly, overseas users in large numbers, while even those living less far away will use a charged service which saves them time and travel costs.

Genealogists also benefit from the ease with which messages and electronic documents can be exchanged around the world at effectively no cost. It is easier than ever to contact people with similar research interests, and even to find distant cousins. It is easier than ever, away from a good genealogy library or bookshop, to find expertise or help with some genealogical problem. And if you need to buy a book, there are genealogy bookshops with on-line catalogues and secure ordering.

Any information stored digitally, whether text or image, can be published on the Web easily and more or less free of cost to both publisher and user. This has revolutionised the publishing of pedigrees and other family history information. It has allowed individuals to publish small transcriptions from individual records, material which it would otherwise be difficult to make widely available. Individual family historians can publicise their interests and publish the fruits of their researches to millions of others.

The internet has enhanced cooperation by making it possible for widely separated people to communicate easily as a group. While collaborative projects did not start with the internet, the internet makes the coordination of vast numbers of geographically distributed volunteers, such as the 6,000 or so involved in FreeBMD (see p. 48), much easier.

Off-line genealogy

Inevitably, however, the explosion of the internet and what it has made possible for family historians has given rise to unrealistic expectations in some quarters. Stories of messages posted to mailing lists or newsgroups asking, 'Where will I find my family tree on-line?' are not apocryphal.[1]

The fact is that if you are only beginning your family tree, you will have plenty to do off-line before you can take full advantage of what is on-line. For a start, because of privacy concerns, you won't find much on-line information about any ancestors born less than a century ago. Scotland has some more recent records on-line for marriages and deaths (see p. 56), but for England and Wales there are only *indexes* to 20th century birth, marriage and death records on-line. This means that in tracing the most recent generations most of the work must be done off-line, though for living people you may well be able to find addresses, phone numbers and perhaps web sites.

But even without all the original records you need on-line, you can still expect to make contact with other genealogists who share your interests. To do this effectively, however, you will need to have established a family tree for the last three or more generations. The reason for this is that if you're going to discover others on the internet who have done research into your ancestors, they are not likely to be close relations. Most people know their first cousins, and at least know of the existence of their second cousins. So on the whole any new relatives discovered via the internet will be no closer to you than third cousins. A third cousin is a descendant of your great-great-grandparents, who were born perhaps 100 or so years before you. So unless you know the names of your great-great-grandparents and where they came from, you will not be in a position to

---

[1] See 'Internet Genealogy' at <**www.cyndislist.com/internet-gen.htm**> for a look at some of the common misconceptions about what the internet can do for the genealogist.

establish that you are in fact related to someone who has posted their pedigree on-line.

Of course, if your surname is unusual, and particularly if you know where earlier generations of your family lived, you may be able to make contact with someone researching your surname and be reasonably certain that you are related. Or you may be lucky enough to find that someone is doing a one-name study of your surname. In this case, they may already have extracted some or all of the relevant entries in the civil registration records, and indeed may have already been able to link up many of the individuals recorded.

But, in general, you will need to do work off-line before you can expect to find primary source material on-line and before you have enough information to start establishing contact with distant relatives.

However, one thing that is useful to every family historian is the wealth of general genealogical information and the huge range of expertise embodied in the on-line community. For the beginner, the internet is useful not so much because there is lots of data on-line, but because there are many places to turn to for help and advice. And this is particularly important for those who live a long way away from their family's ancestral home.

All the same, it is important to remember that, whatever and whoever you discover on-line, there are many other sources for family history, both in print and in manuscript, which aren't on the Web. If you restrict yourself to on-line sources you may be able to construct a basic pedigree, but you will be seeing only the outline of your family's history. On the other hand, if you are one of those who refuses on principle to use the internet (and who is presumably reading this by accident), you are just making your research into your family history much harder than it need be.

History

With the rapid rate at which new developments are taking place, and the relative novelty of the World Wide Web (which has only been widely used beyond a circle of computer buffs for perhaps six or seven years), on-line genealogy might seem to be a new development, but in fact it has quite a history and a number of distinct historical sources.

On the internet itself, on-line genealogy started in the early 1980s with the newsgroup net.roots and with the ROOTS-L mailing list. Net.roots became soc.roots, and eventually spawned all the genealogy newsgroups discussed in Chapter 15; ROOTS-L gave rise to RootsWeb <www.rootsweb.com>, the oldest on-line genealogy co-operative.[2]

---

[2] For a history of the newsgroups, see Margaret J. Olson, 'Historical Reflections of the Genealogy Newsgroups' at <homepages.rootsweb.com/~socgen/Newshist. htm>. For the history of ROOTS-L and RootsWeb, see <www.rootsweb.com/roots-l/>.

But in that period internet access was largely confined to academics and the computer industry, so for many people on-line genealogy meant bulletin boards run by volunteers from their home computers and accessible via a modem and phone line. A system called FidoNet allowed messages and files to be transferred around the world, albeit slowly, as each bulletin board called up its neighbour to pass messages on. The only commercial forums were the growing on-line services which originally targeted computer professionals and those in business, but which gradually attracted a more disparate membership. Of these, CompuServe, with its Roots forum, was the most important. One significant feature of these commercial services was the ability to access them from all over the world, in many cases with only a local call, which we now take for granted.

These systems had the basis of what genealogists now use the internet for: conversing with other genealogists and accessing centrally stored files. But the amount of data available was very small and discussion was the main motivation. Part of this was down to technical limitations: with modem speeds a tiny fraction of what we now take for granted, transferring large amounts of data was unrealistic except for the few with deep pockets or an internet connection at work. No government agencies or family history societies had even contemplated an on-line presence, though genealogical computer groups were starting to spring up by the end of the 1980s.

What changed this was the World Wide Web, created in 1991 (though it was 1995 before it started to dominate the internet), and the growth of commercial internet services. The innovation of the Web made it possible for a large collection of material to remain navigable, even for the technologically illiterate, while at the same time the explosion in public use of the internet was providing the impetus for it to become more user friendly.

The result of these developments is that the internet is now driving developments in access to genealogical information – just as computers had done in the 1980s, and microfilm before that. This in turn is drawing more people to start researching their family tree, which increases the chance of encountering distant cousins on-line, and motivates data holders to make their material available on the Web.

2 First Steps

What your first steps in on-line genealogy are depends on how much research you have already done on your family tree, and what your aim is. If you are just beginning your family history, it is best to regard the internet initially as a source of help and contacts rather than as a source of genealogical information about your most recent forebears. The box below gives a simplified outline of the process of constructing a family tree, which is the foundation on which your family history will be built.

1. Interview your elderly relatives and collect as much first- or second-hand information as you can (and continue doing so, as you find out more in subsequent steps).
2. Get marriage and birth certificates for the most recently deceased ancestors.
3. From these work back to the marriages, and then births of the parents of those ancestors.
4. Keep repeating this process until you get back to the beginning of general registration.
5. Once you have names and either places or actual addresses for a date in the 19th century, refer to the census to see
   a. whole family groups
   b. birth places and approximate birth years.
6. Once you have found in the census an adult ancestor who seems to have been born before general registration, use the birth place and date information in the census to locate his or her baptism in parish registers.
7. From this work back to the marriages, and then baptisms, of the parents of that ancestor in the parish registers.
8. Repeat for all your lines of ancestry until you hit a brick wall.

The first three steps can't be done on-line, and in most cases it's only once you get back 100 years that you will start to find significant amounts of primary source material on the internet. Having done your first century the 'hard' way, you will also have a much better understanding of what's involved in constructing a family tree. The material in the 'Tutorials' and 'Getting help' sections below should help you get going.

If you are not new to family history, but have just started to use the internet, your needs will be rather different. Since you will already be familiar with civil registration and census records, and know what is involved in researching your family tree, your basic questions will be: What's on-line and where do I find it? Who else is working on my family?

Chapter 3 looks at sites that provide collections of links to genealogy resources, while the five subsequent chapters, 4 to 8, look at on-line records. Chapters 11–14 look at internet resources relating to particular aspects of genealogy, while Chapter 16 covers general techniques for finding web sites that have specific information. For making contact with others, look at Chapters 10, 15 and 17.

Whatever stage you are at, it will be worth looking at the discussion groups in Chapter 15, and the information on archives and libraries in Chapter 9.

Tutorials

While the internet cannot match the wealth of introductory books for family historians, there is quite a range of material covering the basics of genealogical research in the British Isles.

One important source for such materials is Genuki (described more fully in Chapter 3, p. 15), which has a page devoted to 'Getting Started in Genealogy and Family History' at <www.genuki.org.uk/gs/>. There are individual pages on major topics, such as that for 'Civil Registration in England and Wales' at <www.genuki.org.uk/big/eng/civreg/>.

Genuki is host to three guides for beginners:

- Roy Stockdill's 'Newbies' Guide to Genealogy and Family History' at <www.genuki.org.uk/gs/Newbie.html>
- Jeanne Bunting's 'What is Genealogy' at <www.genuki.org.uk/gs/Bunting.html>
- Dr Ashton Emery's 'A-Z Of British Genealogical Research' at <www.genuki.org.uk/big/EmeryPaper.html>, presented as a dictionary rather than a connected account.

Genuki also has links to other introductory materials.

The FamilyRecords portal (see p. 14) has a guide for beginners at <www.familyrecords.gov.uk/guides/beginners.htm>, while the National Archives has extensive introductory material on its web site. The 'Education' area of the site at <www.pro.gov.uk/education/> links to 'The Learning Curve', which has historical material for use within the National Curriculum, including a section devoted to the census. 'Pathways to the Past' includes material for grown-ups on local and family history. The family history section at <www.pro.gov.uk/pathways/FamilyHistory/> has pages devoted to the following topics:

Naming Names and Tracing Places
- Civil Registration
- Stand Up and Be Counted
- What About Births, Marriages and Deaths Before 1837?
- Dissenting Voices
- Britons Born, Married or Dying On Board Ship
- Wills and Death Duty Registers
- Finding Taxpayers
- Ancestors as Investors
- Oath Rolls
- Timeline

People at Work
- Apprentices
- Police
- Customs and Excise
- Coastguards
- Lawyers in the Family
- Other Records about People at Work

The Army and Navy
- Soldiers' Papers
- Tracing Army Officers
- Regimental Diaries
- War Medals
- The British Army Before the First World War
- The Royal Navy: Officers
- Tracing Ratings
- Merchant Seamen
- Crew Lists
- Log Books
- Timeline

Migrant Ancestors
- Migrant Ancestors
- Movements of the Poor
- Britons Abroad
- Children on the Move
- Wartime Evacuees
- Immigrants to Britain
- Refugees
- Ships' Passenger Lists

Ancestors and the Law
- Name Changes
- Bankrupts
- Criminal Courts
- Prisoners and Transportation
- Licences and Pardons
- Cases in Chancery
- The Court of Requests

The Society of Genealogists (SoG) has a number of leaflets on-line at <www.sog.org.uk/leaflets/>. Though they are not designed as a coherent introduction to family history, they include 'Starting genealogy' and 'Note taking and keeping for genealogists'. The Federation of Family History Societies (FFHS) has a number of on-line leaflets at <www.ffhs.org.uk/General/Help/>, including 'First Steps in Family History', 'Record Offices', and 'Strays (People who moved)'.

Both the BBC and Channel 4 have areas of their web sites devoted to genealogy. These started life as support materials for particular TV series, but now have an independent existence. The BBC's site will be found at <www.bbc.co.uk/history/your_history/> and includes two comprehensive introductory guides:

- 'Researching your family history', a beginner's guide by Susannah Davis at <www.bbc.co.uk/history/your_history/family/genealogy_1.shtml> and
- Else Churchill's 'Eight-part guide to advanced genealogy' at <www.bbc.co.uk/history/your_history/family/genealogy_guide.shtml>.

There is also material on Afro-Caribbean roots, heraldry, and Victorian studio photographs, as well as an extensive selection of links at <www.bbc.co.uk/history/your_history/family/links_1.shtml>.

Channel 4's Guide to Genealogy is at <www.channel4.com/history/microsites/U/untold/resources/geno/genof.html> with general information about post- and pre-1837 family history, and a particularly strong section on tracing immigrant ancestors, discussed in more detail in Chapter 11.

The on-line history magazine *History in Focus* (see p. 264) has an introductory guide 'Family History on the Internet' in its launch issue at <ihr.sas.ac.uk/ihr/Focus/Victorians/family.html>.

The Church of Jesus Christ of Latter-day Saints (LDS) has extensive introductory material on its FamilySearch web site at <www.familysearch.org/Eng/Search/RG/frameset_rg.asp> (or go to the home page at <www.familysearch.org> and select Search, then Research Guidance). There are separate 'Search Strategy' pages for England, Wales, Scotland and Ireland. Each of these has links to material on looking for births, marriages and

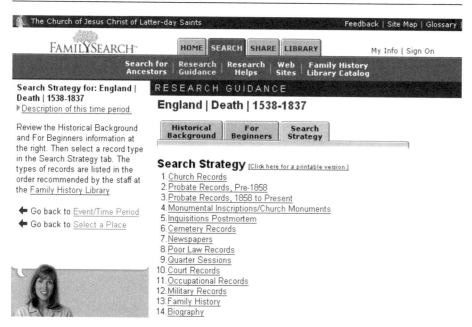

Figure 2.1 FamilySearch's Research Guidance page for English Deaths in the period 1538–1837 at <www.familysearch.org>

deaths in the three main periods for genealogical research: general registration, parish registers, and before parish registers (see Figure 2.1). Clicking on the 'For Beginners' tab will take you to general material on:

- Organising your paper files
- How to find the name of the place where your ancestor lived
- How to find information about the place where your ancestor lived
- How to find maps
- How to find compiled sources.

Origins has a concise one-page guide on 'How to start tracing your family history' at <www.origins.net/howto.html> with many links to on-line material.

Introductory material specific to Scottish research includes the 'Getting Started' section of Scotlandspeople – go to <www.scotlandspeople.gov.uk>, select **Features**, then **Getting Started** – and the Scottish Archive Network's family history pages at <www.scan.org.uk/familyhistory/>. Genuki has an 'Introduction to Scottish Family History' at <www.genuki.org.uk/big/sct/intro.html>.

For Ireland, the Irish Ancestors site has an excellent range of introductory material at <scripts.ireland.com/ancestor/browse/>, including information on the counties and emigration (see Chapter 11) and good pages on the various Irish genealogical records. This is based largely on John Grenham's book *Tracing your Irish Ancestors*. Also by John Grenham is the 'Irish Roots' section of Moving Here (see p. 141) at <www.movinghere.org.uk/galleries/roots/irish/irish.htm>. Irish Origins has an introduction to 'Irish Genealogy on the World Wide Web' by Sherry Irvine at <www.origins.net/art-ireland1.html>.

On Cyndi's List you will find a comprehensive 'Beginners' page at <www.cyndislist.com/beginner.htm>, and a collection of links on 'Researching: Localities & Ethnic Groups' which will be useful if you need to start looking for ancestors outside the UK and Ireland. Cyndi's 'How to: tutorials and guides' page at <www.cyndislist.com/howtotut.htm> provides an outline of all the introductory materials on seven major genealogy sites. These sites are US-based, so much of the material on specific records will not be of use unless you are tracing American ancestors. However, this page should help you find some of the more general information buried in these sites.

About.com has a large collection of introductory articles at <genealogy.about.com>. The best way to find material on particular topics is to go to the list of articles by category at <genealogy.about.com/blresourceindex.htm>. Although many of the articles on specific records are intended for those researching American ancestry, there is useful material on general topics, such as 'Top Ten Genealogy Mistakes to Avoid' at <genealogy.about.com/library/weekly/aa072100a.htm>.

If you are trying to research British or Irish ancestry from overseas, Genuki's 'Researching From Abroad' page at <www.genuki.org.uk/ab/> will be useful. The SoG has a leaflet 'Notes for Americans on tracing their British ancestry' on-line at <www.sog.org.uk/leaflets/americans.html>. Mark Howells' 'Guide to Researching Ancestors from the United Kingdom using the LDS Family History Center Resources' at <www.oz.net/~markhow/uksearch.htm> is also recommended. If you are unfamiliar with the administrative subdivision of Britain into counties and parishes, you should consult Jim Fisher's page 'British Counties, Parishes, etc. for Genealogists' at <homepages.nildram.co.uk/~jimella/counties.htm> and Genuki's pages on 'Administrative Regions of the British Isles' at <www.genuki.org.uk/big/Regions/index.html>. See also the section on 'The counties' on p. 165.

Getting help

Even with these tutorial materials, you may still have a question you can't find an answer to. One solution is to use a search engine to find pages devoted to a particular topic (see Chapter 16). However, this can be a time consuming task, since you may end up following quite a few links that turn out to be useless before you find what you are looking for.

The various discussion forums discussed in Chapter 15 are ideal places for getting help and advice. Before posting a query to one of these, though, make sure you read the FAQ (Frequently Asked Questions) – see p. 207. This will give the answers to the most common questions. There are a number of mailing lists for beginners, notably GEN-NEWBIE-L 'where people who are new to computers and genealogy may interact'. Information on how to join this list will be found at <**www.rootsweb.com/ ~newbie/**>, and past messages are archived at <**archiver.rootsweb.com/ th/index/GEN-NEWBIE**>. This is a very busy list, so for a specifically UK focus and a more manageable number of messages, look at the UK-GENEALOGY-NEWBIES list – details at <**lists.rootsweb.com/index/intl/ UK/UK-GENEALOGY-NEWBIES.html**>. If you are already a member of a family history society, it may have a mailing list where you can turn to other members for assistance.

Ask a Librarian is an 'on-line reference service' run by CoEast, a public library consortium, at <**www.ask-a-librarian.org.uk**>. You can e-mail a question and you will get a reply within two working days. Before asking a family history question, consult the 'tips on asking your question' page, and don't expect them to search original records on your behalf to find your great grandparents' wedding.

However, there is one really important step that will save you a lot of this trouble: get a good book on family history. If you are a relative beginner, you might start with the Reader's Digest volume *Explore Your Family's Past* or Jean Cole and John Titford's *Tracing your Family Tree*; if you have already made some progress, Mark Herber's *Ancestral Trails* should be on your bookshelf. Contrary to the hype, the internet has not made such publications redundant. There is a lot of good reference material on the internet, and an increasing amount of primary data, but tutorial material is still a relatively underdeveloped area despite all the sites listed in this chapter.

Genealogical terms and abbreviations

Whatever your level of experience in family history, you're very likely at some point to come across unfamiliar terms and, especially, abbreviations. Internet resources for legal terms are covered in Chapter 13 (p. 178) while words for obsolete occupations are covered in Chapter 11 (p. 132). But genealogy as a discipline has its own specialist terms, which may baffle at first.

GenealogyPro has a Glossary of Genealogy Terms at <**genealogypro.com/ details/glossary.html**> with around 130 entries, while Sam Behling has a page of about 400 terms at <**homepages.rootsweb.com/~sam/terms.html**>. Gareth Hicks' page on Technical Words/Expressions at <**home.clara.net/ tirbach/hicks3.html**> is arranged under a number of key topic headings, which is useful if you're not sure of the distinction between a vicar, rector and parson, for example.

If you have to read documents written in a language other than English then FamilySearch has wordlists of key genealogical words in fifteen European languages at <**www.familysearch.org/Eng/Search/rg/research/ type/Word_List.asp**>. These lists are not comprehensive but should at least help you identify key words like 'husband', 'parish' and 'baptism'. Web resources for Latin are discussed in more detail on p. 176.

One frequent question from those getting started is about the meaning of phrases like 'second cousin once removed'. To help you with this, About.com has a Genealogy Relationship Chart at <**genealogy.about.com/ library/nrelationshipchart.htm**>. Genealogy.com's article 'What is a First Cousin, Twice Removed?' at <**www.genealogy.com/genealogy/16_cousn. html**> explains all.

For making sense of abbreviations and acronyms, there are a number of sites to help you. Dr Ashton Emery's 'A–Z Of British Genealogical Research' at <**www.genuki.org.uk/big/EmeryPaper.html**> has already been mentioned and this explains some of the more common abbreviations. Mark Howells has a page devoted to 'Common Acronyms & Jargon' found in UK genealogy at <**www.oz.net/~markhow/acronym-uk. htm**>, and RootsWeb has a more general list of abbreviations used in genealogy at <**www.rootsweb.com/roots-l/abbrevs.html**>. But by far the most comprehensive is GenDocs' 'Genealogical Abbreviations and Acronyms' page at <**www.gendocs.demon.co.uk/abbr.html**> with over 2,000 entries.

For links to other on-line dictionaries and lists of abbreviations, look at Glossarist, which has links to around 60 sites at <**www.glossarist.com/ glossaries/family-relationships/genealogy.asp**>, or the page on Cyndi's List devoted to 'Dictionaries & Glossaries' at <**www.cyndislist.com/diction. htm**>.

3 On-line Starting Points

Subsequent chapters in this book are devoted to particular types of genealogical resource or internet tools. This one looks at some of the on-line starting points for genealogy on the internet, sites which provide links to other resources. These go under various names: directory, gateway or portal.

- An internet **directory** is the electronic equivalent of the Yellow Pages, a list of resources categorised under a number of subject headings.
- A **gateway** is a directory devoted to a single subject area, and may also offer knowledgeable annotation of the links provided as well as additional background information. A gateway is not just a directory; it can be more like a handbook.
- A **portal** is a site which aims to provide a single jumping-off point on the internet for a particular audience, bringing together all the resources they might be interested in. Like a gateway, a portal may provide information as well as links.

In genealogy, since the audience is defined by its interest in a particular subject, it is not always possible to maintain a clear distinction between gateways and portals. 'Portal' tends to be the preferred term in the case of a site which has some official status or which aims to be definitive. Both gateways and portals are selective and only include links to recommended resources, whereas directories tend to be all-encompassing. (The term 'gateway' is also used in a quite different sense, see p. 203.)

Directories, gateways and portals are not the only way to find information on the internet: general-purpose search engines such as Google <www.google.com> and AltaVista <www.altavista.com>, discussed in Chapter 16, can also be used to find genealogical material on-line. The differences between directories, gateways and portals on the one hand and search engines on the other are summarised in Table 16.1 on p. 216. The most important is that directories etc. provide lists of web *sites* while search engines locate individual web *pages*, so the former are better for locating significant resources on a particular topic rather than mere mentions of a subject. This makes them preferable for initial exploration. The fact that the entries are selected, and perhaps helpfully annotated makes them even more useful. However, there are certain things they are poor for, notably information published on the personal web sites of individual family historians, and for material relating to individual surnames.

The British Isles

There are two on-line starting points which are essential for British genealogy: the FamilyRecords portal, which is the government's gateway to official web sites of use to family historians; and Genuki, which aims to be comprehensive in its coverage of sites relating to genealogy in the British Isles. In addition, there are a number of other official and unofficial sites which provide starting points for exploring specifically British and Irish internet resources. Sites linking to more general resources are discussed later in this chapter (p. 21ff.).

FamilyRecords

The FamilyRecords portal at <**www.familyrecords.gov.uk**> (Figure 3.1) is run by a consortium made up of the National Archives, Public Record Office of Northern Ireland, National Archives of Scotland, the National Library of Wales, the General Register Office, the General Register Office for Scotland and the British Library India Office, and aims to provide links to the web sites of these bodies and to official information. FamilyRecords provides basic information about the major national repositories, including contact details and links to their web sites – this is in the 'Partners' area of the site at <**www.familyrecords.gov.uk/partners.htm**>. In the 'Topics' area at

Figure 3.1 The FamilyRecords portal at <www.familyrecords.gov.uk>

<www.familyrecords.gov.uk/topics.htm> are brief descriptions of the main types of public record, with links to the bodies that hold them. Although deliberately limited in scope, it provides a good way of locating specific material on the official web sites. The web sites of the individual bodies linked to the FamilyRecords portal are discussed under 'Civil registration' in Chapter 5 and under 'National archives' in Chapter 9 (p. 95ff.).

UKonline

While the FamilyRecords portal is restricted to genealogical coverage, there is also a general-purpose official gateway called UKonline at <www. ukonline.gov.uk>.[3] This site provides access to *all* government information on-line, with links to all branches of local and national government. It therefore covers local authorities, county record offices and the like, which are not linked from FamilyRecords. There is a search facility as well as alphabetical indexes of national and local government services.

There is an unofficial directory of government sites at Tagish <www. tagish.co.uk/links/>, which is in some ways easier to use than UKonline.

Ireland

Obviously, there is no link from FamilyRecords to official bodies in the Republic of Ireland, but the official web site of the Irish government will be found at <www.irlgov.ie>, and this has links to sites of government departments and state organisations.

The National Archives of Ireland have a page of genealogy links at <www.nationalarchives.ie/genealogy5.html>, and Genuki, described in the next section, has a comprehensive collection of links to Irish material on-line at <www.genuki.org.uk/big/irl/>. The Irish Ancestors site has links to the major Irish bodies with genealogical material at <scripts.ireland.com/ancestor/browse/links/index.htm>, with sub-pages devoted to libraries, societies and individual counties, as well as passenger lists and emigration resources. Irish libraries and archives are covered in Chapter 9, while Irish civil registration is covered in Chapter 5.

Genuki

The most comprehensive collection of on-line information about family history for the British Isles, with an unrivalled collection of links, is Genuki, the 'UK & Ireland Genealogical Service' at <www.genuki.org.uk>. Genuki describes itself as 'a virtual reference library of genealogical information that is of particular relevance to the UK & Ireland.' As a reference source, the material it contains 'relates to primary historical material, rather than material resulting from genealogists' ongoing research.' This means it is effectively a handbook of British and Irish genealogy on-line. But Genuki

---

[3] The UKonline (one word) web site is not to be confused with the Internet Service Provider UK Online (two words) at <www.ukonline.net>.

also functions as a gateway, simply because it has links to an enormous number of on-line resources for the UK and Ireland, including every genealogical organisation with a web site.

Genuki has its origins in the efforts of a group of volunteers, centred on Brian Randell at the University of Newcastle and Phil Stringer at the University of Manchester, to set up a web site for genealogical information in 1994, when the World Wide Web was still very young. Genuki has always been an entirely non-commercial and volunteer-run organisation. All the pages are maintained by a group of about 50 volunteers on many different web sites, mostly at UK universities or on the personal sites of the volunteers. Many other individuals have provided information and transcripts of primary data. Genuki started as an entirely informal group, but is now a charitable trust.

There are two distinct parts to Genuki. First, there are a number of pages devoted to general information about family history in the British Isles:

- Frequently Asked Questions (FAQs) – typical queries asked by Genuki users.
- Getting started in genealogy – a range of beginners' guides (or links to them). See 'Tutorials' on p. 6.
- Pages devoted to individual general topics, such as 'Military Records' or 'Immigration and Emigration', all linked from <**www.genuki.org.uk/big/**> (many of these are mentioned in later chapters).
- Researching from abroad – useful links for those who dwell outside the UK, especially in North America.
- World genealogy – a small collection of links for those researching non-British ancestry.
- Genealogical events relating to UK and Ireland ancestry (see p. 263).

 United Kingdom and Ireland

Contents & Search

Guidance for
First-Time Users
of These Pages

**UK & Ireland
Genealogy**

Guidance for
Potential Contributors
to These Pages

Enter this large collection of genealogical information pages for England, Ireland, Scotland, Wales, the Channel Islands, and the Isle of Man.		
Getting started in genealogy	Frequently Asked Questions (FAQs)	Researching UK and Irish genealogy from abroad
World genealogy, newsgroups and bulletin boards, etc.	Recent changes to these pages	Upcoming UK & Ireland Genealogical events (GENEVA)

We recommend subscribing to our associated newsletter, UK-FAMILY HISTORY NEWS.

For the latest GENUKI server status see www.genuki.info
This page gives news of (past, present and future where possible) incidents that may prevent or hinder your access to parts of GENUKI.

Figure 3.2 Genuki <www.genuki.org.uk>

- Information on Genuki itself – how it is run, the principles on which it is structured.

Second, it provides information on and links to on-line resources for all the constituent parts of the British Isles, with pages for:

- England, Wales, Scotland, Ireland, the Isle of Man, and the Channel Islands
- Every individual county in these areas
- Many individual towns and parishes.

The county pages (see Figure 3.3) in turn provide links to the web sites of:

- County record offices and other repositories of interest to family historians (see Chapter 9)
- Local family history societies (see Chapter 18)
- County mailing lists (see Chapter 15)
- County surname lists (see Chapter 10), and
- Other on-line resources relating to genealogy in the county.

   GENUKI Contents Staffordshire Towns & Parishes Information related to all of Staffordshire

STAFFORDSHIRE

"A county of England, bounded by, Shropshire Cheshire, Derbyshire, Warwickshire, and Worcestershire. It is in length about 54 miles, and varies in breadth from 18 to 36. It is divided into 5 hundreds, which contain 1 city, 21 towns, 181 parishes, and 670 villages. The principal rivers are the Trent, Dove, Sow, Churnet, Stour, Penk, and Manifold. The air is reckoned pleasant, mild, and wholesome. The middle and southern parts are level and plain, and the soil is good and rich; the north is hilly, and full of heaths and moors. Staffordshire is famous for its potteries, its inland navigations, and its founderies, blast furnaces, slitting mills, and various other branches of the iron trade. The mines of coals, copper, lead, and iron ore are rich and extensive; and there are also numerous quarries of stone, alabaster, and limestone. Stafford is the county town. Population, 510,504. It sends 17 members to parliament."
[Barclays Complete & Universal English Dictionary, 1842-1852]

INFORMATION RELATED TO ALL OF STAFFORDSHIRE

- Archives and Libraries
- Bibliography
- Business Records
- Cemeteries
- Census
- Church History
- Church Records
- Civil Registration
- Correctional Institutions
- Court Records
- Description and Travel
- Directories
- Genealogy
- Historical Geography
- Maps

- Medical Records
- Military History
- Military Records
- Names, Geographical
- Names, Personal
- Newspapers
- Occupations
- Orphans and Orphanages
- Periodicals
- Poorhouses, Poor Law, etc
- Probate Records
- Societies
- Taxation
- Voting Registers

Figure 3.3 A Genuki county page

Genuki also has central listings of:

- National genealogical organisations and local family history societies at <www.genuki.org.uk/Societies/>
- All mailing lists relevant to British and Irish genealogy at <www.genuki.org.uk/indexes/MailingLists.html>
- All county and other surname lists at <www.genuki.org.uk/indexes/SurnamesLists.html>.

Most material on Genuki will be found on these geographical pages, which are organised hierarchically. Figure 3.4 shows a diagram of the hierarchy.

Because of the enormous amount of material on Genuki – there are almost 45,000 pages – it is well worth taking the time to look at the 'Guidance for First-Time Users of These Pages' at <www.genuki.org.uk/org/>, which gives an outline of what Genuki is. There is a more

The Structure of GENUKI.

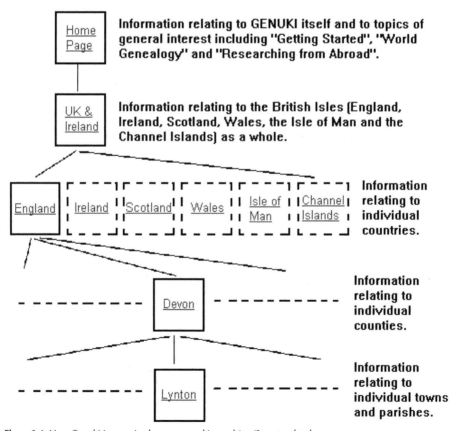

Figure 3.4 How Genuki is organised <www.genuki.org.uk/org/Structure.html>

detailed on-line user guide 'How the information on this server is presented to the user' at **<www.genuki.org.uk/org/user.html>**.

A particular virtue of Genuki is that it uses well-defined subject categories, which are based on those used in the LDS Church's library catalogue and have therefore been designed by genealogically aware librarians. Its coherent coverage of every county, with a long-term aim of covering every parish, is the other feature which makes it useful. The list of categories used on Genuki is shown in Table 3.1.

Table 3.1 Genuki subject headings

Almanacs	Merchant Marine
Archives and Libraries	Migration, Internal
Bibliography	Military History
Biography	Military Records
Business and Commerce Records	Minorities
Cemeteries	*(Monumental Inscriptions – see*
Census	*Cemeteries)*
Chronology	Names, Geographical
Church Directories	Names, Personal
Church History	Naturalisation and Citizenship
Church Records	Newspapers
Civil Registration	Nobility
Colonisation	Obituaries
Correctional Institutions	Occupations
Court Records	Officials and Employees
Description and Travel	Orphans and Orphanages
Directories	*(Parish Registers – see Church*
Dwellings	*Records)*
Emigration and Immigration	Pensions
Encyclopedias and Dictionaries	Periodicals
Ethnology	Politics and Government
Folklore	Poorhouses, Poor Law, etc.
Gazetteers	Population
Genealogy	Postal and Shipping Guides
Guardianship	Probate Records
Handwriting	Public Records
Heraldry	Religion and Religious Life
Historical Geography	Schools
History	Social Life and Customs
Inventories, Registers, Catalogues	Societies
Jewish History	Statistics
Jewish Records	Taxation
Land and Property	Town Records
Language and Languages	Visitations, Heraldic
Law and Legislation	*(Vital Records – see Civil*
Manors	*Registration)*
Maps	Voting Registers
Medical Records	Yearbooks

Some of these categories (for example Handwriting, Politics and Government) will be relevant only at the top, national levels, but topics such as church records, local records and maps should be represented on every county page. Since the list of subject headings pre-dates the internet, there are no specific categories for internet-related subjects such as surname lists and mailing lists, so Genuki places these under the Genealogy heading.

Once you are familiar with how Genuki is organised, there are other quick ways to get where you want to go. The 'List of Genuki Contents Pages' at <**www.genuki.org.uk/mindex.html**> has links to outline pages for the contents of each county page. These pages lack any description of the material they link to, so they are not intended for first time visitors to Genuki, but they provide a quick way of getting to specific material that you know is there. Genuki also has a search facility at <**www. genuki.org.uk/search/**>, discussed on p. 235.

For a detailed guide to Genuki there is a book, simply called *Genuki*, by David Hawgood, one the Genuki trustees, published by the FFHS. The complete text is available on-line at <**www.hawgood.co.uk/genuki/**>.

Because Genuki is very comprehensive, it can be easy to overlook the fact that there are some things it does not do. First, it has some deliberate limitations in its linking policy. It does not link to sites which provide information only on an individual family, pedigree or surname. It does not link to commercial sites, unless they also offer useful information free of charge. And finally, if obviously, its links are strictly confined to sites which are relevant to UK and Ireland genealogy. However, as long as what you are looking for is available on-line and falls within Genuki's scope you should expect to find it listed.

Another service Genuki does not provide is answering genealogical queries from individuals. There is a Genuki e-mail address, but this is intended only for reporting errors on the site or drawing attention to new resources not listed on Genuki. See 'Getting help' on p. 10 and Chapter 15 for places to post genealogical queries.

'Essential Web Sites'

The SoG has a small but useful page of 'Essential Web Sites' at <**www.sog.org.uk/links.html**>. While it only has about three dozen links, these cover the core web sites in the following categories:

- General genealogical sites
- Governmental repositories
- Libraries and other national repositories
- Other organisations
- Major on-line data collections.

General genealogy gateways

If you have ancestors who lived outside the British Isles you will need to look at some of the general genealogy directories and gateways. And even if all your ancestors were British or Irish, there are good reasons to use other gateways and directories. Since FamilyRecords and Genuki take a strictly geographical approach, you need to look elsewhere for genealogical resources, such as computer software, which are not tied to a particular country or region.

Cyndi's List

The most comprehensive genealogy gateway is Cyndi's List at <www.cyndislist.com>, maintained by Cyndi Howells. You can get an idea of the scope of the list, which has over 185,000 links, from the 160 or so main categories in Table 3.2.

Unlike Genuki (p. 15) or Yahoo (p. 27), Cyndi's List has a fairly flat structure: most of these headings lead to a single page, while a few act as indexes to a whole group of pages on their subject (these have the word 'index' in their title). So, for example, the main UK page at <www.cyndislist.com/uksites.htm> acts simply as an index to the sub-pages devoted to the various parts of the British Isles, to general UK sites and to British military sites. The advantage of this flat structure is that you don't have to go deep into a hierarchy to find what you're looking for; the disadvantage is that the individual pages tend to be quite large and can take a while to download.

However, alongside the main home page, Cyndi provides other, quicker ways to get to where you want once you are familiar with the site. There are four other 'home pages':

- The 'No Frills' index at <www.cyndislist.com/nofrills.htm> is essentially the home page, but with just the headings – no descriptions or update information, and no cross references.
- The 'Alphabetical Category' index at <www.cyndislist.com/alpha.htm> is a complete list of all pages and sub-pages in alphabetical order, with cross references.
- The 'Topical Category' index at <www.cyndislist.com/topical.htm> lists all categories under 11 main headings (Localities, Ethnic Groups and People, Religions, Records, Research Tools and Reference Materials, Help from Others, Marketplace, History, Military, Internet Tools for Genealogy, Miscellaneous).
- The 'Text Only Category' index at <www.cyndislist.com/textonly.htm>.

Once you are familiar with the List, it is much quicker to use these alternative entry points – the main home page is over 150k, while these are under 40k. The smallest is the text-only page at about 30k.

Another way to speed up access to Cyndi's List is to save a copy of the

Table 3.2 Categories on Cyndi's List

Acadian, Cajun & Creole
Adoption
African-American
America Online – AOL
Asia & The Pacific
Australia
Austria
The Baltic States – Estonia, Latvia & Lithuania
Baptist
Beginners
Belgium
Biographies
Births & Baptisms
Books
Calendars & Dates
Canada Index
Canals, Rivers & Waterways
Catholic
CD-ROMs
Cemeteries & Funeral Homes
Census Related Sites Worldwide
Chat & IRC
Citing Sources
City Directories
Clothing & Costumes
Correspondence
Cousins & Kinship
The Czech Republic & Slovakia
Databases – Lineage-Linked
Databases – Searchable Online
Death Records
Denmark
Diaries & Letters
Dictionaries & Glossaries
Disasters: Natural & Man-Made
Eastern Europe
Education
Ellis Island
England
Etiquette & Ethics
Events & Activities
Family Bibles
Famous People
Female Ancestors
Finding People

Finland
France
GEDCOM
Genealogy in the Media
Genealogy Standards & Guidelines
Genetics, DNA & Family Health
Germans from Russia
Germany
Greece
Handwriting & Script
Handy Online Starting Points
Heraldry
Hispanic, Central & South America, & the West Indies
Historical Events & People Worldwide
Hit a Brick Wall?
House & Building Histories
How To
How To – Tutorials & Guides
Huguenot
Humor & Prose
Iceland
Immigration & Naturalisation
Internet Genealogy
Ireland & Northern Ireland
Italy
Jewish
Kids & Teens
Land Records, Deeds, Homesteads, Etc.
Languages & Translations
LDS & Family History Centers
Libraries, Archives & Museums
Lookups & Free Searches by Volunteers
Lost & Found
Loyalists
Lutheran
Luxembourg
Magazines, Journals, Columns & Newsletters
Mailing Lists
Maps, Gazetteers & Geographical Information
Marriages

Table 3.2 cont.

Medical & Medicine
Medieval
Mennonite
Methodist
Microfilm & Microfiche
The Middle East
Migration Routes, Roads & Trails
Military Resources Worldwide
Military – World War II
Mining & Miners
Money
Movies, Music, Fiction & Non-
    Fiction
Myths, Hoaxes & Scams
Names
Native American
Netherlands
New Zealand
Newsgroups
Newspapers
Norway
Novelties
Obituaries
Occupations
Odds & Ends
Oral History & Interviews
Organising Your Research
Orphans
Passports
Personal Home Pages
Photographs & Memories
Poland
Poorhouses & Poverty
Ports of Departure
Portugal
Ports of Entry
Postcards
Presbyterian
Preservation & Conservation
Primary Sources
Prisons, Prisoners & Outlaws
Professional Researchers,
    Volunteers & Other Research
    Services

Public Servants
Quaker
Queries & Message Boards
Railroads
Recipes, Cookbooks & Family
    Traditions
Records Preservation
Religion & Churches
Reunions
ROOTS-L & RootsWeb
Royalty & Nobility
Scandinavia & the Nordic
    Countries Index
Scanners
Schools
Scotland
Scrapbooks
Search Engines
Ships & Passenger Lists
Societies & Groups
Software & Computers
South Africa
Spain & the Basque Country
Supplies, Charts, Forms, Etc.
Surnames, Family Associations &
    Family Newsletters
Sweden
Switzerland
Taxes
Timelines
Travel & Research
Unique Peoples & Cultures
United Kingdom & Ireland Index
United States Index
Video & Audio Tapes
Volunteer Online Regional Projects
Voters, Poll Books, Electoral
    Records
Wales
Web Rings for Genealogy
Weights & Measures
Western Europe
Wills & Probate
Writing Your Family's History

home page to your own hard disk. You will find that clicking on the links from this copy (assuming you are on-line!) will take you to the sub-page without having to wait while the main page loads over the Web. Obviously, you will need to check periodically that no new categories have been added to this top-level page. It is also worth bookmarking any part of the site that you regularly refer to.

Even if your genealogical interests are confined to the British Isles, a number of categories and topics on Cyndi's List are worth noting. The pages devoted to individual religious groups will be useful if you have Catholic, Nonconformist or Jewish ancestors (covered in Chapter 11). The 'Software & Computers' page <www.cyndislist.com/software.htm> has a very useful collection of links for genealogy software. The Personal Home Pages section <www.cyndislist.com/personal.htm> lists around 9,000 web sites of individuals, while the Surnames page <www.cyndislist.com/surnames.htm> has over 5,000 sites for individual surnames.

GenWeb

For ancestors from outside the British Isles, you will find a wide coverage of countries and regions on Cyndi's List. But there is also a purely geographical gateway with worldwide coverage in the GenWeb projects. In GenWeb, the world is split into a number of regional projects, each of which has its own web site, and a separate volunteer is responsible for each individual country or island in the region. Apart from USGenWeb at <www.usgenweb.org> and CanadaGenWeb at <www.rootsweb.com/~canwgw/>, which are independent, the remainder are coordinated under the WorldGenWeb project at <worldgenweb.org>.

In all, there are around 100 countries, islands or island groups for which there are actively maintained web sites, grouped as follows:

- Africa (6 countries active)
- Asia (15 countries active)
- British Isles (including the Falkland Islands, Gibraltar, St Helena)
- Canada
- Central Europe (all but Lithuania active) – actually Northern Europe would be a more accurate description
- Caribbean (21 islands active)
- Eastern Europe (12 countries active)
- Mediterranean (8 countries active) – actually more like Southern Europe, since it excludes African and Middle Eastern states, though it includes Turkey
- Middle East (9 countries active)
- North America (all but Nicaragua active) – actually Central America, since it excludes Canada and the USA
- Pacific (4 'areas' active – Australia and 3 groups of islands – though not every individual island has an active page)

- South America (7 countries active)
- United States.

Most of the links to UK and Irish material at <**www.britishislesgenweb. org**> will in fact be found on Genuki, whose county pages are generally more comprehensive. So the real strength of the GenWeb sites, from the point of view of British and Irish family historians, lies in the material relating to former British colonies and those countries from which immigrants came to the UK (see Chapter 11). There is huge variation in the amount of material available: for some countries there is a single page, while for others there are individual pages for administrative subdivisions, for example French *départements*. In general, the level of detail does not go down to the equivalent of individual parishes, though for each US state there are pages for the constituent counties.

While most of the pages are in English, quite a few are maintained by natives of the countries concerned and are in the local language. Some, notably the Caribbean and South American pages, are available in more than one language.

On the WorldGenWeb projects, the topics on each page are sorted under the following headings:

- History
- Resource Addresses (libraries, archives)
- Society Addresses
- Maps
- Geography
- Culture and Religious History
- Query Board
- Mail List
- Reference Materials (census, deeds, biographies).

Beyond this, the pages do not necessarily have the same layout or look. A useful feature to note is that every GenWeb page has a Query Board where readers can post queries. Such a board is often available for countries which have no maintained web page.

Genealogy Resources on the Internet

One of the longest established genealogy directories on the internet is Chris Gaunt and John Fuller's Genealogy Resources on the Internet site at <**www.rootsweb.com/~jfuller/internet.html**>. This differs from Genuki, GenWeb and Cyndi's List in that its main division of material is not by subject or by area but by type of access – web, e-mail, etc. This is really a hangover from its origins at a time before web browsers provided a way of integrating all types of internet resources into a single interface, and when different software was required for each type of resource. This may be the

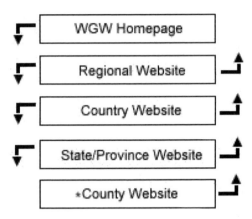

* Not all countries have counties.
The term county is used here in the general sense and
refers to the most common political or administrative district
in a country. Other names include shires, parish, townlands,
states, prefects, rajones, etc.

Figure 3.5 How WorldGenWeb is organised <worldgenweb.org/policy.html>

only place where you'll still see references to Gopher and Telnet sites. One of the great virtues of this site is that the pages are designed for very fast downloading, with very simple layouts and few graphics.

The sections devoted to newsgroups and the Web provide excellent starting points and, in particular, the pages on mailing lists (main page at <www.rootsweb.com/~jfuller/gen_mail.html>) are one of the essential genealogy resources on the Web, and one which is repeatedly referred to in this book. Mailing lists are discussed further in Chapter 15.

Another interesting collection of resources listed here are those accessible by e-mail rather than the Web, at <www.rootsweb.com/~jfuller/gen_email.html>. Although many of these started off as services for people with e-mail but without Web access (which is nowadays almost no one), there are still some interesting things on this page you are unlikely to see mentioned elsewhere.

Other genealogy gateways

While Cyndi's List may be the most widely used general genealogy directory, and Genuki is certainly the pre-eminent gateway for UK material, there are many others. Each has its own particular strengths, though many are US-based and are therefore naturally stronger in US resources. There is not enough space here to list them all, let alone describe them in detail. The following represent a small selection:

- About.com's 'Family Tree and Genealogy Research guide' site at <genealogy.about.com>
- The Genealogy Gateway at <www.gengateway.com>
- Genealogy Links at <www.genealogylinks.net>
- The Genealogy Pages at <www.genealogypages.com>
- The Genealogy Portal at <www.genealogyportal.com>
- The Genealogy SiteFinder at <www.genealogy.com/genealogy/links/>
- I Found It! at <www.gensource.com/ifoundit/>.

Specialist gateways

There are also a number of gateways that are not specifically devoted to genealogy but which have links to sites of interest to genealogists. The National Maritime Museum's Port site at <www.port.nmm.ac.uk>, for example, has links to naval resources on the Web, which may be of interest to those with maritime ancestors. The same is true for several of the military sites mentioned in Chapter 11 – even those with no genealogical information may provide links to other military genealogy sites.

General directories

In addition to the specifically genealogical gateways discussed so far, the general directories of the Web also provide genealogical links. On the whole, anyone who is sufficiently interested in genealogy to be reading this book will probably find them less useful than the dedicated sites already mentioned, not least since they are not edited and maintained by people with expertise in the subject, and cannot aim to be comprehensive.

Yahoo
The best known and most widely used directory is Yahoo <www.yahoo.com>, which also has a UK version at <www.yahoo.co.uk>. This organises subjects in a hierarchical structure, and the main Genealogy area comes under History, itself a subsection of Humanities. However, companies that sell genealogy products will be found under the Business heading, and genealogy resources for individual countries will be found under the relevant country heading. The main page for genealogy is <www.yahoo.co.uk/Arts/Humanities/History/Genealogy>, but you can get a complete list of relevant Yahoo subject pages by doing a search on *genealogy*. There are, of course, many other areas of Yahoo which will have material of interest to a family historian. The list of genealogy categories on Yahoo is shown in Table 3.3.

Although Yahoo, like other directories and gateways, is selective, its basis of selection is not entirely satisfactory since it depends in part on submissions from web sites that want to be listed. This means the selection does not conform to a coherent policy, so, for example, Yahoo's Genealogy Organisations page lists the Northern Ireland Public Record

Office (PRONI) but equivalent bodies in other parts of the UK or the Republic of Ireland, including the National Archives, are not listed. Some family history societies are there, but only a small number.

Table 3.3 Genealogy categories on Yahoo UK <uk.dir.yahoo.com/arts/humanities/history/genealogy>

Beginners' Guides
Chats and Forums
   Mailing Lists
   Usenet
GEDCOM
Heraldry
Lineages and Surnames
   Family Reunions
   Irish Clans
   Publications for Sale
   Scottish Clans
   Web Directories
Magazines
Organisations
   PAF Users Groups
   Regional and Ethnic
      Australia
      British Isles
      Canada
      Germany
      Judaism
      United States
PAF
   User groups
Reference
   Cemeteries
   Census Records
   LDS Family History Centres
   Obituaries
   US Civil War Muster Rolls
Regional and Ethnic Resources
   Acadian
   Armenia
   Australia
   Belgium

Canada
Caribbean
Cuba
Czech Republic
France
Germany
Hispanic and Latino
India
Ireland
Italy
Native American
Netherlands
New Zealand
Poland
Religious
Russia
Scandinavia
Scotland
Sweden
Switzerland
Ukraine
United Kingdom
United States
Royal Genealogies
   European Royalty
Shopping and Services
   Databases
   Family History Publishers
   Heraldry & Name Histories
   Internet Services
   Publications
   Research
   Software
Tombstone Rubbing
Web Directories

The Open Directory Project

The Open Directory Project at <dmoz.org> is a non-commercial web directory, entirely maintained by volunteers. (Yahoo does not, of course, charge users, but it does carry advertising and give prominence on some pages to sponsored links). Genealogy comes under the heading of 'Society' at <dmoz.org/Society/Genealogy/>. The main category headings are:

- Adoption
- Chats and Forums
- Directories
- For Kids and Teens
- Heraldry
- Immigration
- Magazines and E-zines
- Medical
- Military
- Obituaries
- Organisations
- Personal Pages
- Products and Services
- Religions
- Resources
- Reunions
- Royalty
- Shopping
- Surnames
- Web Rings.

There is no UK version, and so the links for some of the categories have a US bias – 'immigration', for example, means immigration into the USA – but many of the other topics such as Heraldry or Software (under Products and Services) are of general relevance. Specifically UK material will be found at <dmoz.org/Regional/Europe/United_Kingdom/>.

4 Using On-line Sources

The aim of Chapters 5 to 8 is to look at what the internet holds in the way of primary source material, while Chapter 11 will look at topics of relevance for tracing particular ancestors – for example, military and emigration – and Chapters 12 to 14 examine non-genealogical material of interest to the family historian. This chapter discusses some of the general issues of using the internet for genealogical sources, and looks at the payment systems on the major commercial data services.

The core of any family history research in the British Isles is the information drawn from the 19th century registrations of births, marriages and deaths, and from the records of christenings, marriages and burials in parish registers starting in the 16th century. Linking these two sources are the census records, which enable an address from the period of civil registration to lead to a place and approximate year of birth in the time before registration. In addition, wills and memorial inscriptions, quite apart from providing additional information, can substitute for missing or untraceable death and burial records.

While the internet is the ideal way of making all this material widely available, particularly to those who are distant from the relevant repositories and major genealogical libraries, the fact is that a huge amount of work is involved in publishing such material on the Web. For example, there may have been as many as 100 million births, marriages and deaths registered between 1837 and 1900, and each census includes a record for every member of the population. Nonetheless, there are already some substantial data collections on-line, described in the following chapters. And in addition to transcriptions by individual genealogists on the Web, there are several large-scale non-commercial projects to put primary data on-line.

There are a number of ways in which such projects can be funded. Volunteer-run projects tend to rely entirely on goodwill and sponsorship, while a number of projects have public funding, usually from the Heritage Lottery Fund. In such cases, access to the data is normally free. Other data holders have taken three main routes to making material available on-line:

- Setting up an in-house data service (e.g. the FFHS's FamilyHistoryOnline site)
- Partnership with a commercial firm for a combined data service (e.g. Scotlandspeople or English Origins)

- Licensing of data to third parties (e.g. the 1891 census on Ancestry.com licensed from the National Archives).

Prior to the release of the 1901 census, there was considerable debate within the on-line genealogical community about the appropriateness of government agencies already funded by the tax-payer seeking income by charging for on-line access to public records. There was a feeling that the limited off-line availability of the 1901 census on microfiche, which cynics viewed simply as a move to safeguard on-line income, took insufficient account of the many people who were not computer-literate or had no internet access.[4]

Leaving aside the matter of principle, however, the fact is that progress on digitising the nation's historical records will be very much slower if it has to be done from existing funds – as if to prove the point, in 2002 Ancestry.com was able to start putting the 1891 census on-line (digitised from the microfilm) within a very short time of licensing it from the National Archives. And for most people the costs of using an on-line service will be very significantly less than the costs in time and travel of visiting a repository.

The issue of the connected being favoured over the non-connected will, presumably, become less significant as more and more homes go on-line and in view of the government's promotion of publicly available internet access. But it should not be forgotten that the traditional modes of access to records are also biased: they favour the mobile over those who are less so, and those who happen to live close to repositories.

Images, transcripts and indexes

There are three main ways in which any historical textual source can be represented digitally:

- As an image – the original document is scanned.
- In a transcription – the full text of a document is held in a file.
- As an index – a list of names, with or without other details, directs you to the relevant place in a transcription or to the relevant scanned image, or provides you with the full reference to an original document.

Ideally, an on-line index would lead to a full transcription of the relevant document, which could then be compared to an image of the original. But for material of any size this represents a very substantial investment in time and resources, and to date very little of the primary genealogical data is so

---

[4] In the event, the microfiche were made more widely available. You can follow part of the debate on the microfiche issue in the minutes of the 1901 Census Advisory Panel at <**www.pro.gov.uk/census/advisory.htm**>.

well served. In particular, because images take up much more disk space than text does, images of original documents are not yet very common on-line. Since a transcription takes so much more time to prepare than an index, and still requires an index to be of any use, indexes are by far the most common option on the internet.

This has important implications for how you use the internet for your research: you simply cannot do it all on-line. Except where you have access to scans of the original documents, all information derived from indexes or transcriptions will have to be checked against the original source.

The perfect index would be made by trained palaeographers, familiar with the names and places referred to and thoroughly at home with the handwriting of the period, working with original documents. Their work would be independently checked against the original, and where there was uncertainty as to the correct reading this would be clearly indicated. However, very little of the genealogical material on the Web has been transcribed in this way. The material on-line has been created either in large-scale projects or by individual genealogists, and often working from microfilms not original records. On large-scale projects the data are input by knowledgeable amateurs such as family history society members or by clerical workers. In the latter case, there will always be a question about the quality of data entry. It is self-evident that adequate levels of accuracy can only be achieved where there are good palaeographical skills, and knowledge of local place names and surnames.

The only area where one can expect a lower error rate is in the transcription of printed sources, such as trade directories, where problems of identifying names or individual letters are less great.

On a more positive note, it is worth remembering that although all indexes are subject to error, the great virtue of on-line indexes is that mistakes can be corrected. In printed or CD-ROM publications this can only be done if and when a subsequent edition is produced.

The upshot of this is that for many types of record the internet is best regarded as a finding aid, just like aids in a genealogical library, not as a substitute for a record office. And what is true of any transcription or index – that a failure to locate an individual does not permit you to draw negative inferences – is particularly true of large on-line projects.

Payment systems

There are major data collections such as FreeBMD and FamilySearch which do not charge for access to their material, and there are smaller free collections which are maintained by volunteer efforts or have some source of public funding. But it is increasingly the case that there is a charge for access to larger datasets. There are three basic ways of paying for this: subscription, pay-per-view, and on-line shop.

The subscription model is in fact not widely used. The reason for this is that it requires people to pay a flat fee up front regardless of how much data they end up using. The only major data service to use this is Ancestry.com at <**www.ancestry.com**>, which can do so because it has an enormously wide range of datasets, which no genealogist is likely to exhaust quickly. Another subscription-based service is Otherdays at <**www.otherdays.com**> which has a very diverse collection of Irish sources.

In pay-per-view systems you pay, in principle, for each item of data viewed. However, it is difficult to collect small amounts of money via credit and debit cards and tedious for users to complete a new financial transaction for every record they want to view. Therefore, all such systems require you to purchase a block of 'units' in advance, which are then used up one at a time. Sometimes these are only available in discrete amounts, and work with either real or virtual vouchers for round sums of money; sometimes you must pay a minimum charge up-front, and at the end of your session a higher charge is made if you have viewed more data than is covered by the minimum. There is usually a time limit, which means you could have units unused at the end of your session. You won't be able to claim a refund, but in some cases you can carry forward unused portions of a payment to a subsequent session.

In an on-line shop, whether it's for genealogical data or for physical products, you add items to a virtual 'shopping basket' until you have everything you want, and pay for all of them. in a single transaction at a virtual 'checkout'. Only then can you download the data you have paid for. Such a procedure would make little sense for individual data entries, but is a good way of delivering entire electronic documents, so it is ideal for the wills available from DocumentsOnline or ScottishDocuments (see Chapter 8). It also allows items to be priced individually, though these two services in fact charge at a flat rate.

An overview of the current charges and facilities for the major commercial data services in the UK is shown in Table 4.1.

Major data collections

The following chapters cover the various types of record and look at sites relevant for each. But there are a number of commercial sites which have datasets for a variety of different records and these are discussed here for convenience.

English Origins
The English Origins site at <www.englishorigins.com> went live at the end of 2000. It contains data from the collections of the SoG, and the on-line service is run by Origins.net. The complete list of datasets either already available or in preparation is:

● Marriage Licence Allegations Index 1694–1850 (670,000 names)

Table 4.1 Commercial on-line genealogy data services in the UK (prices and facilities as of summer 2003)

Service	URL	Type Of System	Minimum Charge	Index Cost	Transcription	Document Image	Duration	Carried Forward
1837online	<www.1837online.com>	credit card	£5 for 50 units	free	–	10p	min. 45 days	yes
1901 census	<www.census.pro.gov.uk>	voucher/credit card	£5	free	50p	75p per page	48 hours	voucher only
DocumentsOnline	<www.documentsonline.pro.gov.uk>	shop	none	free	–	£3 per document	–	–
English Origins	<www.englishorigins.com>	credit card + shop	£6 for 150 units	1 unit per entry	–	£10 per document (postal service)	7 days	yes
FamilyHistoryOnline	<www.familyhistoryonline.net>	voucher/credit card	£5 voucher	free	<10p	–	6 months	no
Scotlandspeople	<www.scotlandspeople.gov.uk>	credit card	£6 for 30 units	1 unit per page (max. 25 entries)	–	5 units per page or £10 per document (postal service)	48 hours	yes
ScottishDocuments	<www.scottishdocuments.com>	shop	none	free	–	£5 per document	–	–

Type of System:

voucher   prepayment by physical voucher
credit card   prepayment on-line by credit card
shop   payment at end of session

- Bank of England Will Extracts Index 1717–1845 (61,000 names)
- Archdeaconry Court of London Wills Index 1750–1800 (5,000 names)
- London Consistory Court Depositions Index 1700–1717 (3,200 names)
- London City Apprenticeship Abstracts 1442–1850 (300,000 names)
- Prerogative Court of Canterbury Wills 1750–1800 (208,000 records)
- Boyd's Marriage Index 1538–1837 (over 6 million records)
- Apprentices of Great Britain 1710–74 (over 600,000 records)
- Boyd's Inhabitants of London 14th–19th centuries (60,000 families)
- Boyd's London Burials (50,000 names).

The first five are already on-line in their entirety at the time of writing. Boyd's Marriage Index, with its six million records, is probably the most significant on-line data collection for England after the 1901 census, and will take some time to complete. The counties with the most substantial coverage in the Index are already available, and the remainder should be on-line by the end of 2003. The datasets on English Origins will mostly be of use to those who have already got some way with their pedigree, as the records only go up to the mid-19th century, but the range of London records makes this site invaluable to those with ancestors from the city.

English Origins is a pay-per-view site. Each payment of the £6 charge gives you access to a maximum of 150 records within a seven-day period. Once you have used your allocation you can pay for a new session, but if you do not use your allowance of 150 records any 'unused' units will be added to the next batch of units you buy. Members of the SoG have one free session per quarter. Before paying, however, you can do initial searches on surname and year range to see how many records there are in each database which contain the surname.

Once you have purchased credits, you can search in individual datasets or across the entire collection. If you do the latter, you will get a screen like that in Figure 4.1, which indicates how many records were found in each dataset. You can then view the results for a single dataset, or refine your search.

Figure 4.2 shows the results of a search in the Bank of England Wills. In this case, since a will is a substantial document, you cannot read the will itself on-line but must order a hard copy from the SoG, so the search results give you only the basic details.

In other cases, such as the City of London Apprentices, most of the genealogically significant information is given in the results (see Figure 4.3).

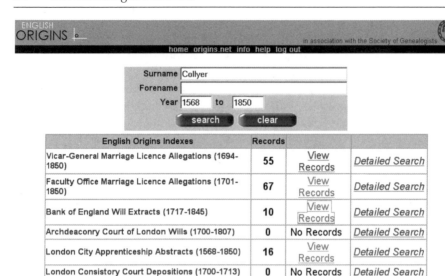

Figure 4.1 General search in EnglishOrigins at <www.englishorigins.com>

Bank of England Will Extracts index: search results

new search?   return to main search page   view images of sample original documents

Surname **Collyer**
Forename
Year **1568** to **1850**

If you are ordering a hard copy of a document, please make a note of the Order Number (on the order button). This number should be quoted in case of any problem.

Description	Book	Date	Reg	Film	Order Extract
COLLYER Andrew. Coach Master of Farnham,Surrey	47 A-I	1836	9934		Order 1006033
COLLYER Ann. Widow of Manchester St,Manchester Sq	37 A-I	1831	7925		Order 1006034
COLLYER Edward. Gent of Church Court,Strand	25 A-I	1826	5518		Order 1006035
COLLYER John Weaver of Covent Garden	5	1760-74	2482	63/2	Order 0005741
COLLYER John. Tailor of Guildford,Surrey	8 A-K	1812	2353		Order 1006036
COLLYER Joseph. Gent of Grays Inn Rd	31 A-I	1828	6606		Order 1006037
COLLYER Margaret Widow of Homerton Hackney	30	1777-81	4442	59/4	Order 0005742
COLLYER Nathaniel. Esq of Park Pl,St James's St	13 A-I	1819	2670		Order 1006038
COLLYER Samuel Carpenter of Crutched	33	1763-1804	390	60/4	Order 0005743

Figure 4.2 Search results in the Bank of England wills at EnglishOrigins

Description
Christian David, son of David, Spitalfields, Middlesex, turner, to William Cowley, 7 Feb 1722/3, Distillers' Company
Christian James, son of James, Old Street (St Luke), Middlesex, labourer, to James Budgen, 10 Apr 1790 [free], Curriers' Company
Christian John, son of Edward, Christ in Aire, Isle of Man, clothier, to Samuel Gunn, 19 Jul 1693 [19 Feb 1694 discharged] Coachmakers' and Coach Harness Makers' Company
Christian Twigden, son of Hugh, Spratton, Northamptonshire, tailor, to Thomas Kente, 13 Jul 1620, Farriers' Company
Christian William, son of Anthony, St Clement Danes, Middlesex, to Joseph Garth, 18 Jun 1772, Coachmakers' and Coach Harness Makers' Company

Figure 4.3 Search results in the apprenticeship records at EnglishOrigins

FamilyHistoryOnline

FamilyHistoryOnline at <www.familyhistoryonline.net> is the data service of the Federation of Family History Societies, which went live at the beginning of 2003. It offers data transcribed by FFHS member societies. The types of record indexed are:

- marriages
- burials (data from the National Burial Index published on CD-ROM)
- monumental inscriptions
- census records.

A full list of datasets is available on the site at <www.familyhistoryonline. net/database/>.

A search of the indexes is free of charge, though you need to log in with a username and password (free) to access the search facility. When you do a search, this provides you with a list of matching entries with details of the dataset in which the match was found and the year of the event (see Figure 4.4). In order to view full entries, you need either to have bought a physical pre-payment voucher (£5 or £10), or you can buy a virtual voucher on-line (£5, £10, £20 or £50). Both types of voucher are valid for six months – in the case of the physical vouchers this means six months from first use.

The charge is made for each individual item retrieved and depends on the nature of the data, as shown in Table 4.2. As you can see from Figure 4.4, on the search results pages the cost of every item is indicated individually.

Table 4.2 FamilyHistoryOnline charges (summer 2003)

indexes	surname only	3p
	other	5p
transcriptions	general	7p
	census from 1851 onwards	
	marriages from July 1837 onwards	9p

Any records not yet checked by the database provider cost 1p less in each case.

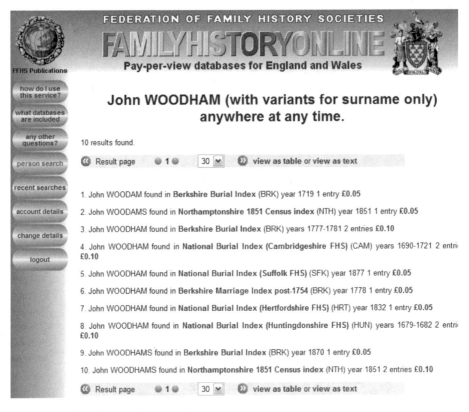

Figure 4.4 Search results in FamilyHistoryOnline

Scotlandspeople

The Scottish civil registration indexes were the first genealogical records in the UK to be put on-line by a government agency, when ScotsOrigins opened its electronic doors in 1998 to provide the data on behalf of GROS. In 2002, the contract for the on-line service was awarded to Scotland Online, who now provide it on the Scotlandspeople site at <**www. scotlandspeople.gov.uk**>. The site makes the following data available:

- Old parish registers from 1553
- Birth, marriage and deaths from 1855 to 1902 or later
- Census records for 1881, 1891 and 1901.

A more detailed description of what material is available for each of these classes of record will be found in the sections on civil registration (p. 56), census (p. 69) and parish registers (p. 76). Work on these data collections is ongoing – all should be available in index form by the time you read this, and the remaining census records are planned for 2004. All index entries will eventually link to images of the original records. Many of these images are already available and the process is due to be completed by early 2004.

This is a pay-per-view system and you purchase access in blocks of 30 credits for £6. An initial search is free of charge, but this only tells you how many hits your search produces. Each page of search results costs you one unit and includes a maximum of 25 entries. For the births and deaths, there is then an option to view an image of the original register page at a cost of five credits. For all events you can order a copy of the relevant certificate for £10. This is paid for separately and does not come out of your pre-paid units. A session lasts 48 hours, timed from when you last bought credits, and any unused units bought are automatically carried forward to a subsequent session. Access to the 1881 census index, incidentally, is free of charge.

The site keeps a record of all search result pages and certificates that you have paid to view and these can be retrieved at any time, not just during the session in which they were first accessed. You therefore don't need to pay to return to the site to review material you have already paid for.

The images are delivered as TIFF format files which are displayed in a special viewer plug-in, which requires Java to be installed on your computer (see p. 43). Images can be enlarged or printed direct from the viewer, and you can save them to your hard disk. TIFF is a standard graphics format, so you should be able to display, manipulate and print the files with any graphics program. Note that the images are black and white,

Figure 4.5 Search results in Scotlandspeople

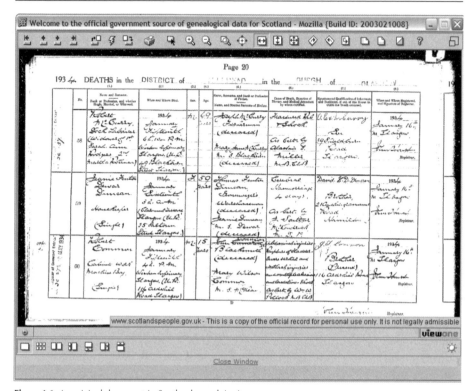

Figure 4.6 An original document in Scotlandspeople's viewer

not greyscale like photographs, and some of the poorer quality originals can be hard to read, particularly as they are scanned at only 200 dots per inch.

The site offers a range of discussion groups with general advice on using the system, hints and tips for the individual types of record, and discussion of technical problems.

On its launch, Scotlandspeople faced a number of problems and met with a great deal of criticism from users. Apart from technical teething problems one might expect for any new system, notably with the payment system, users reported inconsistent search results, missing images, and concern about image quality. Improvements have been made since the launch and a user group has been set up to offer feedback from users and advise on future developments. The minutes for this can be found by looking in the Announcements bulletin board (the first minutes are under February 2003).

Ancestry.com

The Ancestry.com web site <www.ancestry.com> is the largest commercial collection of genealogical data. It holds over 2,000 separate datasets, many of them derived from printed materials which may be more or less difficult to find outside a major genealogical library. For genealogists in the British Isles, however, the UK version of Ancestry at <**www.ancestry.co.uk**> is more convenient as it contains only those records relating to the British Isles or emigrants from them, such as the Australian Convicts Index. For Americans with UK ancestors, there is a subscription option at the main site which includes both US and UK records.

Among the records for the British Isles are:

- Parish register extracts for all counties
- Pallot's Baptism and Marriage Indexes
- 1891 census for England and Wales (currently in progress)
- a number of historic books.

Although Ancestry is a commercial service, some of the material is free of charge (for example, FreeBMD's GRO index data is available here as well as on FreeBMD's own web site). On the main site, there are often free offers where a database which is normally only for subscribers can be accessed free for a limited period (usually a couple of weeks).

The easiest way to see if Ancestry has anything of interest is simply to search across all databases for a particular name, from the search box on the front page (Figure 4.7). You can then inspect more detailed listings.

Figure 4.7 Ancestry UK home page

Figure 4.8 shows an expanded listing with details of the individual databases containing the name George Sealey, along with the number of references in each. Those accompanied by a padlock icon require an Ancestry subscription, while those with a page icon are free and could be looked at immediately. There is also a form at the foot of the page to narrow down your search if you are overwhelmed by the initial numbers of hits. Note that Ancestry is not a pay-per-view system, and a quarterly or annual subscription provides access to *all* paid databases. The subscriptions for UK material as of summer 2003 are £29.95 for a quarter, or £69.95 for a year. The main site has a range of subscription options covering various combinations of the available datasets.

A full list of databases available on Ancestry can be found at <www.ancestry.com/search/rectype/alldblist.asp>, while <www.ancestry.co.uk/search/rectype/alldblist.asp> lists only those for the British Isles.

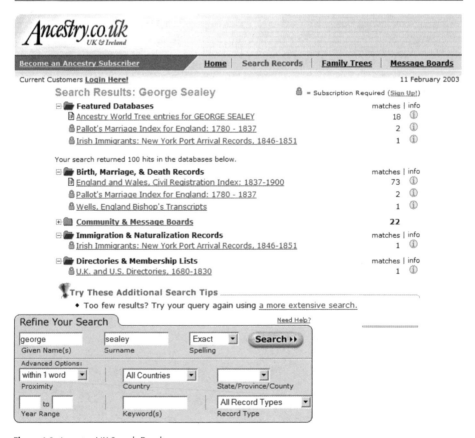

Figure 4.8 Ancestry UK Search Results

Common problems

It is not uncommon for users to experience problems with commercial genealogy sites, as indeed with all e-commerce sites. This is nothing to do with the security concerns people have about on-line payments, which are addressed in Chapter 18, but relate to the web browser and how it is configured. While it is not possible here to cover every eventuality, most of these problems arise from a readily identifiable set of facilities used by commercial web sites, and are more or less straightforward to solve. Sites that use such facilities usually provide information on what is required – see for example the National Archives 'Technical Information' page for DocumentsOnline at **<www.documentsonline.pro.gov.uk/help/ help-technical.asp>** – and you should normally see a warning if some required facility is absent from your configuration (see Figure 4.9).

The main features which cause problems are:

Cookies

A 'cookie' is a piece of information a web site stores on your hard disk for its own future use. This is how a site can 'remember' who you are from one visit to the next – even if you are using a different ISP – or even during a single session.[5] However, browsers can be configured to reject cookies, and some people do this to preserve their internet privacy. This will make pay-per-view sites and on-line shops unusable – in fact any site that requires some sort of login will only work with cookies enabled. See **<www.documentsonline.pro.gov.uk/help/help-technical. asp#cookies>** for information on how to enable cookies.

JavaScript

This is a scripting language which, among other things, makes it possible for a web page to validate what the user enters in an on-line form (checking, for example, that you haven't left some crucial field blank) before the information is submitted to the server. You will be unable to use sites that require this if JavaScript is disabled. The on-line help for your browser should tell you how to check whether JavaScript is enabled, and how to ensure it is. Most sites that require it will also give instructions.

Java

Java is a programming language which allows programs (called 'applets', i.e. small applications) to run on any type of computer as long

---

[5] It may appear to you to be a single session, but it is not like a phone call where a line is allocated exclusively to you for the duration of your call. On the Web, each page requested from the server is a completely separate transaction, and cookies are the main way of identifying continuity.

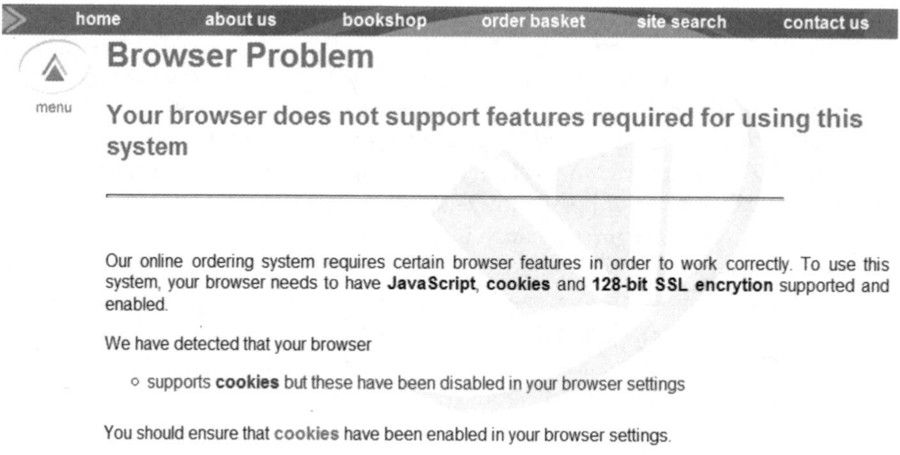

Figure 4.9 A typical browser warning. This one is from the National Archives' on-line shop.

as it has software installed which can understand the language. This allows for programmable web sites. Java facilities (referred to as a 'Java virtual machine') are normally installed and enabled automatically when you install a new browser, but can be disabled. Individual web sites will then download their own applets to your machine – you will often see a grey box saying 'loading' in the browser window while an applet is being downloaded. The on-line help for your browser should tell you how to check whether Java is enabled, and how to ensure it is.

Plug-ins

A 'plug-in' is a small utility program which a web browser uses to display material which it can't handle with its own built-in facilities. A number of plug-ins are fairly standard (for example, Flash, QuickTime, and Shockwave) and may well be on your machine already. But some pay-per-view sites have their own plug-ins for viewing images of documents – this is the case for the 1901 census, Scotlandspeople and 1837online sites. A plug-in needs to be downloaded before it can be run. This will usually take significantly longer than a normal web page to download. Plug-ins sometime also require Java, as on the 1901 census site.

Compatibility

Although the Web is based on open standards, browsers do not all implement these as fully and consistently as they might. Also, some web site designers insist on using features that only work properly on a particular browser (usually Internet Explorer, as that is the most popular). The only way around problems from this source is to have a recent version of your preferred browser and, if that is not Internet

Explorer, a copy of that too. Since all the main browsers can be downloaded free, there's no real reason not to have the latest version, unless your computer is running an old operating system or has limited memory or disk space.

If you have any difficulties with on-line data services, there will always be a variety of help available. Sites selling data should always have a help page, and perhaps a technical help page which spells out hardware and/or software requirements. You are very likely to find a FAQ ('Frequently Asked Questions') page. As a last resort there should always be an e-mail address to contact for assistance and there may also be a telephone helpline.

Incidentally, for a commercial, official or major volunteer-run site, it is a good idea to mail the webmaster if you find that it doesn't display properly in your browser. All government sites should conform to the government's own browser compatibility standards (see 'Guidelines for UK government websites', available in various formats from **<www.e-envoy.gov.uk/ Resources/WebGuidelines/fs/en>**).

5 On-line Sources: Civil Registration

Birth, marriage and death certificates are generally the first official documents the family historian encounters. In an ideal world – for the genealogist at least – all of them would be on-line. But of course privacy concerns make it unlikely that more recent certificates, those which relate to people who may still be living, will ever be freely accessible in this way. Only a small pecentage of the 'historical' certificates are actually on-line so far – those from Scotland – but many of the indexes *are* available on the Web; and there is much information about civil registration, even if you still have to buy most certificates in the traditional way.

England and Wales

Civil registration of births, marriages and deaths started in England and Wales on 1 July 1837, and the original certificates are held in duplicate by the original local register office and by the General Register Office (GRO). The original certificates cannot be seen (for reasons which have been questioned, though not yet legally challenged), but copies can be ordered from the Family Records Centre (FRC). Indexes to the certificates can be consulted at the FRC and on microfiche in county record offices and other genealogical libraries.

The FamilyRecords portal has basic information on birth, marriage and death certificates at <**www.familyrecords.gov.uk/topics/bmd.htm**>: it explains how to get certificates and what information is on each of them. FamilyRecords also hosts the web site of the FRC at <**www.familyrecords. gov.uk/frc/**> (see Figure 5.1) which provides details of its location and opening hours, as well as the records and indexes the FRC holds. The GRO web site at <**www.statistics.gov.uk/registration/general_register. asp**> has comprehensive information about ordering certificates. There is also information about adoptions and overseas records.

Neither the FRC nor the GRO have a data service, and they do not provide on-line access to birth, marriage and death indexes or certificates. However, in July 2003 the GRO launched a trial on-line service for ordering certificates at <**www.col.statistics.gov.uk**> (this covers only England and Wales).

Beyond the FRC, there are a number of unofficial sources of information on general registration and these are probably more helpful for initial orientation. Genuki has a page devoted to civil registration in England and Wales at <**www.genuki.org.uk/big/eng/civreg/**>. Barbara

Welcome to The Family Records Centre website

You can use **access keys** to navigate around this site - use **access key** 0 for the list.

The Family Records Centre (FRC) is jointly run by the **General Register Office** (GRO) and **The National Archives** (NA).

The FRC provides access to some of the most important sources for family history research in England and Wales, including births, marriages and deaths and census returns. This site will help you to plan your **visit** to the FRC with information to help you with your **research**. You can also keep up to date with all the **news** from the FRC and read the latest edition of our quarterly newsletter the *Family Record*.

For information about other UK archives visit the **familyrecords.gov.uk** website.

We hope that you find the site useful and easy to use. Please send your comments to the **webmaster**.

Is the text too small or large for you? You can change the size using the "View" menu in your browser.

All the information on this site is © Crown Copyright 2002. Please read this important information about the **terms of use** for this website.

New This Month

We're Talking To You - a full programme of **talks at the FRC** aimed at helping you with your research is now under way...

 More...

The National Archives

On 2 April 2003 the Public Record Office and the Historical Manuscripts Commission joined forces to become the **National Archives**. the national archives

 More...

Figure 5.1 Family Records Centre home page

Dixon's Registration Web Page at **<home.clara.net/dixons/Certificates/ indexbd.htm>** describes how to order certificates and gives a detailed description of the fields on the three types of certificate. Overseas readers may find it useful to look at Mark Howells' article 'Ordering Birth Registration Certificates from England and Wales. Using the LDS Family History Center's Resources' at **<www.oz.net/~markhow/ukbirths.htm>**.

Register offices and registration districts

Even though, for England and Wales, you will not find certificates on-line, there are some useful on-line resources relating to registration districts which may help in searching the indexes.

For historical information about registration districts, Genuki has a set of pages prepared by Brett Langston at **<www.fhsc.org.uk/genuki/reg/>** which provide details of every registration district in each English or Welsh county, giving:

- Name of the district.
- Date of creation.
- Date of abolition (if before 1930).
- Names of the sub-districts.
- The GRO volume number used for the district in the national indexes of births, marriages and deaths.
- An alphabetical listing of the parishes, townships and hamlets included within its boundaries. If a district covered parts of two or more counties, the areas in each county are listed separately.

- The name(s) of the district(s) which currently hold the records. If two or more offices are listed, the one which holds most records is named first, and the one with least is given last.

There is an alphabetical list of districts at <**www.fhsc.org.uk/genuki/reg/ district.htm**>, and if you are not sure what registration district a particular place is in, consult <**www.genuki.org.uk/big/eng/civreg/places/index.htm**>. FreeBMD has information on the relation between volume/page numbers and registration districts at <**www.freebmd.org.uk/DistrictInfo.html**>.

The names and current contact details of individual register offices will also be found on Genuki, at <**www.genuki.org.uk/big/eng/RegOffice/**>, though this list does not link to the web sites of register offices which have an on-line presence. However, although the site of the Office for National Statistics (ONS) does not have a complete on-line list of register offices it does provide links to those that have web sites at <**www.statistics.gov.uk/ nsbase/registration/LocalServices.asp**>. The ONS site has detailed information about registering present-day births, marriages and deaths at <**www. statistics.gov.uk/nsbase/registration/default.asp**>. Application forms for copies of certificates can be downloaded from this site in Adobe Acrobat format from <**www.statistics.gov.uk/nsbase/registration/certificates.asp**>.

FreeBMD

In the absence of any official programme to digitise either the original certificates or the GRO indexes, in 1999 the ONS gave a volunteer project called FreeBMD permission to digitise the indexes over 100 years old for free on-line access. More recently, the GRO has announced a broader general policy – any organisation which has purchased the microfiche indexes is now free to digitise them and make them available on-line, free or charged, and the more recent indexes are no longer excluded.[6]

FreeBMD has a large group of volunteers, currently around 6,000, who either transcribe the indexes from microfiche in planned extractions or simply submit entries from their own extractions along with the surrounding entries. It has two sites: <**www.freebmd.org.uk**> is the home site and there is also a mirror on RootsWeb at <freebmd.rootsweb.com>.

By summer 2003, the project's database had reached over 50 million entries. The pattern of extractions has concentrated on marriages, with smaller percentages of births and deaths, and for many years the extraction of marriages is already complete. Since the relaxation of the 100-year restriction is relatively recent, FreeBMD's material is overwhelmingly for the period before 1903, though it will be extended to 1983 in due course.

---

[6] The GRO's announcement was posted (unofficially) to the soc.genealogy.britain newsgroup on 13 February 2003 under the heading 'GRO Indexes – England & Wales' and can be found in the archive of the GENBRIT mailing list at <archiver. rootsweb.com/th/index/GENBRIT/2003-02> or on Google groups at <groups. google.com>.

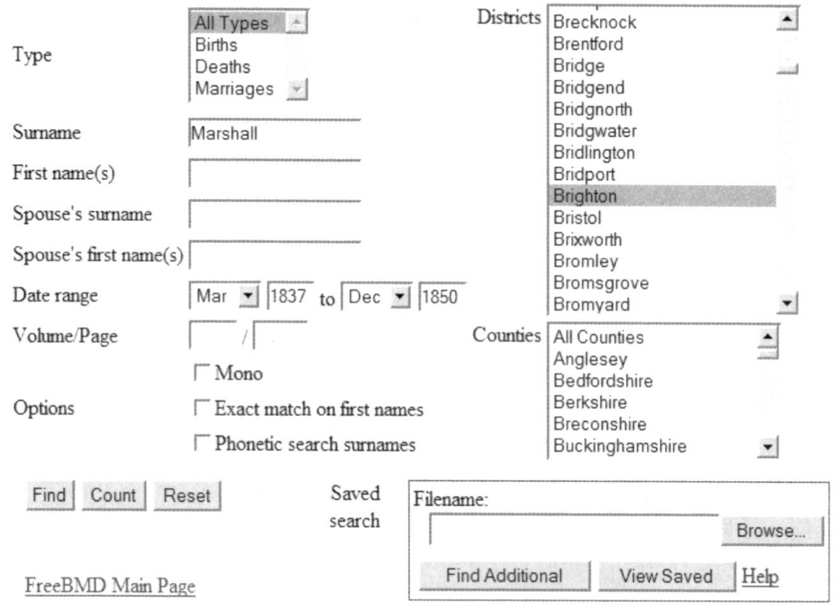

Figure 5.2 Searching FreeBMD

Up-to-date information on the percentage of coverage for each year and each type of event will be found at <freebmd.rootsweb.com/progress. shtml>. At the current rate of progress, it looks as if the 19th century part of the project will be complete by the end of 2005.

The material so far collected can be searched on-line. A comprehensive search page (Figure 5.2) allows you to search for a specific person in a chosen place and date range, or to extract all the entries for a particular surname. Figure 5.2 shows a search for all events for the surname Marshall in the Brighton registration district between 1837 and 1850. Figure 5.3 shows the results of this search. Clicking on the links in the district column will take you to information on the registration district, while following the link in the page column brings up a list of all the events on that page in the original register (*not* the index). Note that the contributor's contact details are provided only for error reporting, and you cannot expect to contact the contributor for full details of the event, since he or she has only looked at the index, not the original certificates. You will need to order any certificate yourself.

A very useful feature is the ability to save a search and re-run it at any time. When you repeat a saved search, you see only new records that have been added since you saved.

FreeBMD is always looking for new volunteers, and details of what is involved can be found on the web site. You can keep up to date with the progress of the project by joining the FreeBMD-News-L mailing list –

| Search for | *Type:* All Types | *Surname:* Marshall | *Start date:* Mar 1837 |
| | *End date:* Dec 1850 | *District:* Brighton | |

Whilst FreeBMD makes every effort to ensure accurate transcription, errors exist in both the original index and the transcription. You are advised to verify the reference given from a copy of the index before ordering a certificate.

Surname	First name(s)	Age	District	Vol	Page	
		Deaths Sep 1837				
Marshall	Eliza		Brighton	7	170	[Info]
Marshall	John		Brighton	7	172	[Info]
		Deaths Dec 1837				
Marshall	Elizabeth		Brighton	7	185	[Info]
		Deaths Jun 1838				
Marshall	Ellen		Brighton	7	19[8]	[Info]
		Marriages Jun 1838				
MARSHALL	John Goddard		Brighton	7	303	[Info]

Figure 5.3 FreeBMD search results

subscription information will be found at <lists.rootsweb.com/index/intl/UK/FreeBMD-News.html>.

1837online

1837online is a commercial site which went live in April 2003 at <www.1837online.com> offering *all* the GRO indexes apart from the most recent 18 months. The material is provided simply as images of the original paper indexes – they are taken from the microfiche – and there is no index of individual entries. You use the index to locate the page on which a given name, alphabetically, should occur. Since this is based on the original index letters at the head of each page it is only accurate to the first three letters of a surname. It may therefore require some guesswork to select the precise place where a particular name occurs if the first three letters are found in many other names. Of course, if entries for a name run across a page boundary, you may need to look at both pages, as I discovered when looking for 'Christian' in the pages for the March quarter of 1900 listed in Figure 5.4.

18		37
FAMILY RESEARCH LINK		
The Key To Family History		

| log off |
| search 1837 to 1983 |
| search 1984 to date |
| browse 1837 to 1983 |
| buy units |
| site tour |
| my account |
| order a certificate |
| download DjVu viewer |
| help |
| home page |
| about us |

THE DEFINITIVE LIST SINCE 1837

Search Results   PRINT

Marriages from Jan-Feb-Mar 1900 to Oct-Nov-Dec 1901 for surname CHR

Quarter	Year	Surname range	Number of pages	
Jan-Feb-Mar	1900	CHA-CHR	1	View
Jan-Feb-Mar	1900	CHR-CLA	1	View
Apr-May-Jun	1900	CHO-CLA	3	View
Jul-Aug-Sep	1900	CHE-CHR	1	View
Oct-Nov-Dec	1900	CHE-CHR	1	View
Oct-Nov-Dec	1900	CHR-CLA	3	View
Jan-Feb-Mar	1901	CHE-CLA	2	View
Apr-May-Jun	1901	CHE-CHU	1	View
Jul-Aug-Sep	1901	CHI-CHU	1	View
Oct-Nov-Dec	1901	CHE-CHU	1	View

Redefine Current Search   Start New Search

Figure 5.4 Initial search at 1837online

However, the material from 1984 onwards is rather different, since the GRO has electronic records from this date: 1837online offers this in a proper searchable database, and you use a search form to locate an individual entry rather than an index page.

The site operates a pay-per-view system. There are various rates depending on how many units you buy at a time. The basic rate is £5 for 50 page views, but heavier users get discounted rates of £60 for 800 and £120 for 2,400 page views. Units are valid for 45 days, unless bought in the larger blocks, in which case they are valid for a year.

A special plug-in, DjVu, needs to be downloaded and installed before any images can be viewed. This allows you to zoom in and out, print and save the images to hard disk (see Figure 5.5). However, the DjVu image format does not seem to be widely supported by graphics programs, so you may not easily be able to edit the saved images.

Local BMD projects

While FreeBMD and 1837online are national in coverage, there are a growing number of projects centred on local register offices. These will be useful if your family comes from one of the parts of the country covered. An important difference between these local projects and FreeBMD, is that they work from the local copies of the original certificates and so should be free of some of the errors that dog the GRO indexes used by FreeBMD.

The first of these projects was CheshireBMD at <**cheshirebmd.org.uk**>, a collaboration between Cheshire County Council, Wirral Metropolitan Borough, the Family History Society of Cheshire and South Cheshire

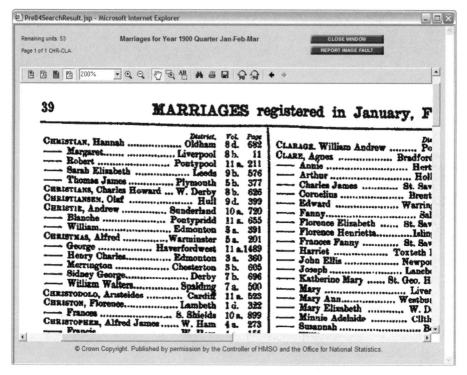

Figure 5.5 A page from the GRO indexes in the DjVu viewer at 1837online

Family History Society. This aims to have all index entries for births, marriages and deaths on-line for the period 1837–1950. The site has detailed information on the coverage so far for each registration district, and makes the ordering of certificates very straightforward – a link from each search result brings up a form for printing off, with the certificate reference (though not the other details) already filled in. The site already has over 2.5 million entries available for searching.

So far three similar projects have taken a lead from the example of Cheshire, and use the same web site design and software:

- YorkshireBMD at <www.yorkshirebmd.org.uk> has around 2 million entries to date.
- LancashireBMD at <www.lancashirebmd.org.uk> contains around 240,000 records, only marriages so far.
- StaffordshireBMD at <www.staffordshirebmd.org.uk> has around 400,000 records, concentrating on births and marriages.

A NorthWalesBMD project is in the pipeline.

Some other local authorities are developing indexes on similar lines in partnership with local family history societies:

Figure 5.6 CheshireBMD at <www.cheshirebmd.org.uk>

- Middlesbrough Indexes covers the register offices of the former county of Cleveland (now replaced by Middlesbrough, Stockton-on-Tees, Redcar & Cleveland, and Hartlepool) and can be found at <**www.middlesbrough-indexes.co.uk**>.
- Cambridgeshire County Council's CAMDEX project at <**www.cambridgeshire.gov.uk/sub/register/cambsindex.htm**> has over 800,000 records, mainly births and marriages.
- Durham County Council has an on-line certificate ordering system based on an index of over 375,000 births and 1.1 million marriages at <**www.durham.gov.uk/DurhamCC/usp.nsf/pws/Registrar+-+purchase+of+registration+certificates**>.

Kent County Council has on-line ordering of certificates at <**extranet.kent.gov.uk/coldfusion/cs/rois/home.html**>.

Links to all local BMD projects will be found on Ian Hartas' UKBMD site at <**www.ukbmd.org.uk**>.

Mike Foster's transcriptions
Mike Foster has created a range of index transcriptions which are available on Genuki:

- Selective transcriptions for South-East England (Suffolk, Essex, East London).
- A complete transcription for the March quarter of 1849.
- Transcription for the year 1856 (ongoing).

- Entries missing from the published indexes: 1856, 1858 and 1861.

Information about this material and links to it will be found on Genuki at <**www.cs.ncl.ac.uk/genuki/StCathsTranscriptions/**>.

Mike Foster is the author of two books about the inaccuracy of the current indexes, *A Comedy of Errors* and *A Comedy of Errors, Act 2*, details of which will be found on his web site at <**homepages.paradise. net.nz/mikefost/**>.

Certificate exchange

The UK BDM Exchange at <**www.ukbdm.org.uk**> is the only project that offers access to the information on certificates without the need to order them. The exchange is a forum for people who have certificates to post the basic details so that others can contact them for more information. Each entry gives surname, forename, town and county, along with the e-mail address of the submitter who must be contacted for details of the information on the certificate. It also indicates any certificates unwanted by their owners and therefore available for purchase. The site includes some material for baptisms, marriages and burials from parish registers. It offers details of over 40,000 events on the site. Incidentally, HMSO forbids the publication of scanned copies of certificates on the Web.[7]

Future developments

While the GRO has relaxed controls over putting the registration indexes on-line, an obvious question is whether England and Wales will be following Scotland (see below) in putting the primary data on-line. The answer would seem to be yes and no: there are no plans for an official data service for civil registration records in England and Wales, but other organisations will be permitted to digitise the 'historical records', which in this case means those relating to people born more than 100 years ago. However, the registration process is to go electronic itself, and the more recent records will be digitised for use by the registration service and government departments. This is the proposal in a government white paper *Civil Registration: Vital Change*, published in January 2002, which is on-line at <**www.statistics.gov.uk/registration/whitepaper/**>.

The freeing up of older records for digitisation is entirely welcome, but the white paper also raises matters of some considerable concern to genealogists. In particular, it proposes to restrict access to some items of information on non-historical certificates. As a result it has been the object of vigorous (and more or less unanimous) criticism both on-line and in print from the whole genealogical community.

A summary of the proposals has been published by the Federation of

---

[7] 'Guidance on the Copying of Birth, Death and Marriage Certificates', HMSO Guidance Note No. 7, on-line at <**www.hmso.gov.uk/copyright/guidance/gn_07.htm**>.

Family History Societies on its web site at <**www.ffhs.org.uk/Societies/ Liaison/WhitePaper.htm**> and details of what information will become restricted are at <**www.ffhs.org.uk/Societies/Liaison/AnnexC.htm**>. For the general reaction to the proposals and reports from some of the consultation meetings, refer to the archives of the GENBRIT mailing list at <**archiver.rootsweb.com/th/index/GENBRIT**>, particularly messages for January and February 2002 (look for the words 'civil registration' in the message subject). Both the FFHS and the SoG have published their own responses to the white paper on-line, the SoG's being at <**www.sog.org.uk/ files/cm5355response1.html** >.

Scotland

In Scotland, general registration dates from 1 January 1855. The web site of the General Register Office for Scotland (GROS) at <**www.gro-scotland.gov.uk**> is the official on-line source of information about these records.

Genuki's 'Introduction to Scottish Family History' at <**www.genuki. org.uk/big/sct/intro.html**> has information on civil registration in Scotland, and GROS has a page 'How can GROS help me research my Scottish ancestors?' at <**www.gro-scotland.gov.uk/grosweb/grosweb.nsf/pages/hlpsrch**>. GROS also has a list of local register offices with contact details at <**www. gro-scotland.gov.uk/grosweb/grosweb.nsf/pages/file1/$file/reglist.pdf** >.

Figure 5.7 The General Register Office for Scotland home page at <www.gro-scotland.gov.uk>

The situation with the Scottish general registration records is much better than that for England and Wales. Currently, the older indexes to births, marriages and deaths are available, along with images of the birth and death certificates, via the pay-per-view system at Scotlandspeople described in the following section.

Not all certificates can be viewed or ordered on-line, and for those that cannot, the GROS web site provides ordering information at <**www.gro-scotland.gov.uk/grosweb/grosweb.nsf/pages/bdm**>. Alternatively, Scots Origins (see below) allows you to order transcriptions of more recent certificates on-line. However, no index information is available on-line for more recent certificates, and you will need to establish the correct entry by referring to the microfilm indexes held in genealogy libraries. But the LDS church has also microfilmed the original registers, and David Wills' guide to the microfilm numbers for this material in Family History Centres will be useful if you want to refer to these films. The main page is at <**www.ktb.net/~dwills/scotref/13300-scottishreference.htm**>.

GROS has a list of registration districts at <**www.gro-scotland.gov.uk/ grosweb/grosweb.nsf/pages/files/$file/old_opr.pdf**>.

Scotlandspeople

Scotlandspeople is the official on-line source for Scottish General Registration records and is described in detail on p. 38. This site offers the following registration records:

- Birth indexes and images of certificates 1855–1902
- Marriage indexes 1855–1927
- Death indexes and images of certificates 1855–1952.

Images of the marriage certificates are due to be added to the site by the end of 2003, but the site currently includes a facility for ordering paper certificates from the on-line indexes. Each year will see the extension of the period covered by one year.

Scots Origins

While Scots Origins at <**www.scotsorigins.com**> ceased to host the GROS's own pay-per-view service in September 2002, it now offers instead the 'Scots Origins Sighting Service'. This allows you to request a transcription of a number of different types of record, including the Statutory Registers. A search in the Statutory Registers costs £8, and the results are e-mailed to you with 10 days.

One reason why you might sometimes want to use this service rather than Scotlandspeople is that it covers events up to 1990, and therefore allows on-line access to more recent certificates (on-line ordering of certificates direct from the GROS is only possible for the period covered by Scotlandspeople). On the other hand the Sighting Service requires reasonably accurate information, including the registration district and the year ±2 so that the correct entry can be identified.

Ireland

In Ireland, registration of Protestant marriages dates from 1 April 1845, while full registration began on 1 January 1864. The records for the whole of Ireland up to 31 December 1921 are held by the Registrar General in Dublin, who also holds those for the Republic of Ireland from that date. The equivalent records for Northern Ireland are held by the General Register Office (Northern Ireland). The relevant web sites are at <www.groireland.ie> and <www.groni.gov.uk/index.htm> respectively. The National Archives of Ireland have information on records of births, marriages and deaths at <www.nationalarchives.ie/birthsmarrdeaths. html>.

Almost none of these records, nor indexes to them, are on-line. According to its consultation document *Bringing Civil Registration into the 21st Century* at <www.groireland.ie/images/consultation.pdf>), the Irish government is, in principle, committed to digitising historical registration records, but there have been no outward signs of progress since the first edition of this book in 2001, and it is in any case far from clear that it will eventually lead to an on-line service.

A very useful site by Sean Murphy at <homepage.tinet.ie/~seanjmurphy/gro/> covers all aspects of civil registration in Ireland. The introduction at <homepage.tinet.ie/~seanjmurphy/gro/intro.htm> discusses what little he has been able to discover from officials about the progress of digitisation. The Genealogical Society of Ireland's page devoted to the consultation document at <www.dun-laoghaire.com/genealogy/civreg.html> provides a highly critical account of the Irish Government's proposals.

No plans to place records or indexes on-line have been announced by GRONI. However, certificates can be ordered on-line via a secure e-commerce system, or you can print off blank forms in PDF format. The web site does promise 'many more exciting developments', which for genealogists can only mean one thing.

The only Ireland-wide material on-line will be found at FamilySearch <www.familysearch.org>, where the IGI (see p. 72) includes the births for the first five years of registration in Ireland, 1864–1868.

Local transcripts

In the absence of a visible national programme of digitisation for Irish registration records, there are however some local and partial transcription projects.

The only coherent project I am aware of is Waterford County Library's on-line index to local death registrations 1864–1901, with full transcriptions of the original certificates, at <193.193.166.161/death.html> as part of its on-line catalogue. This site requires Java – a program has to be downloaded before you can view the material.

Otherwise there are a number of sites which have small collections of registration data transcribed:

- Among its User Submitted Databases, RootsWeb includes some death records for County Tipperary at <**userdb.rootsweb.com/regional. html#Irl**>. There is no indication of the dates covered, and this database cannot be selected for searching, though its records will be included when you specify 'Ireland' and 'deaths' as the country and type of record to be searched.
- Margaret Grogan has a range of transcriptions for County Cork, mostly for individual places, at <**www.sci.net.au/userpages/mgrogan/cork/ a_civil.htm**>, compiled from submissions to the Cork mailing list. You need to check each one as there is no overall search facility.
- The Ireland CMC Genealogy Record Project at <**www.cmcrp.net**> has user-submitted data which includes civil registration records, though these are mostly individual entries rather than systematic extractions. There are separate pages for Clare, Cork, Kerry, Limerick, Mayo, Tipperary, Waterford, Wicklow, and a single page for all other counties.

Offshore

The Isle of Man, Jersey, Guernsey, Alderney and Sark have their own civil registration, starting from various dates.

The Isle of Man Civil Registry seems to have no web site, but contact details, including an e-mail address, will be found on the Isle of Man government site at <**www.gov.im/deptindex/reginfo.asp#registries**> and the Genuki pages for the Isle of Man <**www.genuki.org.uk/big/iom/**> provide some further information.

Alex Glendinning has a 'Research in the Channel Islands FAQ' at <**user.itl.net/~glen/genukici.html**> with information on civil registration, but I am not aware of any registration data on-line for these islands. The relevant authorities for the individual islands do not seem to have web sites. However, John Fuller's 'Channel Islands Genealogy' page at <**www. rootsweb.com/~jfuller/ci/volunteers.html**> mentions some volunteers prepared to do look-ups in the Guernsey death registers.

Overseas

If you have ancestors who were immigrants or emigrants, you may need access to other countries' civil registration services. There is no single way of getting this information for every country, but the most likely to succeed are:

- See if there is a GenWeb page for it – the index of countries at <**www.worldgenweb.org/countryindex.html**> will take you to the relevant regional GenWeb site, which may have the information, and should at least point you to a message board where you can ask.
- Check the relevant country or regional page on Cyndi's List at <**www.cyndislist.com**>.

Don't expect other countries to be as far on the road to complete digital records as Scotland is, but you may be lucky. Some states in English-speaking parts of the world have indexes on-line. For example, New South Wales has an on-line index to historic registration records at <**www.bdm. nsw.gov.au**>, and British Columbia has a similar service at <**www. bcarchives.gov.bc.ca/textual/governmt/vstats/v_events.htm**>. For births, both of these sites list only events over 100 years ago, but more recent marriages and deaths are included. For the USA, Cyndi's List has detailed information for each state (under the heading Records).

6 On-line Sources: Census

A census has been taken every 10 years since 1801, except for 1941, and names of individuals are recorded from the 1841 census onwards. The significance of these records for genealogists is that they provide snapshots of family groups on a 10-year basis. More importantly, for individuals born before the start of general registration, they give, from 1851 onwards, a place of birth. Since an approximate date of birth can be calculated from the person's age, this makes it possible to trace the line back to the parish registers.

General information

The census data which is on-line for the British Isles comprises:

- England & Wales
  - The 1901 census available on the National Archives site (pay-per-view)
  - The 1891 census being made available by Ancestry.com (subscription)
  - The 1881 census at FamilySearch (free)
  - Local census indexes and transcriptions made by family history societies on the FamilyHistoryOnline site (pay-per-view)
- Scotland
  - The 1881 census at Scotlandspeople (free)
  - The 1891 and 1901 censuses at Scotlandspeople (pay-per-view).

Each of these is discussed in detail below.

There are two starting points for official information on the census. The FamilyRecords Portal 'Census' page at <**www.familyrecords.gov.uk/topics/census.htm**> has basic details and links to other official web sites with census information and data. The FRC's site has a number of factsheets on the census in PDF format at <**www.familyrecords.gov.uk/frc/research/censusmain.htm**>.

Genuki has pages on the census for:

- England and Wales: <**www.genuki.org.uk/big/eng/CensusR.html**>
- Scotland: <**www.genuki.org.uk/big/sct/Census.html**>
- Ireland: <**www.genuki.org.uk/big/irl/#Census**>

It also has a searchable database of places in the 1891 census at

<www.genuki.org.uk/big/census_place.html>, which gives the county, registration district, registration sub-district, National Archives piece number and LDS film number (see p. 107) for any place in England, Wales and the Isle of Man.

The GenDocs site shows exactly what information was recorded for each census from 1841 to 1901 at <www.gendocs.demon.co.uk/census.html>, and gives the date on which each census was taken. The British-Genealogy site has similar information and explains piece, folio and schedule numbers at <www.british-genealogy.com/resources/census/>.

For Scotland, a useful tool is the on-line index of census microfilms at <www.ktb.net/~dwills/scotref/13311-censusfilms.htm>, which gives the relevant enumeration district(s) and LDS microfilm number for each parish.

1901 Census for England and Wales

The National Archives unveiled the 1901 census for England and Wales in January 2002, on a pay-per-view basis from the census web site at <www.census.pro.gov.uk>. The digitisation was carried out by Qinetiq, which is also responsible for running the service.

Access to the material is initially via a free search facility, and there are a number of different things you can search for: a person, a place, a vessel or an institution. The person search is shown in Figure 6.1. There is also an advanced person search which allows you to specify additional data items such as occupation and marital status.

Once you have identified the record you want to look at (Figure 6.2), you can pay 50p to see the full census entry for the person found (Figure 6.3) or 75p to view an image of the relevant page in the original enumeration book (Figure 6.4). From the full entry for a person, you have an option to view the details of other people in the same household or, again, go to the page image.

It is always a good idea to view the page image, as this allows you to see fuller details than are included on the transcription (where some long entries are truncated). You will also need to check that the transcription is correct. The image will normally include the remainder of the household, so you probably will not often want to pay for the separate household transcription.

You do not need to view the full record for the person; you can if you wish go straight to the page image. But viewing the person and household transcription may be necessary if you are not sure you have the right individual. The software utilities described below help to identify household groups from the search results pages and can also be useful in identifying the right person before viewing a page.

If you already know piece and folio number from previous research, you can use the direct search.

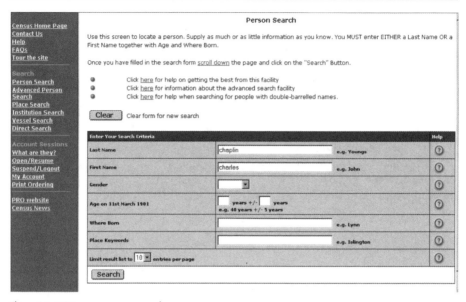

Figure 6.1 1901 census: person search

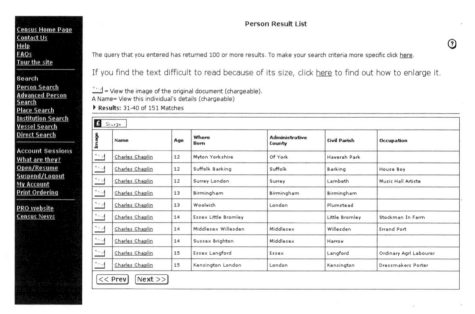

Figure 6.2 1901 census: Results of the individual search in Figure 6.1

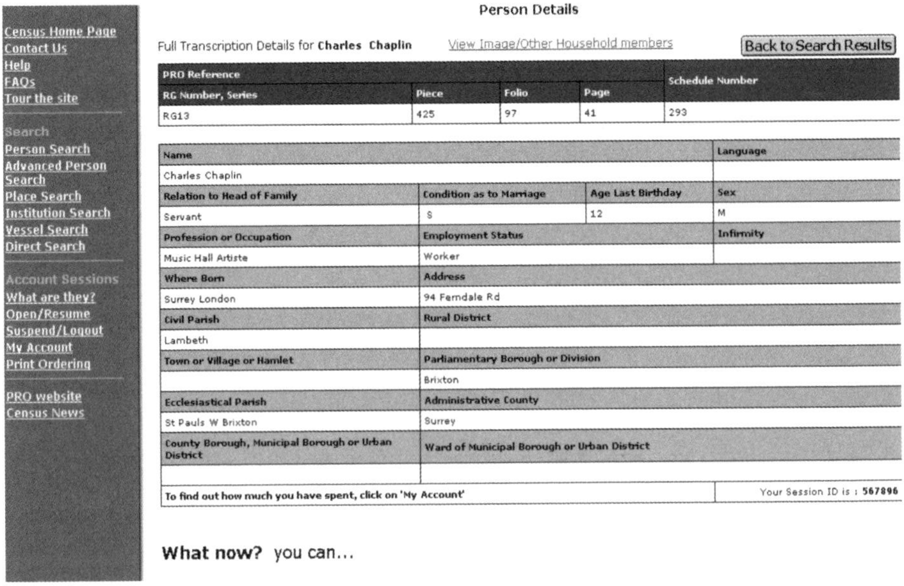

Census Home Page
Contact Us
Help
FAQs
Tour the site

Search
Person Search
Advanced Person Search
Place Search
Institution Search
Vessel Search
Direct Search

Account Sessions
What are they?
Open/Resume
Suspend/Logout
My Account
Print Ordering

PRO website
Census News

Person Details

Full Transcription Details for **Charles Chaplin** View Image/Other Household members Back to Search Results

PRO Reference				Schedule Number
RG Number, Series	Piece	Folio	Page	
RG13	425	97	41	293

Name			Language
Charles Chaplin			
Relation to Head of Family	Condition as to Marriage	Age Last Birthday	Sex
Servant	S	12	M
Profession or Occupation	Employment Status		Infirmity
Music Hall Artiste	Worker		
Where Born	Address		
Surrey London	94 Ferndale Rd		
Civil Parish	Rural District		
Lambeth			
Town or Village or Hamlet	Parliamentary Borough or Division		
	Brixton		
Ecclesiastical Parish	Administrative County		
St Pauls W Brixton	Surrey		
County Borough, Municipal Borough or Urban District	Ward of Municipal Borough or Urban District		

To find out how much you have spent, click on 'My Account' Your Session ID is : 567896

What now? you can...

Figure 6.3 1901 census: full census record for an individual

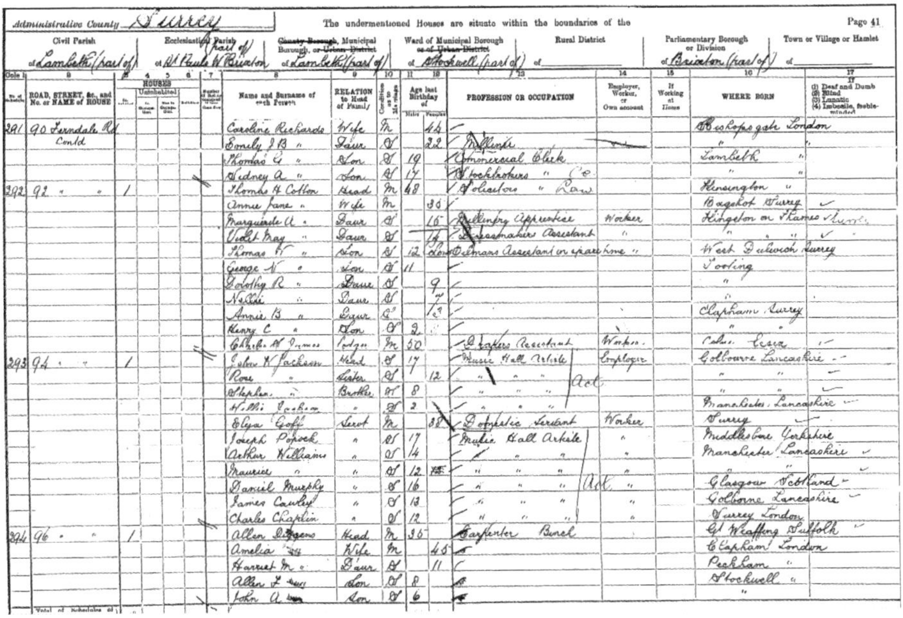

Administrative County Surrey — The undermentioned Houses are situate within the boundaries of the — Page 41

Civil Parish of Lambeth (part of) — Ecclesiastical Parish (part of) of St Pauls W Brixton — ~~County Borough~~, Municipal Borough, or ~~Urban District~~ of Lambeth (part of) — Ward of Municipal Borough ~~or of Urban District~~ of Stockwell (part of) — Rural District of — Parliamentary Borough or Division of Brixton (part of) — Town or Village or Hamlet of

No. of Schedule	Road, Street, &c., and No. or Name of House	Houses Inhabited	Name and Surname of each Person	Relation to Head of Family	Condition as to Marriage	Age last Birthday Males	Age last Birthday Females	Profession or Occupation	Employer, Worker, or Own account	If Working at Home	Where Born	(1) Deaf and Dumb (2) Blind (3) Lunatic (4) Imbecile, feeble-minded
291	90 Ferndale Rd Contd		Caroline Richards	Wife	M		44				Bishopsgate London	
			Emily J B "	Daur	S		22	Milliner			"	
			Thomas G "	Son	S	19		Commercial Clerk			Lambeth "	
			Sidney A "	Son	S	17		Stockbrokers " Co			" "	
292	92 " "	1	Thomas H Cotton	Head	M	48		Solicitors " Law			Kensington "	
			Annie Jane "	Wife	M		36				Bagshot Surrey	
			Marguerite A "	Daur	S		15	Millinery Apprentice	Worker		Kingston on Thames Surrey	
			Violet May "	Daur	S		14	Dressmakers Assistant	"		" "	
			Thomas W "	Son	S	12		Oilmans Assistant on spare time	"		West Dulwich Surrey	
			George W "	Son	S	11					Tooting	
			Dorothy R "	Daur	S		9				"	
			Nellie "	Daur	S		7				"	
			Annie B "	Daur	S		3				Clapham Surrey	
			Henry C "	Son	S	2					" "	
			Charles W James	Lodger	M	50		Drapers Assistant	Worker		Colne Essex	
293	94 " "	1	John W Jackson	Head	S	17		Music Hall Artiste	Employer		Golbourne Lancashire	
			Rose "	Sister	S		12	" " "			" "	
			Stephen "	Brother	S	8		" " "			" "	
			Willie Jackson	"	S	2		" " "			Manchester Lancashire	
			Eliza Goff	Servt	M		38	Domestic Servant	Worker		Surrey	
			Joseph Popock	"	S	17		Music Hall Artiste	"		Middlesbro Yorkshire	
			Arthur Williams	"	S	14		" " "	"		Manchester Lancashire	
			Maurice "	"	S	12		" " "	"		" "	
			Daniel Murphy	"	S	16		" " "	"		Glasgow Scotland	
			James Cawley	"	S	13		" " "	"		Golborne Lancashire	
			Charles Chaplin	"	S	12		" " "	"		Surrey London	
294	96 " "	1	Allen Diggens	Head	M	35		Carpenter Bench			Gt Weafting Suffolk	
			Amelia "	Wife	M		45				Clapham London	
			Harriet M "	Daur	S		11				Peckham "	
			Allen F "	Son	S	8					Stockwell "	
			John A "	Son	S	6					"	

Figure 6.4 1901 census: image of a page from the original census record

There is also an address search. By default this allows you to search on two fields, the house or street name, and the place name. For more advanced address searching, there is an option to specify a whole range of place fields – County, Civil Parish, Parliamentary Borough, etc. This will be particularly useful with common place names, though you may need good knowledge of 1901 administrative geography to exploit it fully. Unlike the other searches, the address search only links to a page image, not to a transcription. If you are working from a present-day address, rather than one taken from contemporary documents, don't assume that the 1901 house number applies to the same building as it does now.

You pay for access to the data by purchasing physical vouchers or by making a credit card payment on-line (the minimum is £5). This covers an account session of 48 hours. However, if you are using a voucher, you can use remaining time left at the end of a session on a subsequent session. If you pay by credit card, any unused units at the end of the session are lost. Vouchers can be bought on-line and from many genealogy suppliers, and are valid for six months from first use.

Problems and issues

On its release, the 1901 census was by far the most complex on-line project in British genealogy, combining images of the original records with transcriptions and an index. Not surprisingly, therefore, there were some initial problems. The most notable of these, the failure of the system to cope with the level of demand at launch, meant that it was November 2002 before it was running full-time. There are, however, some outstanding issues which affect the user's ability to find individuals.

Since the beginning there were doubts about the likely quality of the transcriptions, largely on the basis that much of the work was being done by non-English speakers without local knowledge. After the project went live, systematic failings of quality control and assurance were discovered. Of course, there will be errors in every major transcription project, and the original census records themselves are not free from error, but problems which raised more general worries about quality control included:

- people with Ditto or Do as a surname
- individuals who were recorded with spectacular ages in three figures
- gender errors (e.g. implausible numbers of female Johns).

These are all serious because they reduce the possibility of finding an individual. The first two of these problems have now been dealt with (see <www.census.pro.gov.uk/changes_index.html>), and there is a programme for correcting other errors reported by users. There also seem to be many errors in the transcription of occupations (e.g. 'fuel grower' for 'fruit grower', 'carman' for 'barmaid') but these will only cause difficulties if you specify occupation in the advanced person search. An unofficial list of errors is also being collected and published on the UK Surnames site at <www.county-surnames.co.uk/1901list.mv>, from which these occupation examples were taken.

The result of the errors is that some imagination must be used when searching for a surname if normal spellings fail to retrieve an expected individual. The corollary is that it is best to search on as few fields as you can get away with. It is probably better to use the standard person search rather than the advanced person search, unless the results of a standard search are really too numerous to be manageable.

Another issue is that of standardisation. The transcription is intended to represent accurately what is written on the original enumeration form, but this can give rise to problems in searching, particularly with the names of counties, where abbreviations and variant spellings may have been used by the enumerators for what is a clearly defined set of data items. An additional field has been promised for standard names of counties, and other standardisation fields may be added at a later date.

There has been extensive discussion of the 1901 census in the soc.genealogy.britain newsgroup and the UK-1901-CENSUS mailing list. The latter is a forum for discussing any aspect of the project, and details of how to subscribe will be found at <lists.rootsweb.com/index/intl/UK/UK-1901-CENSUS.html>, which also has a link to the list archives, where you can look at past messages. Past messages from soc.genealogy.britain will be found in the newsgroup archive at Google Groups (<groups.google.com>) or in the archive for the equivalent mailing list GENBRIT-L at <archiver.rootsweb.com/th/index/GENBRIT>. Alongside the serious discussion, there is also some lighter material: Not the 1901 Census at <www.staithes.demon.co.uk/census.html> presents a gently satirical look at the whole business.

The minutes of the National Archives' Census Advisory Panel at <www.pro.gov.uk/census/advisory.htm> provide information about the progress of the project. In summer 2002, this was transformed into the National Archives Online Services Advisory Panel with a broader brief, whose minutes are at <www.pro.gov.uk/online/advisory.htm>.

Hints and tips

Some basic search tips are provided on the 1901 site itself (from a link on the home page), but if you are looking for a wider range of advice on making the most of the 1901 census on-line, the UK-1901-CENSUS mailing list is a useful unofficial resource. The list archives can be searched or browsed from <lists.rootsweb.com/index/intl/UK/UK-1901-CENSUS.html>. Bryan Wetton has collected some of the most useful tips from this list at <www.wetton.net>, and there are further tips at <www.web-community.co.uk/census/tips.html>.

There can be problems where an ancestor is in an institution or on-board ship, because the page on which he or she is listed may not name the ship or institution. To assist you in identifying these, there are two helpful lists compiled by Jeffery Knaggs. The page at <homepage.ntlworld.com/ jeffery.knaggs/RNShips.html> lists Royal Navy ships that were at sea or in ports abroad on census night, while the page at <homepage.ntlworld.com/ jeffery.knaggs/Instuts.html> does the same for all institutions. The piece, folio and page numbers given here should enable you to work out where your ancestor was living.

Some transcriptions from the 1901 census are discussed on p. 68.

Software utilities

There are a number of software programs which aim to enhance your use of the site by managing the data collected from it. The essential feature that all of these have in common is that they make it possible to store the results of searches in a more convenient way than just saving or printing out the web pages of search results.

But they also allow you to extract other information from the searches that is not apparent on the results pages. Every entry in the on-line database has a Page ID and a Person ID. Since the Person IDs run consecutively through the census, they can be used to group members of the same household together (see Figure 6.5). Because these programs save this data from the free search pages, you can examine your initial results much more carefully before paying to see the full record for a chosen individual. Particularly for common names, this will help you avoid paying to see the wrong records.

All the programs mentioned below are for Windows and are shareware or freeware. They are described more fully in my article on 'Software Utilities for the 1901 Census' in the December 2002 issue of *Ancestors*. However, since they can all be downloaded free of charge there's no reason not to try all of them.

- Get1901Data: <www.genuki.org.uk/big/eng/CensusSoftware/>
- Census Manager: <uk.geocities.com/kgnsheffield/Html/CensusManager/ Census1.html>
- 1901 Census Extractor/Guesstimator: <leedsindexers.co.uk/Main-Internet%20Tools.htm>
- Web Tabular Garner: <mysite.freeserve.com/webtabgarner>

Note that the last of these is not designed specifically for the 1901 census – it will attempt to extract *any* tabular data.

Other censuses

The National Archives have promised further censuses to join the 1901, and the 1891 census for Norfolk was available briefly in 2001 as part of a pilot project. It seems likely that the full 1891 census will be the next one available.

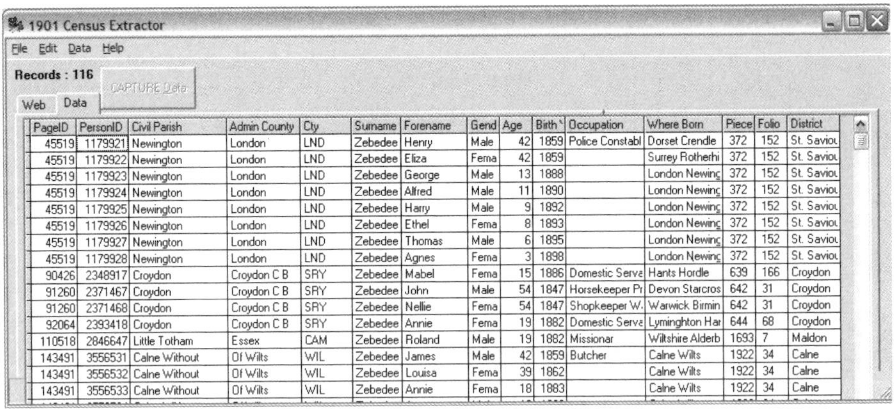

PageID	PersonID	Civil Parish	Admin County	Cty	Surname	Forename	Gend	Age	Birth	Occupation	Where Born	Piece	Folio	District
45519	1179921	Newington	London	LND	Zebedee	Henry	Male	42	1859	Police Constabl	Dorset Crendle	372	152	St. Saviou
45519	1179922	Newington	London	LND	Zebedee	Eliza	Fema	42	1859		Surrey Rotherhi	372	152	St. Saviou
45519	1179923	Newington	London	LND	Zebedee	George	Male	13	1888		London Newinc	372	152	St. Saviou
45519	1179924	Newington	London	LND	Zebedee	Alfred	Male	11	1890		London Newinc	372	152	St. Saviou
45519	1179925	Newington	London	LND	Zebedee	Harry	Male	9	1892		London Newinc	372	152	St. Saviou
45519	1179926	Newington	London	LND	Zebedee	Ethel	Fema	8	1893		London Newinc	372	152	St. Saviou
45519	1179927	Newington	London	LND	Zebedee	Thomas	Male	6	1895		London Newinc	372	152	St. Saviou
45519	1179928	Newington	London	LND	Zebedee	Agnes	Fema	3	1898		London Newinc	372	152	St. Saviou
90426	2348917	Croydon	Croydon C B	SRY	Zebedee	Mabel	Fema	15	1886	Domestic Serva	Hants Hordle	639	166	Croydon
91260	2371467	Croydon	Croydon C B	SRY	Zebedee	John	Male	54	1847	Horsekeeper Pr	Devon Starcros	642	31	Croydon
91260	2371468	Croydon	Croydon C B	SRY	Zebedee	Nellie	Fema	54	1847	Shopkeeper W.	Warwick Birmin	642	31	Croydon
92064	2393418	Croydon	Croydon C B	SRY	Zebedee	Annie	Fema	19	1882	Domestic Serva	Lymington Har	644	68	Croydon
110518	2846647	Little Totham	Essex	CAM	Zebedee	Roland	Male	19	1882	Missionar	Wiltshire Alderb	1693	7	Maldon
143491	3556531	Calne Without	Of Wilts	WIL	Zebedee	James	Male	42	1859	Butcher	Calne Wilts	1922	34	Calne
143491	3556532	Calne Without	Of Wilts	WIL	Zebedee	Louisa	Fema	39	1862		Calne Wilts	1922	34	Calne
143491	3556533	Calne Without	Of Wilts	WIL	Zebedee	Annie	Fema	18	1883		Calne Wilts	1922	34	Calne

Figure 6.5 1901 census entries sorted into family groups with 1901 Census Extractor

The 1881 census index for England and Wales was a joint indexing project between the Genealogical Society of Utah (GSU) and the FFHS, which gave rise first to an index on microfiche and then, with Scotland, on CD-ROM. (There is a history of the project on the FFHS site at <**www.ffhs.org.uk/General/Projects/1881.htm**>.) In October 2002, the data for England and Wales was made available on the FamilySearch site at <**www.familysearch.org**>. It is automatically included in any search on 'All Resources', but there is also the possibility of searching only this dataset, by selecting 'Census' instead. Those who have access to the CD-ROM edition of this data should note that this remains more comprehensive both in its data and its search facilities than the on-line version.

The GSU/FFHS project produced only an index, but it seems likely that the National Archives will be making images of this census available for England and Wales in due course, and Scotlandspeople plans to do the same for Scotland (see p. 69).

In 2002, Ancestry.com (see p. 40) began to put digitised images of the 1891 census on-line, a county at a time, as part of a major project to make all pre-1901 census material available electronically. It is worth noting that the page images are much larger than those on the 1901 census site (over 2Mb) and will take quite a while to download if you have a modem connection. On the other hand, the quality is exceptional. Like the other material on Ancestry, this data requires a subscription.

There is a great deal of census material being published on CD-ROM. While that in itself falls outside the scope of this book, S&N Genealogy (see p. 266) are developing on-line indexes to the census images on their CDs. Access to the indexes is by 90-day or 1-year subscription, with a separate subscription required for each county. Details of the project and the material already available will be found at <**www.thegenealogist.co.uk**>.

Census extracts

Alongside the official projects there are, as with civil registration, volunteer projects as well as many efforts of individuals.

FreeCEN at <freecen.rootsweb.com> is a comprehensive volunteer project which aims to include all English and Welsh census data from 1841 to 1891. At the time of writing, transcription is well under way, starting with 1891, and the database should be on-line by the time you read this. The database aims to support the following types of search:

- Search by surname across census years and counties
- Search by place or address
- Display of individual and household details
- 'Neighbourhood scan' – the ability to display adjacent households
- Statistical enquiry – e.g. numbers of carpenters by place name.

The site has a status page for each county currently being transcribed. For Devon, which was the pilot county for the project, some of the material has been put on-line (just as text, not in a searchable database) at <**www.cs.ncl.ac.uk/genuki/DEV/Census.1891/**>.

FamilyHistoryOnline (see p. 37) has an increasing number of census indexes for individual countries, transcribed by local family history societies. Most complete is Cornwall, which has some material for each of the released censuses except 1881. There is data for Berkshire, Hampshire, Northamptonshire and Rutland, as well as some individual towns in other countries. The complete list can be seen at <**www.familyhistoryonline.net/database/**>.

There are probably quite a lot of other small collections of census material on the Web, but no major collections. The 2% sample of the 1851 census, originally created as part of an academic research project, was available on-line for a while but was removed for copyright reasons, though it is available on CD-ROM from S&N Genealogy (see p. 266).

The best way to find any locally-based transcriptions is via the relevant Genuki county and parish pages. For example, there are many transcriptions for individual parishes, such as:

- Veryan in Cornwall from 1841 to 1891 <freepages.genealogy.rootsweb. com/~dtrounce/veryan.html>
- Bovingdon in Hertfordshire for 1841 and 1871 at <**www.geocities.com/ mellowsbrown/introcen.html**>
- a number of small communities in Ross and Cromarty at <freepages. genealogy.rootsweb.com/~coigach/index.htm>
- Corfe, Somerset for 1841 at <**www.parkhouse.org.uk/transcr/ corfe1841.htm**>
- Wirksworth, Derbyshire, <**www.wirksworth.org.uk**> 1841–1891.

Also, you may find that genealogists with web pages devoted to particular surnames include extracts from census records on their sites, though usually only for their own surnames of interest.

Scotland

The Scotlandspeople site at <www.scotlandspeople.gov.uk>, discussed in Chapter 4, p. 38, has the 1881, 1891 and 1901 censuses for Scotland. The 1881 is an on-line version of the index created by the GSU (see p. 66) and can be accessed free of charge, though you need a username and password to reach the search page. The 1891 and 1901 data is not just an index but includes digitised images of the original enumeration books. There is an important difference between these and the National Archives' 1901 census service – the Scottish data does not include a transcription. As with the civil registration data on Scotlandspeople, an initial search indicates how many hits your search produces, and you then need to spend one of your pre-purchased units to see each page of the full search results. At that point, you can choose to view a census image at a cost of five units.

Although this may be cheaper than the National Archives' system, it does have the disadvantage that if a household is split over a page break, it may be difficult to identify the remainder of the family.

In the long term, the site is intended to host all earlier Scottish census data for on-line access, and images for the 1881 census are due to be added to the site by Spring 2004. Indexes for earlier census are planned for the same time.

Ireland

For Ireland, the National Archives of Ireland have a brief page of information at <www.nationalarchives.ie/censusrtns.html>, as has the PRONI at <www.proni.gov.uk/records/census19.htm>. A good guide to the Irish censuses, detailing what is missing and what has survived, is available on the Fianna site at <www.rootsweb.com/~fianna/guide/census.html>.

Unlike England, Wales and Scotland, there are no national datasets on-line for the Irish census. One of the reasons for this is that almost all 19th century census returns for Ireland have been destroyed. However, there seem to be no plans to put the 1901 census, the earliest one to survive in its entirety, on-line. In Ireland the 1911 census has also been available for many years, but there is no sign of any project to make it available on-line.

However, there are a number of sites with census data for individual counties. In the Republic of Ireland some data from the 1901 census is on-line at <www.leitrim-roscommon.com/1901census/>. Available data covers all or part of the following six counties: Roscommon, Leitrim, Mayo, Sligo, Westmeath and Galway. Data for Leitrim and Roscommon are essentially complete, but for the others, only small amounts of material are present. A table gives detailed information about which individual parishes are wholly or partly covered.

Because of the amount of Irish census material destroyed, the so-called 'census substitutes' are important. Fianna has a useful guide to these at <**www.rootsweb.com/~fianna/guide/cen2.html**>, while the National Archives of Ireland has a briefer description at <**www.nationalarchives.ie/ titheapplprimvalu.html**>. The PRONI has similar information at <**www.proni.gov.uk/records/census18.htm**>. One of the most important census substitutes, Griffiths Valuation, is discussed in Chapter 8, p. 86.

Overseas

It is not possible to deal here with census data for countries outside the British Isles, but Cyndi's List provides links to census sites around the world at <**www.cyndislist.com/census2.htm**>.

The census data on FamilySearch includes the 1880 US census and the 1881 Canadian census, and there is a large amount of US census data on-line at Ancestry.com <**www.ancestry.com**>, which requires a special subscription.

Another site that may be useful is Census Links at <**www.censuslinks. com**>, which lists census transcriptions for a number of countries.

7 On-line Sources: Parish Registers

Before the introduction of General Registration in 1837, church records of baptisms, marriages and burials are the primary source for the major events in our ancestors' lives. Unfortunately, there is very much less data on-line for parish registers than for the civil registration and census records covered in the previous chapters, and there are good reasons why this should be so.

The national records are centrally held and recorded on forms which ensure that the structure of the data is consistent and very obvious; they all date at the earliest from the 1830s; and they have generally been kept in fairly good conditions. All this makes digitising and indexing them a manageable, if mammoth, task.

But for parish registers, there is much more variety. First, in England and Wales, at least, they are not held centrally, so no one body can be approached to put them on-line. Second, there is huge variation in their format and preservation, the more so since they cover 300 years up to general registration. And, third, while most genealogists can become accurate readers of 19th-century handwriting, the same cannot be said when it comes to the writing in some of the 18th-century registers, never mind those from the 16th century. Although many parish registers have been transcribed and published in print or typescript, getting the requisite permissions simply to digitise and index these from the hundreds of individuals and groups concerned would be a substantial task. Indeed, the right to transcribe and publish parish register material seems to be legally unclear, with some dioceses refusing to allow transcription. All this conspires to make the prospect of a comprehensive collection of on-line parish registers for England and Wales much more distant than it is for civil registration and census records. Nevertheless, some data is available on-line, as well as information that will help you to identify what parish registers remain.

If you are unfamiliar with parish register material, Rod Neep has some useful pages on English Parish Registers at <**www.british-genealogy.com/ resources/registers/indexf.htm**>. These describe the information given for baptism, marriage and burial entries at different periods and have some examples of original documents. The tutorials discussed in Chapter 2 will also have information on using parish registers. For help with the handwriting found in registers, refer to the material on p. 174 ff.

For parish maps, maps of counties showing the parishes, and resources to help you locate parishes see Chapter 12.

The material in this chapter refers mainly to the records of the established Church (i.e. of England, Wales, Scotland and Ireland). Other religious denominations are discussed in Chapter 11.

FamilySearch

The major on-line resource for all parish records is the LDS Church's FamilySearch site at <www.familysearch.org>. The material on this site is drawn from a number of sources, and it is important to note that not all of it is from transcriptions of parish registers ('controlled extractions', as the LDS calls them). Two of the data collections on the site, Ancestral File and Pedigree Resource File, consist of unverified material submitted by individual genealogists, which is therefore secondary material and of variable reliability – these datasets are discussed in Chapter 10. The collection that contains British parish register extractions is the International Genealogical Index (IGI), originally published on microfiche and then on CD-ROM. A further collection, the Vital Records Index (VRI), has been published on CD-ROM but at the time of writing no data for the British Isles has been put on-line, though no doubt it will be in due course. (If you are thinking of buying the VRI CD-ROM, there is a useful listing of the parishes covered at <www.genoot.com/downloads/BVRI2/> – the site has two PDF files for each county, detailing marriage and birth coverage.)

The IGI on FamilySearch is the only substantial collection of parish register records for England and Wales on-line, and as such is one of the essential tools for UK genealogy on the Web. There is also much material for other countries. The majority of the IGI material is for baptisms and marriages, though with some births and a few deaths and burials.

The exact nature of the search options on FamilySearch depends on whether you choose to search in 'All Resources' or in one of the individual data collections. A good reason for choosing the IGI search (see Figure 7.1), apart from the quality of the data, is that it allows you to select not only a country, but also a UK county. You can also choose to look for all events or for just, say, marriages; you can leave the year blank, give a precise year or a range of years. If you are looking for a specific individual, you can also enter the name of the father and/or mother.

When the search has been completed, you are presented with a list of search results (see Figure 7.2), with sufficient detail to identify the most plausible matches, and you can then click on the name to get the full details of the record (Figure 7.3).

You can select an individual record or a group of records to download in GEDCOM format (see p. 239), ready to be imported into your genealogy database. Of course, you can also simply save the web page for

Figure 7.1 IGI search page on FamilySearch <www.familysearch.org>

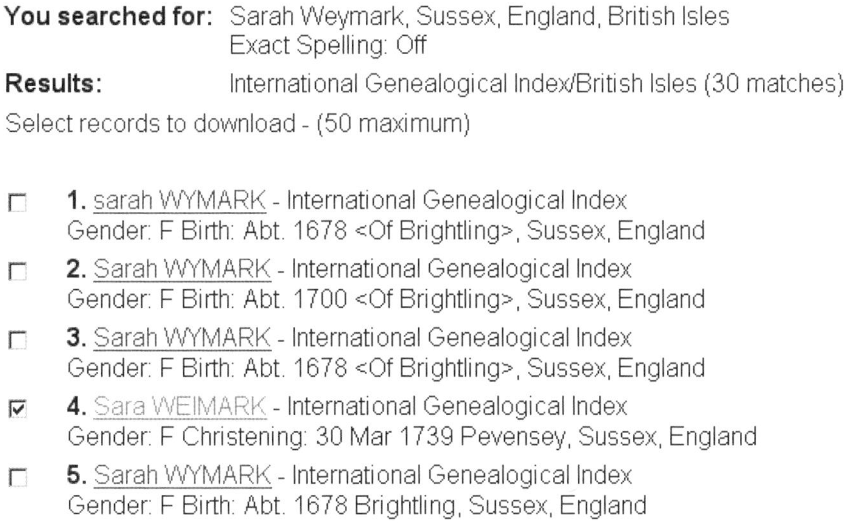

You searched for: Sarah Weymark, Sussex, England, British Isles
Exact Spelling: Off

Results: International Genealogical Index/British Isles (30 matches)

Select records to download - (50 maximum)

☐ **1.** sarah WYMARK - International Genealogical Index
Gender: F Birth: Abt. 1678 <Of Brightling>, Sussex, England

☐ **2.** Sarah WYMARK - International Genealogical Index
Gender: F Birth: Abt. 1700 <Of Brightling>, Sussex, England

☐ **3.** Sarah WYMARK - International Genealogical Index
Gender: F Birth: Abt. 1678 <Of Brightling>, Sussex, England

☑ **4.** Sara WEIMARK - International Genealogical Index
Gender: F Christening: 30 Mar 1739 Pevensey, Sussex, England

☐ **5.** Sarah WYMARK - International Genealogical Index
Gender: F Birth: Abt. 1678 Brightling, Sussex, England

Figure 7.2 Initial search results for the search Figure 7.1

Individual Record

FamilySearch™ International Genealogical Index v4.01

British Isles

Select record to download - (50 maximum)

☐ **Sara WEIMARK**
    Sex: F

Event(s):
    Christening: 30 Mar 1739
                     Pevensey, Sussex, England

Parents:
    Father: Edward WEIMARK
    Mother: Jude_

Source Information:

Batch number:	Dates	Source Call No.	Type	Printout Call No.	Type
C042501	1569-1837	0504417	Film	0933425	Film
Sheet:					

Figure 7.3 An individual record in FamilySearch

---

individual records or the list of search results, though these will have to be saved in text or HTML formats and the data will have to be added to your database manually.

If you are not just looking for a single individual but want to look at a surname in a whole parish, then the information at the bottom of the screen in Figure 7.3 will be useful. This identifies the particular transcription from which this record comes. You can take the batch number, and enter it in the batch number field on the search form (Figure 7.1) to restrict the search to a particular source document – in the example in Figure 7.3 'C042501' indicates the parish registers for Pevensey in Sussex (the link from the 'Source Call No.' takes you to this information). The batch number is also important because it indicates whether a record comes from controlled extractions – in general, batches that start with a digit are from submissions by Church members, while those starting with a letter are from controlled extractions.

Of course, it would be useful to be able to select the parish straight off without having to run a preliminary search and decode an individual record. You can do this by doing a 'Place Search' in the Family History Library Catalogue, as explained on p. 107. Genuki has detailed instructions on how to find out batch numbers by this method at <**www.genuki. org.uk/big/FindingBatchNos.html**>. The Global Gazette has a detailed article by Fawne Stratford-Devai, 'The LDS FamilySearch Website: Using The Batch Numbers', at <**globalgenealogy.com/globalgazette/gazfd/gazfd36. htm**>, which explains what the batch numbers are and how to use them.

Also, there are a number of sites that list batch numbers for particular counties. The most extensive, at <**freepages.genealogy.rootsweb.com/ ~hughwallis/IGIBatchNumbers.htm**>, has a comprehensive listing based on trying out each possible number. Others can be found by looking under the 'Church records' heading on the Genuki county pages. The Global Gazette page, mentioned above, has links to batch number information for a number of counties.

Bear in mind that all these listings are unofficial, and should not be regarded as authoritative. Also note that for many parishes there will be more than one batch number.

The facilities on the FamilySearch site can be quite complex to use, but because of the importance of the data it is well worth spending time experimenting and trying out different types of search. You can find more detailed guidance in David Hawgood's *FamilySearch on the Internet* (details at <**www.hawgood.co.uk/fs.htm**>).

FamilyHistoryOnline

The FamilyHistoryOnline site at <**www.familyhistoryonline.net**>, which is described in detail on p. 37, has a growing body of parish register transcriptions from local family history societies, and will no doubt eventually rival FamilySearch for this material. A fuller list of the datasets available is provided at <**www.familyhistoryonline.net/database/**>.

In particular, entries from the National Burial Index for England and Wales, which was published by the FFHS in May 2001 on CD-ROM, has already been added for many counties. Details of the counties and parishes covered in the NBI will be found at <**www.ffhs.org.uk/General/Projects/ NBIcounties.htm**>.

FreeReg

FreeReg is another volunteer project, like FreeBMD and FreeCEN, which aims to put UK genealogy data on-line 'to provide free internet searches of baptism, marriage, and burial records, which have been transcribed from parish and nonconformist church registers in the UK.' The project, which can be found at <**freereg.rootsweb.com**>, is still a fairly new one and the number of records it contains compared to the total amount of potential material is still tiny.

Marriage Witness Index

Ted Wildy's UK Marriage Witness Index is a well-known pre-Web index, started in 1988. Until recently, the only on-line access to the index has been via e-mail to the maintainer, Faye Guthrie, but early in 2003 it was put on the Web as one of RootsWeb's user-submitted databases at

<userdb.rootsweb.com/uki/>. It has around 80,000 entries, which include the names of witnesses, groom and bride, together with the date and place of the marriage and the name and address of the genealogist who submitted the information.

Unfortunately, you cannot search RootsWeb specifically for this database, but data from it will be included in any search for UK marriage records. There is, however, still an advantage in e-mailing the maintainer – the RootsWeb version of the material does not include the contact details of the original submitter, who may well be someone researching the family involved. Further information about the MWI will be found at <members.optushome.com.au/guthrigg/mwi.htm>.

Scotland

Unlike England and Wales, Scotland has collected most of its parish registers in one place, the GROS, and the births/baptisms and banns/marriages dating from 1553 to 1854 (the start of general registration) are all available on-line at Scotlandspeople <www.scotlandspeople. gov.uk>, described above (p. 38).

The GROS web site provides a 'List of the Old Parochial Registers' at <www.gro-scotland.gov.uk/grosweb/grosweb.nsf/pages/opr_cov/>.

A Scottish National Death and Burial Index, aiming to index all recorded pre-1855 deaths and burials in Scotland, is being created by the Scottish Association of Family History Societies in conjunction with its member societies and the GROS. It is not yet clear whether this will be made available on-line. Some very basic information is available at <www.gwsfhs.org.uk/projects.html>.

Ireland

There is almost no Irish parish register material on-line apart from a small amount at FamilySearch. However, there are a number of places to look for the little other material that is available:

- RootsWeb has a small number of user-submitted databases with Irish parish register material listed at <userdb.rootsweb.com/regional.html> – note there are *two* sections for Ireland, one of which is under 'United Kingdom'.
- The Irish Ancestors site has links to on-line resources for individual counties at <scripts.ireland.com/ancestor/browse/links/counties/>, which includes some parish register material.
- The Genuki county pages for Ireland, linked from <www.genuki. org.uk/big/irl/>, have sections devoted to Church Records.

There is, however, useful information on-line about the location of church records. IrelandGenWeb at **<www.irelandgenweb.com>** and NorthernIrelandGenWeb at **<www.rootsweb.com/~nirwgw/>** have county pages which often include details of the parishes whose registers have been filmed by the LDS. PRONI has details of its microfilm holdings of Church of Ireland and Presbyterian records at **<www.proni.gov.uk/records/ USING/using.htm>**.

Other indexes

Two important and rare paper collections are being made available on the SoG's English Origins site.

- Boyd's Marriage Index 1538–1837 (over 6 million records)
- Boyd's London Burials (50,000 names).

English Origins is described in detail on p. 33.

Many individual genealogists also have computerised indexes, particularly for marriages. Little of this material has made its way on-line as yet, and most is accessible only for postal searches. However, this situation may improve, if any of the pay-per-view sites are prepared to host material collected by individuals as well as societies.

Genuki has many links to on-line indexes and transcriptions for individual counties and places.

8 Other Records On-line

There are, of course, many types of record of interest to the family historian other than those discussed in the foregoing chapters. This chapter looks at some of the most important, but there is much more than can be covered here. Where these are official records, the web sites of the national archives will give details of any large-scale plans for digitisation (see p. 95 ff.). But even where there are no such plans, many individuals and groups are publishing small collections of data from such records on-line. These tend to be piecemeal digitisations, rather than the publication of complete national datasets, and some are discussed under the relevant topic in Chapter 11 or under 'Local and social history' in Chapter 13.

RootsWeb has a facility for users to upload data into its user-submitted data area. There are about three dozen small datasets for the British Isles, details of which are at <userdb.rootsweb.com/contributors.html>.

Wills

Wills are an important source for family historians and there has been a considerable increase in the number of wills available on-line in the last few years. Wills have been proved in many different places, and locating the right source for the potential will of a particular ancestor can sometimes be difficult, so it is important to look at the general information about probate records before looking for a specific will.

England and Wales
Very basic information about wills in England and Wales can be found on the FamilyRecords gateway at <www.familyrecords.gov.uk/topics/wills. htm>. But for more detail, consult the National Archives' three leaflets relating to wills:

- Wills before 1858: where to start <catalogue.pro.gov.uk/Leaflets/ ri2302.htm>
- Wills and Death Duty Records after 1858 <catalogue.pro.gov.uk/ Leaflets/ri2301.htm>
- Wills, Probate Records <catalogue.pro.gov.uk/Leaflets/ri2241.htm>.

Probate records since 1858 are under the jurisdiction of the Probate

Service which has pages on the Court Service web site at <www. courtservice.gov.uk>. It includes a useful page on Probate Records and Family History at <www.courtservice.gov.uk/cms/3800.htm>, which explains wills and probate, and an on-line leaflet at <www.courtservice. gov.uk/cms/3724.htm> gives details of how to obtain copies of post-1858 wills.

For pre-1858 wills, the most important site is DocumentsOnline at <www.documentsonline.pro.gov.uk>. This offers images of 850,000 wills from the Prerogative Court of Canterbury, the largest probate court for England and Wales, for the period 1670–1858. Detailed information on coverage is given at <www.documentsonline.pro.gov.uk/wills.asp>. At the time of writing, almost all wills from 1780 were available, and those going back to 1710 are partially available. Each will costs £3 to download, regardless of length.

Another source of wills for England and Wales is the English Origins site at <www.englishorigins.com> (see p. 33), which has the following currently available:

- Bank of England Will Extracts Index 1717–1845 (61,000 names)
- Prerogative Court of Canterbury Wills Index, 1750–1800 (208,000 names, incomplete)
- Archdeaconry Court of London Wills Index 1700-1807 (5,000 names).

There is a page with information on each of these collections which should enable you to see whether they will be worth checking in a particular instance.

Most pre-1858 wills were proved in local diocesan courts, whose records are now in County Record Offices. It is, therefore, a good idea to check the web site of a likely CRO for information on the relevant court or courts for parishes in the county. Among CRO-based projects to digitise wills are:

- Cheshire Wills at <www.fhsc.org.uk/wills/>
- The Wiltshire Wills project at <www.wiltshire.gov.uk/heritage/html/ wiltshire_wills.html>.

Scotland

The official source for Scottish wills is ScottishDocuments at <www. scottishdocuments.com>. The site offers an index of around half a million entries to the testaments (wills) of Scots recorded in the Registers of Testaments from the 16th century to 1901, with on-line ordering of copies at £5 each.

The site also has some examples of wills from each 50-year period covered by the index. For those unfamiliar with Scottish probate records and terminology, the FAQ pages at <www.scottishdocuments.com/

content/research_faq.asp> provide a comprehensive introduction to all aspects of the records. Further help is available from a 'Research Tools' menu, which includes material on abbreviations found in wills, occupations, and lists of forename and surname variants.

Ireland

General information about wills and probate in Ireland will be found on the Irish Ancestors site at **<scripts.ireland.com/ancestor/browse/records/ wills/>**. Ancestry.com has two articles on Irish wills by Sherry Irvine at **<www.ancestry.com/library/view/news/articles/2515.asp>** and PRONI has basic information about wills for Northern Ireland at **<www. proni.gov.uk/records/wills.htm>**.

There are no national sites for Irish wills, but as always, you can expect to find local transcriptions done by volunteers. For example, there is an index to wills for the Diocese of Raphoe, Donegal at **<freepages. genealogy.rootsweb.com/~donegal/wills.htm>**, while Ginni Swanton has scanned images of the published index to Irish Wills for the Dioceses of Cork and Ross at **<www.ginnisw.com/Indexes%20to%20Irish%20Wills/**

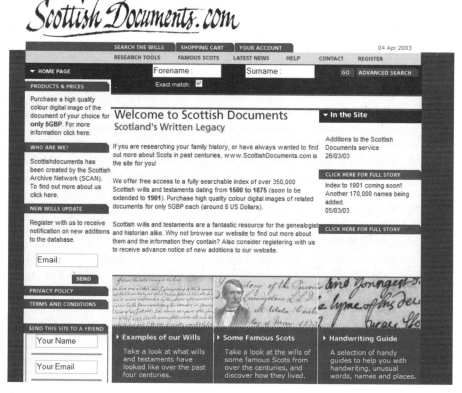

Figure 8.1 ScottishDocuments.com home page

Thumb/Thumbs1.htm>. Other sites with Irish wills can be found from the 'Locality Specific' section on the 'Wills and Probate' page of Cyndi's List at <www.cyndislist.com/wills.htm> or by using a search engine.

Cemeteries and monumental inscriptions

While monumental inscriptions (MIs) are not official records, their close connection with the deceased means that they can provide family information not given by a death certificate, and can make up for a missing entry in a burial register. Similar information can come from obituaries, which are covered on p. 89, below.

The best starting point for cemeteries and MIs is the Tombstones & Monumental Inscriptions site at <gye.future.easyspace.com>. This aims to 'provide a photographic record of the various churches, churchyards and cemeteries for the benefit of those genealogists who live some distance away', but it also has a comprehensive collection of links to related sites for the UK and other English-speaking countries. The site also has links for war memorials. Cyndi's List has a 'Cemeteries & Funeral Homes' page at <www.cyndislist.com/cemetery.htm> with a number of links for UK sites and many general resources for cemeteries.

Quite a few family history societies have projects to transcribe monumental inscriptions, and this material is starting to find its way on-line via the FamilyHistoryOnline site (see p. 37) at <www. familyhistoryonline.net>, which already has extensive MI material for Cornwall, Glamorgan and Wiltshire.

Examples of other county-based projects are:

- Dyfed FHS's list of Burial Grounds in Cardiganshire, Carmarthenshire and Pembrokeshire with links to a number of MI transcriptions, at <www.dyfedfhs.org.uk/register/burials.htm>.
- Cornish Cemeteries at <freepages.genealogy.rootsweb.com/~chrisu/ cemeteries.htm> with material for around a dozen cemeteries and churchyards in Cornwall.

As with all local resources, there are countless small volunteer transcriptions. For example, the England Tombstone Project at <www. rootsweb.com/~engcemet/> has transcriptions for a number of cemeteries, including four from London. Interment.net at <www.interment.net> has collections of MI transcriptions for some UK cemeteries. These are individual user-submitted records, and only some of the materials represent complete transcriptions for a cemetery or churchyard.

Apart from the general resources mentioned above, good ways to see if there is anything for a particular place or church is to look at the relevant Genuki parish page if there is one, or simply use a search engine to find pages with the place name and the phrase 'monumental inscriptions'.

Figure 8.2 Interment.net home page

Rod Neep has pages on recording and publishing memorial inscriptions at <www.neep.demon.co.uk/mis/>. The Welsh Family History Archive has a useful page on Welsh Words and Phrases on Gravestones at <home.clara.net/wfha/wales/welsh-phrases.htm>. For help with Latin inscriptions, see p. 176.

There are many mailing lists relating to cemeteries and monumental inscriptions. Those most relevant to the British Isles are:

● MI-ENGLAND, subscription details at <lists.rootsweb.com/index/intl/ENG/MI-ENGLAND.html>

- SCOTLAND-CEMETERIES at <lists.rootsweb.com/index/intl/SCT/SCOTLAND-CEMETERIES.html>
- SCT-TOMBSTONE-INSCRIPTIONS at <lists.rootsweb.com/index/intl/SCT/SCT-TOMBSTONE-INSCRIPTIONS.html>
- IRELAND-CEMETERIES at <lists.rootsweb.com/index/intl/IRL/IRELAND-CEMETERIES.html>
- IRL-TOMBSTONE-INSCRIPTIONS at <lists.rootsweb.com/index/intl/IRL/IRL-TOMBSTONE-INSCRIPTIONS.html>.

Debt of Honour Register

One of the first important collections of genealogical data for the UK to go on-line was the Debt of Honour Register on the web site of the Commonwealth War Graves Commission at <**www.cwgc.org**>. This is a database of the names of 1.7 million members of the Commonwealth forces who died in the First or Second World Wars.

For all those listed there is name, rank, regiment and date of death, with details either of place of burial or, for those with no known grave, of commemoration. The burial information gives not only the name of the cemetery but also the grave reference and instructions on how to get to the

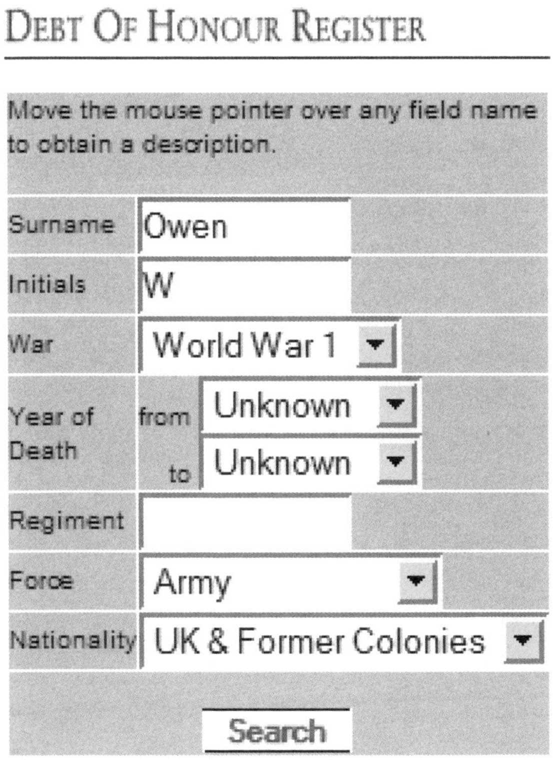

DEBT OF HONOUR REGISTER

Move the mouse pointer over any field name to obtain a description.

Surname	Owen
Initials	W
War	World War 1
Year of Death	from Unknown
	to Unknown
Regiment	
Force	Army
Nationality	UK & Former Colonies

Search

Figure 8.3 Debt of Honour Register search form

cemetery. Some records have additional personal information, usually including the names of parents and the home address. With many cemeteries holding the dead from particular battles and campaigns, there is often historical information which puts the death in its military context. The database also includes information on 60,000 civilian casualties of the Second World War, though without details of burial location.

The initial search box on the home page allows you to specify surname, initials, war or year of death, force (i.e. army, navy, etc.) and nationality. Unless you are looking for an unusual name, it is best to enter as much detail as possible. Figure 8.3 shows a search for the record of the war poet Wilfred Owen. From the details given, the database reports there are 163 records, which can be viewed 25 to a page (Figure 8.4). If you know the regiment and approximate rank of the person you're looking for, it should not take too long to identify the relevant record. Knowing that Wilfred Owen was an officer, and that he was killed near the end of the war, it is relatively easy to identify him as the lieutenant in the Manchester Regiment who died on 4 November 1918.

The list of search results links to a page giving the details for each soldier listed. In the case of Wilfred Owen (see Figure 8.5), in addition to the basic details of rank, regiment and date of death, the record shows the names of his parents and their address, along with some further biographical information. The bottom part of the screen gives details of the cemetery

COMMONWEALTH
WAR GRAVES
COMMISSION

Latest News
The Task
Sir Fabian Ware
Member Countries
Commissioners
Addresses
Global Commitment
Horticulture
Architecture
Publications
Education
Services & Links
Home & Search

SEARCH RESULTS

Here are the results of your enquiry. There are 149 records which match your search criteria.

Select a name to see more details or search again.

Surname	Rank	Service	Date of Death	Age	Regiment	Nationality
OWEN, W C	Private	26249	12 May 1917		Welsh Regiment	United Kingdom
OWEN, W C	Private	25839	30 April 1918	22	Duke of Wellington's (West Riding Regt.)	United Kingdom
OWEN, W C	Private	681810	2 April 1918	21	London Regiment	United Kingdom
OWEN, W D	Second Lieutenant		11 October 1918		Welsh Regiment	United Kingdom
OWEN, W D	Sapper	149631	13 November 1917		Royal Engineers	United Kingdom
OWEN, W E	Private	3/34516	23 July 1916		South Wales Borderers	United Kingdom
OWEN, W E	Private	767340	23 March 1918	19	London Regt (Artists' Rifles)	United Kingdom
OWEN, W E	Private	18281	7 September 1917	23	Lincolnshire Regiment	United Kingdom
OWEN, W E	Lance Serjeant	46631	24 August 1918	19	Durham Light Infantry	United Kingdom
OWEN, W E	Lance Corporal	24560	2 December 1917	30	King's Own Yorkshire Light Infantry	United Kingdom
OWEN, W E	Private	15473	21 September 1917	21	King's Shropshire Light Infantry	United Kingdom
OWEN, W E S	Lieutenant		4 November 1918	25	Manchester Regiment	United Kingdom
OWEN, W F	Private	20814	7 June 1917		Royal Fusiliers	United Kingdom
OWEN, W G	Private	202670	25 November 1917	21	Welsh Regiment	United Kingdom

Figure 8.4 Debt of Honour Register search results

	DEBT OF HONOUR REGISTER
	In Memory of
	WILFRED EDWARD SALTER OWEN MC
	Lieutenant 5th Bn., Manchester Regiment
	who died on Monday 4 November 1918 . Age 25 .

Additional Information:	Son of Mr. and Mrs. Tom Owen, of "Mahim", Monkmoor Rd., Shrewsbury. Native of Oswestry. Enlisted in The Artists' Rifles in October 1915. Commissioned into the Manchester Regiment in June 1916. Was a poet of repute, although during his lifetime, only a few of his poems appeared in print. The 'Atheneum' of December 1919, nominated Owen's work "Strange Meeting" as the finest of the war.
Cemetery:	ORS COMMUNAL CEMETERYNord, France
Grave or Reference Panel Number:	A. 3.
Location:	The village of Ors is between Le Cateau and Landrecies. The Communal Cemetery lies to the north-west of the village. It should not be confused with Ors British Cemetery which is 1 kilometre north-east of the church.
Historical Information:	Ors was cleared by the 6th Division on the 1st November, 1918. There are now over 60, 1914-18 war casualties commemorated in this site. Of these, a small number are unidentified. The plot covers an area of 189 square metres.
	Display Record of Commemoration

Figure 8.5 Debt of Honour Register individual record

and grave, as well as information about the campaigns from which the cemetery holds the dead.

Because the search results give only the initials of the individuals, it can be quite time-consuming to search for someone without any idea of regiment, though in some cases an age is given. Unfortunately, next of kin are not always named, so you may need to look at army records to confirm the identity of a particular entry.

Property records

Property records are important in showing a place of residence before the start of the census or where, as in Ireland, census records are missing. Even those too poor to own property may be recorded as occupiers, though of course only a head of household will be given. Many of the records are held at local level, so it is worth checking the relevant county record office web site for information. There are few national projects in this area, but many small transcriptions for individual parishes.

Tithes

Tithe records, and in particular the 19th-century tithe maps, are important for both owners and occupiers of land. A very thorough discussion of tithe records will be found in the National Archives' leaflet 'Tithe Records: A Detailed Examination' at <catalogue.pro.gov.uk/Leaflets/ri2148.htm>. The National Library of Wales also has comprehensive pages on this topic at <www.llgc.org.uk/dm/dm0030.htm>. County Record Office web sites often give information about tithe maps and schedules in their collections, and Devon CRO has a project to index the county's tithe maps – see <www.devon.gov.uk/dro/tithepack.html>.

There are many individual transcriptions of tithe schedules. The best way to find them is probably to search on the word 'tithes' or the phrase 'tithe map' and the relevant place name. A major tithe records project is the University of Portsmouth's Tithe Survey of England and Wales at <tiger.iso.port.ac.uk:7778/pls/www/web.html?p=tithe_intro>, which also offers data for seven parishes.

Griffiths Valuation

For Ireland, the 19th-century property records are all the more important because of the absence of census records. The sites referred to for Irish census material in Chapter 6 have information on these records. Among the most important is Griffiths Valuation, and there is a range of material from this source on-line.

The Irish Origins site at <www.irishorigins.com> has an index to Griffiths Valuation and images of the original documents, in a joint venture with the National Library of Ireland and Irish CD-ROM publisher Eneclann. Another subscription site for Irish genealogy, Otherdays, has the Valuation on-line at <www.otherdays.com>, and offers correlation of entries with the Ordnance Survey maps.

There are also a number of small local transcriptions, for example:

- the LEITRIM-ROSCOMMON Griffiths database at <www.leitrim-roscommon.com/GRIFFITH/> has a selection of material for parishes in Galway, Leitrim, Limerick, Mayo and Roscommon
- <freepages.genealogy.rootsweb.com/~tyrone/parishes/griffiths/> has some material for Co. Tyrone
- <www.fermanagh.org.uk/fermanaghpresents/griffiths.htm> has some material for Co. Fermanagh
- From-Ireland has material for Carlow, Laois and Leitrim at <www.from-ireland.net/gene/griffithsval.htm>, which also has links to other sites with Griffiths data.

The PRONI has a guide to using Griffiths Valuation at <www.proni.gov.uk/research/family/griffith.htm>.

Newspapers

While most historical editions of newspapers must be read in the libraries discussed in Chapter 9, whose catalogues will provide details, there is some material on-line. The Genuki county pages are a good way of finding links to local newspapers on-line, and Cyndi's List has a 'Newspapers' page at <www.cyndislist.com/newspapr.htm>. There are, of course, many sites relating to present-day newspapers including Kidon Media-link, which has links to the web sites of UK newspapers at <**www.kidon.com/media-link/unitedkingdom.shtml**>, and All the World's Newspapers, which has comprehensive listings for all countries at <**www.onlinenewspapers.com**>.

The British Library Newspaper Library web site has a lot of information about British newspapers at <**www.bl.uk/collections/newspapers.html**>, and under the heading 'Newspaper, Journalism, and Media Internet Resources' on this page it has links for present-day newspapers on-line including: London National Newspapers, Scottish Newspapers, Irish Newspapers, English and Welsh Newspapers, Channel Islands and Isle of Man Newspapers, Newspapers Around the World, and Other Newspaper Libraries and Collections. The BL Newspaper Library Catalogue is on-line at <**prodigi.bl.uk/nlcat/**>, and the web sites for other major libraries and archives discussed in Chapter 9 will have sections on their newspaper holdings.

British Library Online Newspaper Archive is a pilot project at <**www.uk.olivesoftware.com**>, which has digitised copies of a number of editions of:

- *Daily News*
- *News of the World*
- *Penny Illustrated*
- *Manchester Guardian*
- *Weekly Despatch.*

There are a number of short runs of each paper for individual years. Each newspaper page comes up as a separate image in the browser window. In this view, only the headlines are easily legible but clicking on an article brings up an enlarged version so you can read the body text (Figure 8.6). There is also a text search facility.

After the Newspaper Library, the most important site for historical newspapers is Gazettes On-line at <**www.gazettes-online.co.uk**>. This is a major project to make the entire archive of the London, Edinburgh and Belfast Gazettes available on the Web – these are the UK's official newspapers of record, stretching back to 1665. The first material went on-line in January 2003, and the initial offering in the archive consists of all *London Gazette* editions from the war years (1914–1920, 1939–1948), and all London Gazette Honours and Awards in the 20th century. The ultimate aim is to have all 56,000 editions on-line, starting with the remaining 20th-century editions. Among the material in the wartime editions are announcements of military appointments. The site has a link to a BBC4 radio programme in the 'Making History' series which covers the history of the *London Gazette*.

To access this archive go to the Gazettes On-line site and select 'Archive' on the navigation bar. Each page of each edition comes as a separate PDF

Figure 8.6 British Library Online Newspaper Archive. The pop-up window shows an enlarged version of the highlighted article.

file. To date, the site seems to be designed to work only in Internet Explorer on the PC – some Mac users have reported the site to be unusable, and it does not display properly in some other PC browsers.

Another on-line collection of historical newspaper material is the Internet Library of Early Journals at <**www.bodley.ox.ac.uk/ilej/**>, a joint project by the universities of Birmingham, Leeds, Manchester and Oxford to place on-line digitised copies of 18th- and 19th-century journals, in runs of at least 20 years. The project comprises:

- *Gentleman's Magazine*
- *The Annual Register*
- *Philosophical Transactions of the Royal Society*
- *Notes and Queries*
- *The Builder*
- *Blackwood's Edinburgh Magazine.*

Alongside these projects there are some on-line indexes to individual editions of newspapers. These are generally the work of individuals and therefore inevitably limited in scope. Examples include the *Belfast*

Newsletter for 1737–1800 at <www.ucs.louisiana.edu/bnl/>, the *Surrey Advertiser* for 1864–1867 at <www.newspaperdetectives.co.uk>; and selected years for 12 West Country newspapers at <freespace.virgin.net/paul.mansfield1/paul001.html>.

Obituaries

There are a number of sites with information about newspaper obituary notices. Cyndi's List has a page devoted to obituaries at <www.cyndislist.com/obits.htm>, though almost all the sites listed relate only to the USA.

Free Obituaries On-Line at <www.king.igs.net/~bdmlhm/obit_links6.html> has links to sites providing obituaries – many are newspaper sites – for Australia, Canada, England, Ireland, Jamaica, New Zealand, Scotland, and the USA.

The Obituary Daily Times is a daily index of published obituaries at <www.rootsweb.com/~obituary/>, which has over 8 million entries, mainly from US newspapers. The site is an index only – you need to refer to the original newspaper to see the text. A database of the Irish extracts from this service is provided by the Irish Ancestral Research Association site at <tiara.ie/obframe.htm>.

Obituary Lookup Volunteers at <freepages.genealogy.rootsweb.com/~obitl/> holds lists of those prepared to look up obituaries in particular newspapers or libraries. There are separate pages listing volunteers for England, Wales, Scotland and Ireland, as well as a number of other countries.

Directories

Alongside newspapers the other major printed source, particularly for ancestors who were in trade, are 19th-century directories. These are increasingly being digitised and published on CD-ROM, but a number are available either complete or in part on the Web.

There are three approaches to putting this material on-line. The simplest is a name index to the printed volume, such as that for Pigot's *Commercial Directory for Surrey* (1839), which is on the Genuki Surrey site at <homepages.gold.ac.uk/genuki/SRY/>. This provides text files with page references for names and places. While not a substitute for on-line versions of the directories, these listings at least indicate whether it is worth locating a copy of the directory in question.

Another approach is to place scanned images on the Web, along with a name index, as on Nicholas Adams' site, which provides Pigot's 1830 and 1840 directories for Herefordshire at <freepages.genealogy.rootsweb.com/~nmfa/genealogy.html>.

Finally, some sites offer a full transcription, with or without a name index, such as Rosemary Lockie's pages devoted to the 1835 Pigot's *Commercial Directory for Derbyshire* at <www.genuki.org.uk/big/eng/DBY/Pigot1835/about.html>.

The major site for directories is the Digital Library of Historical Directories site at <www.historicaldirectories.org>. This is the result of a Heritage Lottery Fund project based at the University of Leicester. The aim of the project is to place on-line digitised trade directories from all parts of the UK since the 18th century. It is intended to be representative rather than comprehensive, with one directory for each of six time periods for each the counties and each major town.

For browsing, the best starting point on the site is the list of counties at <www.historicaldirectories.org/HistDir/HTML/counties.htm>, but there is also a search facility covering the whole collection, which can used to search for surnames, place names, occupations and the like. The search lists all matching directories, but does not list the pages with individual hits. You therefore have to browse through the matching pages, which can be very time-consuming. The directories themselves are displayed a page at a time in a special viewer, and the pages can be printed or saved (see Figure 8.7).

There are also some partial transcriptions, usually for individual towns or cities, such as Brian Randell's material for Exeter at <www.cs.ncl.ac.uk/genuki/DEV/Exeter/White1850.html> taken from White's *Devonshire* directory of 1850, or Ann Andrews' extracts for a group of Derbyshire parishes from Kelly's 1891 directory at <ds.dial.pipex.com/town/terrace/pd65/dby/kelly1891_index.htm>.

David Foster's Direct Resources site at <www.direct-resources.uk.com> has brief extracts from a large number of directories on-line, with the full

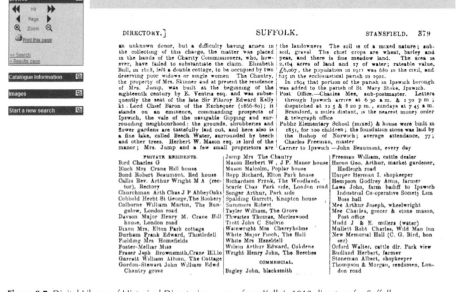

Figure 8.7 Digital Library of Historical Directories: a page from Kelly's 1912 directory for Suffolk

transcriptions available on CD-ROM. Familia (see p. 104) has details of the trade directory holdings of public libraries.

Since directories were compiled on a county basis, the easiest way to find them on-line is to look at the relevant county page on Genuki. Alternatively, you could use a search engine to search for, say, [Directory AND Kelly AND Norfolk] or [Directory AND Pigot AND Lancashire] to locate the publications of the two main 19th-century directory publishers. You may also find information about county directories on county record office web sites. (See Chapter 16 for information on search engines and formulating searches.)

9 Archives and Libraries

Archives and libraries are often seen as the antithesis of the internet, but this is largely illusory, certainly from the genealogical point of view. Only a small number of British genealogical resources are reproduced as images on the Web, and most of the material currently available is in the form of indexes. This means that you will need to go to the relevant archive or a suitable library to check the information you have derived from on-line sources against original documents (or microfilms of them). It will be years before all the core sources are completely available on-line. Technologically, it is in fact a trivial matter to take records which have already been microfilmed and put images of them on-line. But to be usable, such on-line images need to be supported by indexes, if not transcriptions, and the preparation of these requires substantial labour and investment.

If you are going to look at paper records, then catalogues and other finding aids are essential. Traditionally, these have been available only in the reading rooms of record offices themselves, so a significant part of any visit has to be spent checking the catalogues and finding aids for whatever you have come in search of. But the Web has allowed repositories to make it much easier to access information about their collections and facilities. At the very least, the web site for a record office will give a current phone number and opening times. Larger sites will provide descriptions of the holdings, often with advice on how to make the most of them. Increasingly, you can expect to find catalogues on-line and, in some cases, even place orders for documents so that they are ready for you when you visit the repository.

All this means you can get more out of a visit to a record office, because you're able to go better prepared. You can spend more time looking at documents and less trying to locate them. And if you can't get to a record office, you will be able to give much more precise information than previously to someone visiting it on your behalf.

This chapter looks at what the major national repositories and the various local bodies provide in the way of on-line information.

Guides to archives

The ARCHON (Archives On-line) site at <**www.hmc.gov.uk/archon/ archon.htm**> acts as a gateway for all British archives. The site is hosted by the Historical Manuscripts Commission (see p. 99) and its intention is to provide 'information on all repositories in the United Kingdom and all those repositories throughout the world which have collections of manuscripts which are noted in the indexes to the UK National Register of Archives.' The ARCHON Directory at **<www.hmc.gov.uk/archon/ archondirectory.htm>** has a page devoted to each archival repository in the UK *and* the Republic of Ireland. In addition to basic details such as contact information, opening times, and a link to a web site, it also provides links to catalogue entries in the National Register of Archives (see p. 99). In addition, there are search facilities which make it possible to search across the directory, so, for example, you could search for all archives in a given town or county. Although it is probably easier to use Genuki's listing to find County Record Offices (see p. 103), the ARCHON directory is better for locating other archives with relevant material.

The development of electronic sources and finding aids is being taken seriously by all those involved with historic documents. Access to Archives (A2A) is a national project, funded by government and the Heritage Lottery Fund, to 'create a virtual national archives catalogue, bringing together a critical mass of information about the rich national archival heritage and making that information available globally from one source

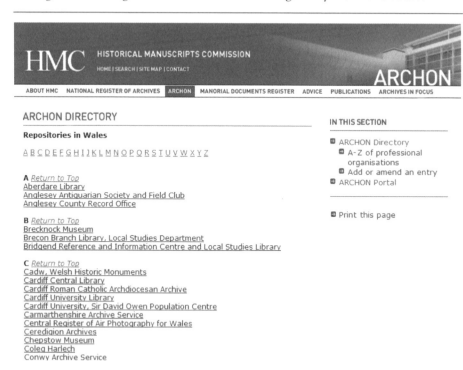

Figure 9.1 The listing of Welsh repositories in the Archon Directory, home page at <www.hmc.gov.uk/ archon/archondirectory.htm>

via the World Wide Web.' Information about A2A will be found at <**www.a2a.pro.gov.uk**>. At the time of writing the site offers search facilities across 300 catalogues.

North of the border, the Scottish Archive Network (SCAN) at <**www.scan.org.uk**> has a similar remit – among its aims are 'the linking of archives large and small, public and private, throughout Scotland, and the creation of a unique knowledge base on Scottish history and culture.' Its directory provides contact details for all Scottish repositories at <**www. scan.org.uk/directory/contactdetails.htm**>, while its Online Catalogues area will provide a consolidated access to the catalogues of around 50 archives in Scotland. This is not yet available as I write, but is promised for later in 2003. The Research Tools pages at <**www.scan.org.uk/ researchrtools/**> include examples of documents, a glossary of Scottish terms, and material on handwriting. There is also a Knowledge Base with answers to questions frequently asked in Scottish archives. Oddly, this does not have its own page but is available as a pop-up link from pages such as the Site Map at <**www.scan.org.uk/aboutus/sitemap.htm**>.

Archives in Focus on the HMC's web site at <**www.hmc.gov.uk/ focus/**> has a different purpose from the sites mentioned so far, aiming not to provide links to archives or archive material but to explain to the non-specialist what archives are and why they are useful. The 'Your History' section of the site has material relating to the use of archives in family history. The 'Teaching Resources' section offers an annotated list of some of the best digitised material on UK archive web sites by way of example.

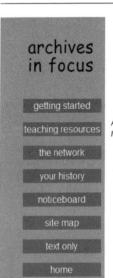

welcome to archives in focus

Archives in Focus is your introduction to archives in the UK. It is maintained by the Historical Manuscripts Commission (HMC). On these pages you will find information about:

- What archives are and how they might be of use to you. Go to getting started
- Using archives in the classroom. Go to teaching resources
- Links to sites relating to education and learning through archives. Go to the network
- Archives for popular lifelong learning topics like family history. Go to your history
- Events and courses featuring archives in your area. Go to noticeboard

© Copyright 2001 Gwynedd Archives

Figure 9.2 Archives in Focus at <www.hmc.gov.uk/focus.htm>

National archives

The Family Records Centre

The Family Records Centre (FRC) is not strictly an archive but rather a service run jointly by the National Archives and the GRO, but from the genealogist's point of view it is effectively an archive – a place where you go to get access to records. Particularly if you are just starting to research your genealogy, its web site at <www.familyrecords.gov.uk/frc/> will be worth a visit. Bear in mind that the records held there are not on-line, so the web site does not provide access to birth, death and marriage indexes or certificates, but it does include a list of the computer databases available at the Centre (see <www.familyrecords.gov.uk/frc/research/ databasesmain.htm>) and the records which can be consulted. There are a number of leaflets in PDF format.

The General Register Office for Scotland is at <www.gro-scotland.gov.uk> and the General Register Office (Northern Ireland) at <www.groni.gov.uk>. These bodies are discussed in more detail under 'Civil registration' in Chapter 5 (p. 46 ff.).

The National Archives

The National Archives web site at <www.nationalarchives.gov.uk> has a number of sections relevant to genealogists. There is a main 'Family History' page at <www.pro.gov.uk/research/familyhistory.htm>, with an

Figure 9.3 The new home page of the National Archives in April 2003

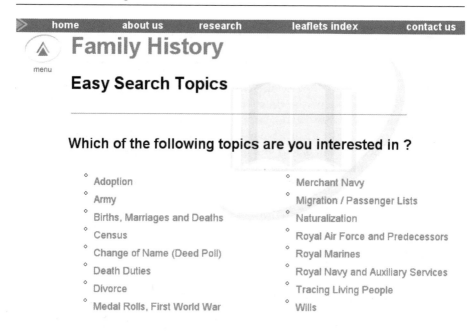

Figure 9.4 The National Archives' Easy Search

'Easy Search' facility at <**www.pro.gov.uk/research/easysearch/**> to help you find relevant material.

For detailed information on the National Archives' records for individual areas of interest, there are over 300 Research Information Leaflets, all of which are on-line, all linked from an alphabetical index at <**www. pro.gov.uk/leaflets/Riindex.asp**>. For a more informal introduction to family history research at the National Archives, see the 'Family History' section of the 'Pathways to the Past' pages at <**www.pro.gov.uk/pathways/ FamilyHistory/**>. A list of the topics in this area is given on p. 6 ff.

The site has links to the FRC and offers an on-line bookshop. In addition, you can expect to find links to any major projects relating to records of genealogical interest. The 'Introduction for New Users' page at <**www.nationalarchives.gov.uk/about/new/**> covers all you need to know when visiting the National Archives, including details of opening hours. Advice on planning your visit will be found at <**www.pro.gov.uk/about/ access/planning.htm**>.

There is much on the site that is relevant to genealogists and these resources are not described here but in the relevant chapters.

The on-line catalogue

One of the most important facilities on the National Archives web site is PROCAT, the on-line catalogue, at <**www.pro.gov.uk/catalogues/**>, with

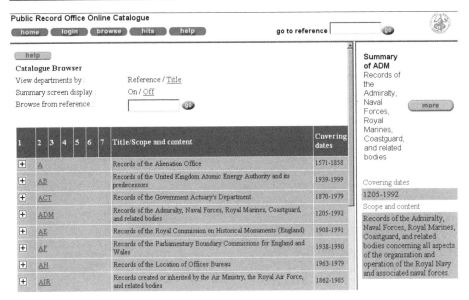

Figure 9.5 List of the National Archives (PRO) Lettercodes

well over eight million entries. There are two ways to use the catalogue: you can browse or you can search.

In browsing, you start from the list of all the Lettercodes denoting the various government departments which created the records in question, and you will then get a list of all the individual document classes from that department. Figure 9.5 shows the start of the list of Lettercodes, and Figure 9.6 shows the start of the list of all the document classes for Admiralty Records (Lettercode ADM), which would be of interest if you had an ancestor who served in the Royal Navy. The titles of the classes are sometimes rather terse, but clicking on the classmark will bring up a description of the class in the right-hand frame of the browser window. Clicking on the link from the class title brings up a list of all the individual pieces within that class – Figure 9.7 shows the start of the list for ADM 11, Officers' Service Records.

Of course, this is all very well if you are familiar with the records in question, or are working with a reference book. If not, it is probably easier to enter the catalogue via the Search option. You can search on up to three keywords, and the results will show all the classes whose titles or descriptions contain the relevant words. Each of these entries will link to a detailed list of piece numbers, as in Figure 9.7.

It itself, the on-line catalogue is very straightforward to use, but it cannot simplify the organisation of the actual records, which have been created independently by individual government departments over 900 or so years. In order to make the most of the catalogue, you will need to be

Public Record Office Online Catalogue

| home | login | browse | hits | help | | go to reference | | GO |

⊟ ADM	Records of the Admiralty, Naval Forces, Royal Marines, Coastguard, and related bodies	1205-1992		
⊞ Division within ADM	Records of the Navy Board and the Board of Admiralty	1563-1985		
⊞ ADM 1	Admiralty, and Ministry of Defence, Navy Department. Correspondence and Papers	1660-1976	31024	
⊞ ADM 2	Admiralty. Out-Letters	1656-1859	1756	
⊞ ADM 3	Admiralty. Minutes	1657-1881	286	
⊞ ADM 4	Admiralty. Letters Patent, Lord High Admiral and Lords of Admiralty Appointments	1707-1964	410	
⊞ ADM 5	Admiralty and predecessors: Letters Patent, Navy Board, Transport Board, Vice-Admiralty and Commissi ...	1746-1890	85	
⊞ ADM 6	Admiralty. Service Records, Registers, Returns and Certificates	1673-1960	476	
⊞ ADM 7	Admiralty. Miscellanea	1563-1953	1005	
⊞ Division within ADM	Records of HM Ships	1669-1971		
⊞ ADM 8	Admiralty. List Books	1673-1909	174	
⊞ Division within ADM	Records of Service	1660-1972		
⊞ ADM 9	Admiralty. Survey Returns of Officers' Services	1817-1848	61	
⊞ ADM 10	Admiralty. Officers' Services, Indexes and Miscellanea	1660-1851	16	
⊞ ADM 11	Admiralty. Officers' Service Records (Series I)	1741-1897	89	
⊞ Division within ADM	Records of the Navy Board and the Board of Admiralty	1563-1985		

Summary of ADM 11
Admiralty: Officers' Service Records (Series I)   [more]

Covering dates
1741-1897

Scope and content
This series includes some original returns of officers' services (including surgeons, chaplains, etc.) in addition to various entry books and compilations of the same and of the appointments of commissioned and warrant officers. It includes also some registers of commissions and warrants entered under the

Figure 9.6 Class list for Admiralty Records

1	2	3	4	5	6	7	Title/Scope and content	Covering dates	Last Piece Ref.
⊟ ADM							Records of the Admiralty, Naval Forces, Royal Marines, Coastguard, and related bodies	1205-1992	
	⊟ Division within ADM						Records of Service	1660-1972	
		⊟ ADM 11					Admiralty. Officers' Service Records (Series I)	1741-1897	89
			⊞ Subseries within ADM 11				*Pieces without a sub-series parent*		
				⊞ ADM 11/1			Commission Branch precedents and draft statements of services of candidates for promotion.	c.1841-1861	
				⊞ ADM 11/2			Survey of Masters' Services, Nos.3-249.	1833-1835	
				⊞ ADM 11/3			Survey of Masters' Services, Nos.250-492.	1833-1835	
				⊞ ADM 11/4			Analysis of masters' eligibility for half-pay.	c.1831	
				⊞ ADM 11/5			Analysis of masters' half-pay list.	1819	
				⊞ ADM 11/6			Analysis of masters' services, annotated to 1847.	1822	
				⊞ ADM 11/7			Survey of Masters' Services, Nos.4168-4400.	1851	

Figure 9.7 List of piece numbers for the class ADM 11

familiar with the way in which the records you are looking for are organised. There are Research Information Leaflets for all the major classes of records of interest to genealogists, as well as the National Archives' *Tracing Your Ancestors in the Public Record Office* and specialist publications on individual classes of record. A useful feature of the on-line catalogue search is that the search results pages start with a list of relevant Research Information Leaflets.

In addition to PROCAT, there are a number of other specialist catalogues on the site. Those of most interest to genealogists are:

- the E179 database – this catalogues tax records relating to lay people in England, c.1200–1688, with over 25,000 documents
- the Equity Pleadings database – this currently contains details of around 30,000 Chancery Pleadings
- the Hospital Database – this includes the location and covering dates of administrative and clinical records.

Links to all of these will be found from the main 'Catalogues' page at <www.pro.gov.uk/catalogues/> and there is a detailed description of each database.

Historical Manuscripts Commission
The Royal Commission on Historical Manuscripts became part of the National Archives in April 2003. At the time of writing, it retains a distinct web site in its own internet domain at <**www.hmc.gov.uk**>, but by April 2004 this should have been fully integrated into the National Archives web site at <**www.nationalarchives.gov.uk**>.

In addition to ARCHON, mentioned on p. 92, the HMC site has two resources of interest to family historians. The National Register of Archives (NRA) has an on-line index at <**www.hmc.gov.uk/nra/nra2. htm**>. This contains reference details for around 150,000 people, families and corporate bodies relating to British history, with a further 100,000 related records. The materials themselves are held in record offices, university libraries and specialist repositories. The NRA catalogue gives details of location and availability. The search engine allows you to search by:

- Name – combined search of the Business Index and the Organisations Index
- Personal Name – combined search of the Personal Index and the Diaries and Papers Index
- Family Name
- Place Name – lists businesses, organisations and other corporate bodies by place.

Historical Manuscripts Commission

UK National Register of Archives

Simple Search

About Simple Search

Corporate Name

Personal Name

Family Name

Place Name

NRA Home

HMC Homepage

Place Name Search for : **Pevensey East Sussex**

Bexhill and Battle Conservative Association: Pevensey Bay branch, Pevensey East Sussex (1)

East Kent and South Pevensey Volunteers, Pevensey Sussex (1)

Pevensey and Hastings levels Commissioners of Sewers, Pevensey Sussex (3)

Pevensey Borough Coroner, Pevensey Sussex (1)

Pevensey parish, Pevensey Sussex (1)

Pevensey Rape land tax, Pevensey Sussex (1)

Plumley family, Pevensey (1)

Robert Plumley, coal merchant, Pevensey Sussex (1)

John Thatcher of Westham and Pevensey, Pevensey Sussex (1)

9 records found.

Figure 9.8 Place name search in the National Register of Archives

Historical Manuscripts Commission

UK National Register of Archives

Robert Plumley, coal merchant
Pevensey, Sussex

1844-70 : memorandum book
East Sussex Record Office
Reference : PLU
NRA 6462 Plumley

1 record noted.

Where reference is made to an NRA number, a catalogue is filed in the National Register of Archives and may be consulted in our public search room.

Figure 9.9 Full entry for a record in the NRA

Figure 9.8 shows the results of a place name search in the NRA, while Figure 9.9 shows the full details for one of the search results. Note that it not only gives the repository but also the reference number used by the record office in question.

Of more specialist interest is the Manorial Documents Register (MDR) at <**www.hmc.gov.uk/mdr/mdr.htm**>, which provides a record of the whereabouts of manorial documents in England and Wales. Although most of the MDR is not computerised, certain sections are available on-line, including Wales and some counties of England.

National Archives of Scotland

The National Archives of Scotland has a web site at <**www.nas.gov.uk**>, with a Family History section at <**www.nas.gov.uk/family_history.htm**>. At the time of writing there is no on-line catalogue, but one is being developed as part of the Scottish Archive Network (see p. 94), and the latest information about the project can be found at <**www.scan.org.uk/ aboutus/indexonline.htm**>. The site offers a comprehensive collection of Fact Sheets in Adobe Acrobat (PDF) format, covering: adoption, buildings, crafts and trades, crime and criminals, customs and excise, deeds, divorce, education, emigration, estate records, inheriting lands and buildings, lighthouses, military records, the poor, sasines, taxation records, valuation rolls, and wills and testaments. There is also a Family History FAQ page covering the National Archives' holdings and services relevant to family historians.

The Public Record Office of Northern Ireland

The Public Record Office of Northern Ireland (PRONI) has a web site at <**www.proni.gov.uk**>. The site offers extensive information for genealogists, including descriptions of the major categories of record and about two dozen leaflets on various aspects of Irish genealogical research. Links to all these aids are provided on the 'Records Held' page at <**www.proni.gov.uk/records/records.htm**>. The 'Introductions to the Major Collections' page at <**www.proni.gov.uk/records/listing.htm**> links to descriptions of the main collections of private papers held by PRONI. There is also an FAQ page at <**www.proni.gov.uk/question/question. htm**>.

The site does not offer a full on-line catalogue, but has four on-line indexes of use to genealogists:

- the Geographical Index (for locating any administrative geographical name, with Ordnance Survey Map reference number)
- the Prominent Person Index
- the Presbyterian Church Index
- the Church of Ireland Index.

The last two cover only those records which have been microfilmed by PRONI. There are plans to add other church records, school records and pre-1858 wills.

National Archives of Ireland

The National Archives of Ireland web site at <**www.nationalarchives.ie**> has no on-line catalogue, but there are several on-line databases of interest to genealogists:

- Ordnance Survey Parishes Index
- Ireland–Australia Transportation
- National School Roll Books and Registers.

All these can be accessed from <**www.nationalarchives.ie/govpapers. html**>. There is a collection of guides to various aspects of Irish genealogy at <**www.nationalarchives.ie/genealogy.html**>.

The national libraries

The British Library has a number of collections of interest to genealogists. The home page of the BL web site is at <**portico.bl.uk**>, while the library catalogue is at <**blpc.bl.uk**>. The catalogue is also included in COPAC, discussed on p. 106. The British Library Newspaper Library at Colindale has a web site at <**www.bl.uk/catalogues/newspapers.html**> and its on-line catalogue at <**prodigi.bl.uk/nlcat/**> includes over 50,000 newspaper and periodical titles from all over the world, dating from the 17th to the 21st century. Each entry in the web catalogue contains full details of the title (including any title changes), the place of publication (the town or city and the country) and the dates which are held. The results can be sorted by any of these fields, which means you can get a historical list of newspapers for a particular town (see Figure 9.10). Further information about the BL's newspaper collection will be found on p. 86.

The India Office Records held by the British Library do not have their own on-line catalogue, but a description of holdings will be found at <**www.bl.uk/collections/orientaloffice.html**>, and some of the material can be found on Access to Archives <**www.a2a.pro.gov.uk/search**> – select 'British Library, Oriental & India Office' from the 'Location of Archives' field. The HMC's ARCHON directory at <**www.hmc.gov.uk/archon/ archondirectory.htm**> also contains entries for material in the India Office Records, including around 1,400 for individuals involved in Indian trade or administration.

The National Library of Scotland has a web site at <**www.nls.uk**> with a number of on-line catalogues linked from <**www.nls.uk/catalogues/ online/**>, though not all of its material is included in these as yet. The Scots Abroad catalogue at <**www.nls.uk/catalogues/online/scotsabroad/**> will be of interest to those descended from Scottish emigrants.

Search Results 🔎

Date ranges show the earliest and latest copies held, but this does not necessarily mean that we hold all intervening copies.
Select the title for its full details

Search hits may be on details which are not shown on this summary screen

Number of hits: 98

Place	Title	Dates
Derby; Derbyshire; England	Drewry's Derby Mercury	1732-1787
Derby; Derbyshire; England	Derby Mercury (The)	1788-1933
Newark-on-Trent; Nottinghamshire; England	Newark Times, and Weekly Advertiser for the Counties of Nottingham, Lincoln, York, Derby, and Leicester	1830-1830
Derby; Derbyshire; England	Derby & Chesterfield Reporter, and General Advertiser for Derbyshire and the Midland Counties (The)	1831-1842
Derby; Derbyshire; England	Derby and Chesterfield Reporter, Derbyshire Chronicle, etc (The)	1842-1853
Derby; Derbyshire; England	Derbyshire Advertiser and Journal (The)	1846-1848
Derby; Derbyshire; England	Derbyshire Advertiser and Ashbourne, Uttoxeter and North Staffordshire Journal (The)	1848-1949
Derby; Derbyshire; England	Derby and Chesterfield Reporter	1854-1930

Figure 9.10 Search results for 'Derby' in the British Library Newspaper Library catalogue

The National Library of Wales web site at <**www.llgc.org.uk**> provides links to a number of on-line catalogues at <**www.llgc.org.uk/cronfa/index_s.htm**>. The most important of these is the ISYS free text-search system, as it includes an index of applicants for marriage licences from 1616 to 1837. The search page for ISYS is at <**www.llgc.org.uk:81**>.

The National Library of Ireland has a web site at <**www.nli.ie**>, with a family history section at <**www.nli.ie/fr_servfamily.htm**>. There are several on-line catalogues, searchable separately or combined, all linked from <**www.nli.ie/fr_cata2.htm**>. Information on 'Family history research in the National Library' will be found at <**www.nli.ie/family_hr.htm**>. The site also hosts the web pages of the Office of Chief Herald at <**www.nli.ie/fr_offi2.htm**>.

For access to on-line catalogues of the UK national libraries, see the information on COPAC, p. 106, below.

County record offices

There are several ways to locate a county record office (CRO) web site. Each Genuki county page provides a link to relevant CROs, and may itself give contact details and opening times. Mark Howells has links to record office web sites for:

- England at <**www.oz.net/~markhow/englishros.htm**>
- Wales at <**www.oz.net/~markhow/welshros.htm**>
- Scotland at <**www.oz.net/~markhow/scotsros.htm**>.

The ARCHON directory (see p. 92) allows you to locate a record office by county or region. Finally, CROs can be found via the web site of the relevant county council (you may even be able to make a guess at its URL, as it will often be something like <**www.essexcc.gov.uk**>) or via the UK government portal at <**www.ukonline.gov.uk**> (see p. 13), which links to the web sites of all arms of national and local government.

There is a wide variation in what CROs provide on their web sites. At the very least, though, you can expect to find details of location, contacts, and opening times, along with some basic help on using their material. However, increasingly they offer background material on the area and specific collections, and even on-line catalogues. Even better, a number of CROs are engaged on major digitisation projects, many of which are mentioned elsewhere in this book. Much of the material held by CROs is catalogued on ARCHON (see p. 92).

The FFHS has a leaflet 'You And Your Record Office: A Code Of Practice For Family Historians Using County Record Offices' at <**www. ffhs.org.uk/General/Help/Record.htm**>, which offers advice on preparing for a visit and what to expect.

Public libraries

Public libraries, although they cannot vie with county record offices for manuscript material, have considerable holdings in the basic sources for genealogical research.

The UK Public Libraries Page at <**dspace.dial.pipex.com/town/square/ ac940/ukpublib.html**> is a general site devoted to Public Libraries. At <**dspace.dial.pipex.com/town/square/ac940/weblibs.html**> it provides links to library web sites, and to their OPACs (On-line Public Access Catalogues) where these are available over the internet.

For public libraries in the Irish Republic, Ireland's public library portal has links to the web sites and on-line catalogues at <**www.library.ie/ public/**>.

However, for genealogists, a more useful starting point is the Familia web site at <**www.familia.org.uk**>. This is designed to be a comprehensive guide to genealogical holdings in public libraries, with a page for every local authority in the UK and the Republic of Ireland, listing the principal public libraries within the authority which have family history resources, along with contact details, opening times, etc. It then outlines the genealogical holdings under the following main headings:

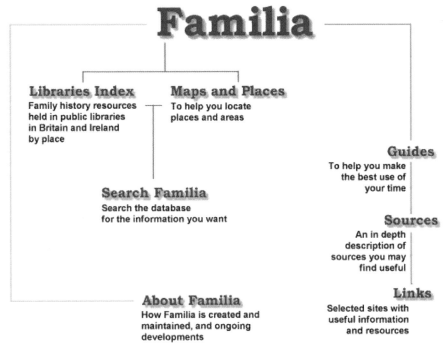

Figure 9.11 Familia home page

- Births, deaths and marriages
- Census records
- Directories
- Electoral registers
- Poll books
- International Genealogical Index
- Unpublished indexes
- Parish registers
- Periodicals
- Published transcripts
- Other materials.

There are also details of any research services offered. While not all local authorities have provided detailed information on their family history material via Familia, over 80% of them have. Figure 9.12 shows part of the entry for the London Borough of Bromley, with details of its directory and electoral register holdings.

6. Directories

6(a) County and Regional Directories

Kent (and some Home Counties) 1840-1938 - incomplete series

6(b) City and Town Directories

Bromley 1866-1962
Beckenham 1897-1939 (some including Anerley and Penge)

6(c) Telephone Directories

Bromley 1952 to date
Orpington 1967-1970. Included in Bromley 1972-

7. Electoral registers and polls books

7(a) Electoral Registers

Beckenham 1925- last non-current year
Bromley 1905-70 (continued as Ravensbourne 1971-)
Chislehurst 1912-
Orpington 1939-
Penge 1899-1947 (continues as part of Beckenham)
N.B. The Reference Library has current registers

7(b) Poll Books

Kent: 1791, 1803
West Kent: 1835, 1837, 1847, 1852, 1857, 1865, 1868

Figure 9.12 Part of the Familia page for the London Borough of Bromley

University libraries

While university libraries are not of major importance for genealogical research, all have special collections which may include personal papers of notable individuals; and many have collections of local material which, while probably not of use in constructing a pedigree, may be of interest to the family historian looking for local topographical and historical information.

There is no single central index to university library holdings but COPAC is a major consortium of, currently, 23 university libraries, including three of the four copyright libraries (Cambridge University Library, the Bodleian in Oxford, and Trinity College, Dublin), as well as the British Library. The COPAC web site at <**www.copac.ac.uk**> provides access to a consolidated catalogue for all member institutions. At the time of writing, there is an additional experimental interface which includes access to the catalogues of the National Libraries of Scotland and Wales (see p. 102).

All university libraries are included on the ARCHON site at <**www. hmc.gov.uk/archon/archon.htm**>, which provides contact details and has catalogue entries for archival material (i.e. not books or periodicals) relating to individuals, families and organisations. The Archives Hub at <**www.archiveshub.ac.uk**> is a site which offers descriptions of archive material in 50 academic libraries.

Bear in mind that university libraries are not open to the general public and that you will normally need to make a written application in advance in order to have access, particularly in the case of manuscript material.

Family History Centres

The LDS Church's Family History Centres (FHCs) are valuable not just because they hold copies of the IGI on CD-ROM, microfiche copies of the GRO indexes, and other materials, but because any UK genealogical material which has been microfilmed by the Church can be ordered for viewing in an FHC, and this includes many parish registers.

Contact details for FHCs are available at the FamilySearch site at <**www.familysearch.org**> – clicking on the Library tab (at the top of most main screens) and then selecting Family History Centres will lead to a search page. Genuki provides a quick way to get listings from this search facility: the page at <**www.genuki.org.uk/big/LDS/**> has links which will search automatically for all FHCs in England, Scotland, Ireland and Wales on the FamilySearch site. There is also an unofficial list, maintained by an

Place Details	FAMILY HISTORY LIBRARY CATALOG	THE CHURCH OF JESUS CHRIST OF LATTER-DAY SAINTS

View Related Places

Place:	England, Kent, Lenham
Topics:	England, Kent, Lenham - Census England, Kent, Lenham - Church records England, Kent, Lenham - Church records - Indexes England, Kent, Lenham - Land and property England, Kent, Lenham - Manors England, Kent, Lenham - Manors - Court records England, Kent, Lenham - Occupations England, Kent, Lenham - Poorhouses, poor law, etc. England, Kent, Lenham - Taxation

Figure 9.13 Search results for Lenham, Kent in the FHL catalogue

Topic Details	FAMILY HISTORY LIBRARY CATALOG	THE CHURCH OF JESUS CHRIST OF LATTER-DAY SAINTS
Topic:	England, Kent, Lenham - Church records	
Titles:	Archdeacon's transcripts, 1564-1813; Bishop's transcripts, 1611-1905 Church of England. Parish Church of Lenham (Kent)	
	Births and baptisms, 1779-1837 Independent Church (Lenham)	
	Bishop's transcripts, 1874-1908 Church of England. Chapelry of Charing Heath (Kent)	
	Churchwarden accounts and vestry minutes, 1681-1918 Church of England. Parish Church of Lenham (Kent)	
	Parish register extracts, 1559-1905 Church of England. Parish Church of Lenham (Kent)	
	Record of members, 1849-1860 Church of Jesus Christ of Latter-day Saints. Lenham Hill Branch (Kent)	
	Record of members, ca. 1795-1877 Church of Jesus Christ of Latter-day Saints. Bromley Branch (Kent)	

Figure 9.14 Search results for Lenham, Kent in the FHL catalogue – Church Records

individual member of the LDS Church, at <www.lds.org.uk/genealogy/fhc/>, which appears to be more up to date. This has a complete listing of towns on the main page, making a search unnecessary.

The key to exploiting this immense wealth of material is the Family History Library (FHL) catalogue, which can be consulted on-line at the FamilySearch site. The search page at <www.familysearch.org/Eng/Library/FHLC/frameset_fhlc.asp> offers searches by place, surname, or, for published works, author. If you search by place, you will get a list of the various types of records available for it. Figure 9.13 shows the initial results of a place search for Lenham in Kent, while Figure 9.14 shows the expanded entry for Church Records, with descriptions of the various items available.

In order to find the microfilm reference for one of the entries, you need to click on it to bring up the 'Title Details' screen (Figure 9.15). This tells you the repository where the material is held (or was at the time of filming), together with the repository's reference for the material. This means you could even use the FHL catalogue as a partial catalogue to county record offices.

Finally, clicking on the 'View Film Notes' button at the top left brings up detailed information on the microfilms relating to this item (Figure 9.16), with an exact description of what is on each film, together with the film reference which you can now use to order the film at an FHC.

The Society of Genealogists

The Society of Genealogists is home to the premier genealogical library in the country. Its library catalogue has been converted to an OPAC system with the aid of a Heritage Lottery Fund grant. At present, this catalogue is

Title Details	FAMILY HISTORY LIBRARY CATALOG	THE CHURCH OF JESUS CHRIST OF LATTER-DAY SAINTS

View Film Notes

Title:	Archdeacon's transcripts, 1564-1813; Bishop's transcripts, 1611-1905
Authors:	Church of England. Parish Church of Lenham (Kent) (Main Author)

Notes:	Microreproduction of original records housed at the Canterbury Cathedral Archives, Canterbury, Kent.
	Some early pages damaged.
	The church was named for St. Mary.
	Canterbury Cathedral Archives no.: DCa/BT/112; DCb/BT1/141; DCb/BT2/174

Subjects:	England, Kent, Lenham - Church records

Format:	Manuscript (On Film)
Language:	English
Publication:	Salt Lake City : Filmed by the Genealogical Society of Utah, 1991-1992
Physical:	on 4 microfilm reels ; 35 mm.

Figure 9.15 FHL catalogue search – Title Details

Film Notes	FAMILY HISTORY LIBRARY CATALOG	THE CHURCH OF JESUS CHRIST- OF LATTER-DAY SAINTS

View Title Details

Title:	Archdeacon's transcripts, 1564-1813; Bishop's transcripts, 1611-1905
Authors:	Church of England. Parish Church of Lenham (Kent) (Main Author)

Note	Location Film
Archdeacon's transcripts: Baptisms, marriages and burials 1564-1813 (missing: 1565/6, 1570/1, 1573/4, 1578/9, 1594/5, 1629/30, 1633/4, 1640/1-1660/1, 1664/5, 1665/6, 1670/1, 1774/5, 1775/6)	FHL BRITISH Film 1751918 Item 3
Bishop's transcripts: Baptisms, marriages and burials 1611-1813 (missing: 1613/4, 1621/2, 1627/8, 1631/2, 1640/1, 1642/3-1662/3, 1716/7, 1795/6)	FHL BRITISH Film 1736839 Item 3
Bishop's transcripts contd.: Baptisms,marriages and burials 1813-1824	FHL BRITISH Film 1786623 Item 6
Bishop's transcripts contd.: Baptisms and burials 1824-1873, 1876-1882, 1897-1898, 1904-1905 Marriages 1824-1837	FHL BRITISH Film 1786624 Item 1

Numbers 1-4 of 4 film notes

Figure 9.16 FHL catalogue – Film Notes

only available in the Society's library, but may be put on-line at some point in the future, possibly as part of the English Origins site (though no doubt access will be free of charge).

However, the Society already has details of one important section of its holdings on-line on its own web site: the list of more than 11,000 parish register copies in its library can be found at <www.sog.org.uk/prc/>. There is a page for each county which lists each parish and gives the dates for which there are copies along with the shelf mark in the Society's library.

Beyond the British Isles

If you need to consult archives outside the UK and Ireland the best general starting points will be the pages for individual countries on Cyndi's List – each of these has a section headed 'Libraries, Archives & Museums'. This will have links to not only the national archives, but also major provincial archives. Of course, if the country is not English-speaking you may not be able to make full use of the site, but you will often find at least some basic information in English and e-mail address for enquiries.

The Family History Centres have microfilmed records from many countries, and searching on a country in the Family History Library Catalogue will list the various types of record and what has been filmed (see p. 107).

Future developments

The ARCHON Portal on the HMC web site at <www.hmc.gov.uk/ archon/archonportal/archonportal.htm> has details of current archival projects. Many of these are not of direct relevance to genealogists, but the following areas from the keywords directory at <www.hmc.gov.uk/ archon/archonportal/keywords.htm> are likely to include projects which relate to topics covered in this book:

● Digitisation
● Directories
● Online national library catalogues and portals
● Online resources for history.

While it may be a very long time before all genealogical records are on-line, it looks as if there will be a comprehensive network of catalogues for the repositories that hold them within the fairly near future.

10 Surname Interests and Pedigrees

The resources discussed in Chapters 4 to 8 contain direct transcriptions of, or indexes to, primary genealogical sources. But alongside these are 'compiled' sources, the material put together by individual genealogists. Many people are now putting their pedigrees on the internet on a personal web site – Chapter 17 explains how to do this yourself, and Chapter 16 looks at how to locate such material. But there are a number of sites to which people can submit details of the surnames they are interested in, or even entire pedigrees, so that others can contact them. Sites devoted to surname origins and distribution are discussed in Chapter 13.

Surname interests

One of the best ways to make progress with your family tree is to contact others who are interested in the same surnames. In some cases you will end up encountering cousins who may have considerable material relating to a branch of your family, but at the very least it is useful to discover what resources others have looked at. If you find someone who is doing a one-name study, they may even have extracts from primary sources which they might be prepared to share with you.

Before the advent of the internet, finding such contacts was quite difficult. It involved checking a range of published and unpublished sources, looking through the surname interests in family history magazines and consulting all the volumes of directories such as the annual *Genealogical Research Directory*. You will still need to do all this, of course, not least because many genealogists are still not on-line and this is the only way to find out about *their* researches. The SoG's leaflet 'Has it been done before?' at <www.sog.org.uk/leaflets/done.html> provides a comprehensive overview of the various off-line resources to check. But the internet now offers a much easier way both of locating and inviting such contacts.

County surname lists

If you have already made some progress with your family history and have got back far enough to know where your ancestors were living 100 or so years ago, then you should check the relevant county surname list – a directory of genealogical research interests for a particular county.

Surname lists do not provide genealogical information as such: they are just registers of interests, like a printed research directory, and give for each surname the e-mail address of the researcher who submitted it, and usually a date range for the period of interest (see Figure 10.1). Some lists also have links to the web sites of submitters.

There is at least one surname list for almost every county in the UK and Ireland, and Genuki keeps a central list of these at **<www.genuki.org.uk/indexes/SurnamesLists.html>**. Many of these are run by Graham Jaunay on behalf of Genuki, covering around 60% of the British Isles. These all have the same interface and organisation. Figure 10.1 shows a page from the Buckinghamshire list. The underlined name of the contributor provides the e-mail address of the person to contact – clicking on it will bring up a mail window in your browser, or you can read the e-mail address from the status bar at the bottom of the browser when you move your mouse over the link. As well as the lists for individual counties, there are also general lists for England, Scotland, Ireland and Wales. These are useful where you don't know the county or where you are conducting a one-name study and are interested in all parts of the UK. Incidentally, Graham Jaunay also maintains surname lists for Australia and New Zealand as part of the same system.

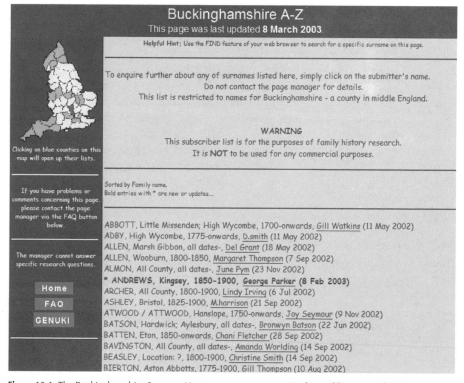

Figure 10.1 The Buckinghamshire Surname List at <www.users.on.net/proformat/bkmnames1.html>

Alongside the Genuki lists, there are around 90 other county-based surname lists, with a few for smaller areas. Although these lists are not formally part of Genuki, many of them have long-standing links with the relevant Genuki county page. Links to any lists relevant to a county will be found on the Genuki county page as well as on the central surname list page.

For other countries, Cyndi's List has links to further surname lists at <www.cyndislist.com/database.htm#Locality>, but do not expect to find the same level of coverage as there is for the UK.

In addition to the county surname lists, there are a number of surname lists relevant to UK emigration and immigration. These are discussed in Chapter 11 (see p. 141 ff).

You should consider submitting your surname interests to the relevant county lists so that other people can contact you. The exact method of doing this varies from list to list: on some there is a web page with a submission form; on others you will need to e-mail the list-maintainer. Be sure to follow the instructions, as many list maintainers expect you to submit your interests in a particular format (to make processing of submissions easier to automate) and may ignore something sent in the wrong format.

One problem with surname lists is that someone who has made a submission may forget to update their entries if they subsequently change their e-mail address, so you will occasionally find contact details that are no longer valid. Unfortunately there is nothing you can do about this – it is a fact of life on the internet – and there is no point in asking the surname list manager where a particular submitter can be contacted if their stated e-mail address is no longer valid. Obviously if you change your own e-mail address, you'll need to contact the owner of any surname list you have submitted to. For Graham Jaunay's lists, there are on-line forms for changing an e-mail address.

The Guild of One-Name Studies

The Guild of One-Name Studies at <www.one-name.org> is an organisation for those who are researching all people with a particular surname, rather than just their own personal pedigree. It has a searchable Register of One-Name Studies on-line at <www.one-name.org/register.shtml>, which gives a contact address (not necessarily electronic) for each of the 7,000 or so surnames registered with the Guild.

Unlike the county lists, the surname interests registered with the Guild cover the whole world – this is, in fact, a requirement for membership. So, even though the person who has registered a particular one-name interest may not have ancestors in common with you, there is still a good chance that they have collected material of interest relating to your surname. In particular, a Guild member is likely to have a good overview of the variants of their registered surname. This makes the Guild's list of

Introduction to the Guild and its benefits.

How and where to join the Guild.

2003 AGM and Conference

The next Guild Regional Seminar

Members events

The on-line searchable Register of One-Name Studies.

Journal of One-Name Studies

Services available to members.

Research facilities for members and non-members.

1881 Distribution Map

WWW.ONE-NAME.ORG

Figure 10.2 The Guild of One-Name Studies at <www.one-name.org/register.shtml>

surnames worth checking even, or especially, if you are only just starting your researches, whereas the county surname lists are probably not very useful until you have got back at least three generations.

RootsWeb

One of the most useful sites for surname interests is RootsWeb at <**www.rootsweb.com**>, which has a wide range of surname-related resources, all linked from <**resources.rootsweb.com/~clusters/surnames/**>. There is a separate page for each listed surname with:

- links to personal web sites at RootsWeb which include the name
- search forms for a number of databases hosted by RootsWeb
- links to any mailing lists for the surname (see below).

The most general surname resource at RootsWeb is the Roots Surname List (RSL) at <**rsl.rootsweb.com**>. This is a surname list attached to the

ROOTS-L mailing list, the oldest genealogy mailing list on the internet, and contains about a million entries submitted by around 200,000 individual genealogists. You can enter a geographical location to narrow your search, using Chapman county codes and/or three-letter country codes (see Figure 10.3 for some examples) – there is a list of standard codes at <helpdesk.rootsweb.com/codes/>. However, you may need to do a couple of searches to make sure you find all relevant entries as some people spell out English counties in full or use the two-letter country code UK instead of ENG. If you check the list regularly, a useful feature is that you can restrict your results to those added or updated recently. As you can see from Figure 10.3, the submitter details are not given on the search results page, but there is a link to them from the user ID given in the 'Submitter' column.

Discussion forums

Mailing lists, newsgroups and other types of discussion forum are described in detail in Chapter 15, but it is worth noting here that there are many groups devoted to individual surnames. Even if you do not participate in any of them, it will still be well worth your while to look through the archives of past messages to see if anyone else is working on the same family or on the same geographical area.

Surname	From	To	Migration	Submitter
Marshall	1000	1889	"SouthBank,ENG>Cleveland,OH"	lindonm
Marshall	1126	1248	WLS>ENG	mcgraw
Marshall	1500	1641	Ilminster,ENG>Exeter,ENG>NewHaven,CT,USA	brucew
Marshall	1500	1600	ENG	seejay
Marshall	1500s	1619	Quarrington,LIN,ENG	edharr
Marshall	1502	1641	ENG	varya
Marshall	1502	1641	"SOM>DEV,ENG>NewHaven,CT"	ktonks
Marshall	1576	1641	ENG>MA,USA	silvie
Marshall	1580	----	LIN,ENG	bchapman
Marshall	1584	now	BKS, ENG	shanan
Marshall	1595	now	LND,ENG>MA,USA>AnnapolisCo,NS,CAN	behall
Marshall	1595	1636	ENG>MA,USA	spencer
Marshall	1596	now	ENG>MA,USA	horvat1
Marshall	1598	1650	ENG>MA	maryl
Marshall	1600	now	LIN,ENG	lkfergus
Marshall	1600	1733	ENG>Westfield,MA,USA	mrstamil
Marshall	1600	now	ENG>VA>JohnsonCo>CarterCo,KY	af15469

Figure 10.3 Search results for MARSHALL and ENG in the Roots Surname List

John Fuller's list of mailing lists has information on those dedicated to individual surnames at <www.rootsweb.com/~jfuller/gen_mail.html#SURNAMES>. Many of these surname lists are hosted by RootsWeb and can also be found from the general list of mailing lists at <lists.rootsweb.com> or via the individual surname pages at <resources.rootsweb.com/~clusters/surnames/>.

Alongside the surname mailing lists, there are Web-based message boards or discussion forums for individual surnames. One of the largest sites hosting such discussion lists is GenForum at <genforum.genealogy.com>, which must have message boards for at least 10,000 surnames. Ancestry.com and RootsWeb also have a common set of surname message boards at <boards.ancestry.com> or <boards.rootsweb.com> – follow the link to 'United Kingdom and Ireland', and then the link to the relevant part of the UK.

In many cases, these boards relate to a surname mailing list hosted by RootsWeb. This means that you can contribute your own query, via the Web, without having to subscribe to a mailing list. A particularly useful feature is that the individual boards can be searched, which makes it possible to find messages and queries relating to particular places, something which is essential for common and widespread surnames.

On the other hand, newsgroups, discussed in Chapter 15, are of little use for finding surname interests. Although there are newsgroups devoted specifically to the posting of surname interests – the group for British surnames is soc.genealogy.surnames.britain – these seem to be defunct. There are 150 or so groups in the hierarchy alt.family-names (e.g. alt.family-names.johnson), but these have few messages and are unlikely to be useful to you.

Family history societies

Every family history society has a register of members' interests, and it will be worthwhile checking the societies which cover the areas where your ancestors lived. If you're lucky, the list will be available on-line. For example, the Shropshire FHS offers a database of 20,000 members' interests at <www.sfhs.org.uk/memberinterests.asp>, which can be browsed, or searched for a specific surname. The Sussex Family History Group at <www.sfhg.org.uk> has both a public members' interests area and a more extensive one for members only. Bear in mind that not all these members will be contactable by e-mail and societies often do not publish members' postal addresses on-line, so you may need to consult the society's journal for contact details. For a list of FHS web sites consult the 'Family History and Genealogy Societies' page on Genuki at <www.genuki.org.uk/Societies/>.

Pedigree databases

The surname-interest resources do not provide genealogical information, they simply offer contact details for other genealogists who may share your interests. But there are several sites which allow genealogists to make their pedigrees available on the Web. You can, of course, do this by creating your own web site, as discussed in Chapter 17, particularly if you want to publish more comprehensive information. But if you just want to make your pedigree available on-line, these sites provide an easy way to do it. Even if you do not make your own pedigree available, many others have, and it is worth checking these sites for overlap with your own family tree. There are two ways of getting your own pedigree into one of these databases. Some of them have facilities for you to create your pedigree entirely on-line, while the commoner method is to upload a GEDCOM file containing your pedigree. Information about GEDCOM files and how to create them will be found on p. 239, Chapter 17.

There is not space here to give more than a brief account of some of the most important sites, but for a comprehensive list of pedigree databases consult the 'Databases – Lineage-Linked' page on Cyndi's List at <www.cyndislist.com/lin-linked.htm>.

Free databases

FamilySearch at <www.familysearch.org> has been discussed as a source of record transcriptions in Chapter 7 (p. 72), but the site also includes two data collections with user-submitted information. Ancestral File goes back to 1978, starting life as a CD-ROM collection, initially as a way for members of the LDS Church to deposit the fruits of their researches but in fact open to submission from anyone with genealogical information. The Pedigree Resource File is a more recent database compiled from submissions to the FamilySearch web site and also published on CD-ROM. In Ancestral File a successful search on an individual name brings up an individual record with links, on the left, to a full pedigree, a family group record and submitter details (see Figure 10.4). Unfortunately, there is only a postal address for the submitter, no e-mail address.

In the Pedigree Resource File a search produces a similar individual record with details of the submitter, but no link to a pedigree. A useful feature is that it gives you the submission number – clicking on this will do a search for all individuals in the same submission. The submitter details will include a postal address, and may also have a link to the submitter's web site. As discussed in Chapter 7, you can search all four FamilySearch databases at once by selecting All Resources from any of the search pages (see Figure 7.1), and the results are then listed separately for each database.

Probably the largest collection of pedigrees is on RootsWeb, whose WorldConnect data has a home page at <worldconnect.genealogy.rootsweb.com>. It currently contains around 250 million names,

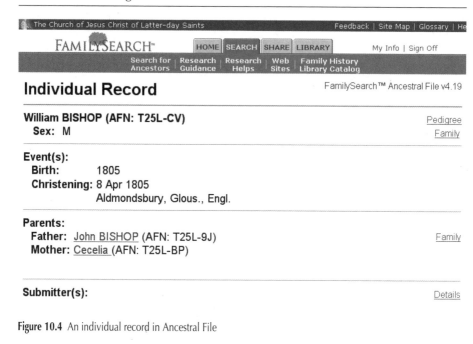

Figure 10.4 An individual record in Ancestral File

submitted by about a quarter of a million users. Ancestry's World Tree provides access to the same database at <**www.ancestry.myfamily.com/trees/awt/**> (this is freely accessible and does not require a subscription to Ancestry).

The initial search page form provided on RootsWeb allows you to search by surname and given name, and the search results pages then list each matching entry with further details and offer a link to the home page for the database in which the entry is found or to the specific person. If you get too many results to cope with, a more detailed search form provides options to narrow down your search with dates, places, names of parents, etc.

Figure 10.5 shows a page of search results on WorldConnect. Clicking on the name of the individual takes you to their data, while the link on the right takes you to details of the submitted database in which this individual is found, including the e-mail address of the submitter. On the Ancestry site you need to register with your name and e-mail address, free of charge, before you can search. However, the initial search form is more comprehensive. Data from World Tree are also included in general searches carried out on the Ancestry site at <**www.ancestry.myfamily.com/search/main.htm**>.

GenCircles at <**www.gencircles.com**> is a fairly new site, started by Cliff Shaw in 2001 (see Figure 10.6). It is a free service that currently has about 45 million individuals. You need to register before using, but there's no

RootsWeb's WorldConnect Project
Global Search

FREE Download!
Ancestry's new family tree software

Names: 255494045 Surnames: 2983869 Databases: 257986

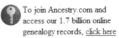

To join Ancestry.com and access our 1.7 billion online genealogy records, click here

Results 1-7 of 7

| Name | Birth/Christening | | Death/Burial | | Database |
	Date	Place	Date	Place	
Christian, Christopher	1799	Pevensey, Sussex, England	1837	Pevensey, Sussex, England	maternal
🔍 📧	Father: Henry Christian Mother: Mary Gearing				
Christian, Cornelius	7 Jun 1797	Pevensey, Sussex, England	3 Jun 1883	Frederickton, NSW Australia	maternal
🔍 📧 ❓	Father: Henry Christian Mother: Mary Gearing Spouse: Harriet Hollebone				
Christian, George	1807	Pevensey, Sussex, England	Unknown	Unknown	maternal
🔍 📧	Father: Henry Christian Mother: Mary Gearing				
Christian, Henry	26 Apr 1764	Pevensey, Sussex, England	8 Feb 1821	Pevensey, Sussex, England	maternal
🔍 ❓	Spouse: Mary Gearing				
Christian, Jane Elizabeth	Abt 1837	Pevensey, Sussex, England	Unknown	N.S.W. Australia	maternal
🔍 📧	Father: Cornelius Christian Mother: Harriet Hollebone				

Figure 10.5 Search results on WorldConnect

subscription. GenCircles offers a facility called SmartMatching, which compares the individuals in your file against all other individuals submitted to detect any matches.

Another free service is GeneaNet, a French-run site at <www.geneanet. org> which started in 1996. This allows you to upload a GEDCOM file, but it also has its own free software GeneWeb, which you can either use on the site or download. It has more than 200 million individuals submitted by over 200,000 genealogists. Additional facilities are available as part of 'privileged membership' for 40 per year.

A very simple way to make your pedigree available on-line is provided by Dave Wilks in his free GEDCOM server at <www.my-ged.com>. This does not provide its own search facilities, and is just for uploading your GEDCOM file. The material on the site is indexed by Gendex (see p. 122).

Subscription databases
Alongside the free pedigree databases, there are a number of commercial services, all of which require a subscription.

GenServ, started by Cliff Manis in 1991 as an e-mail only service – this was before the invention of the Web – is among the oldest pedigree databases on the internet. It is a subscription system at <www.genserv. com>, with over 25 million individuals in around 17,000 GEDCOM files.

It is a slightly unusual service in that you *must* submit some of your own

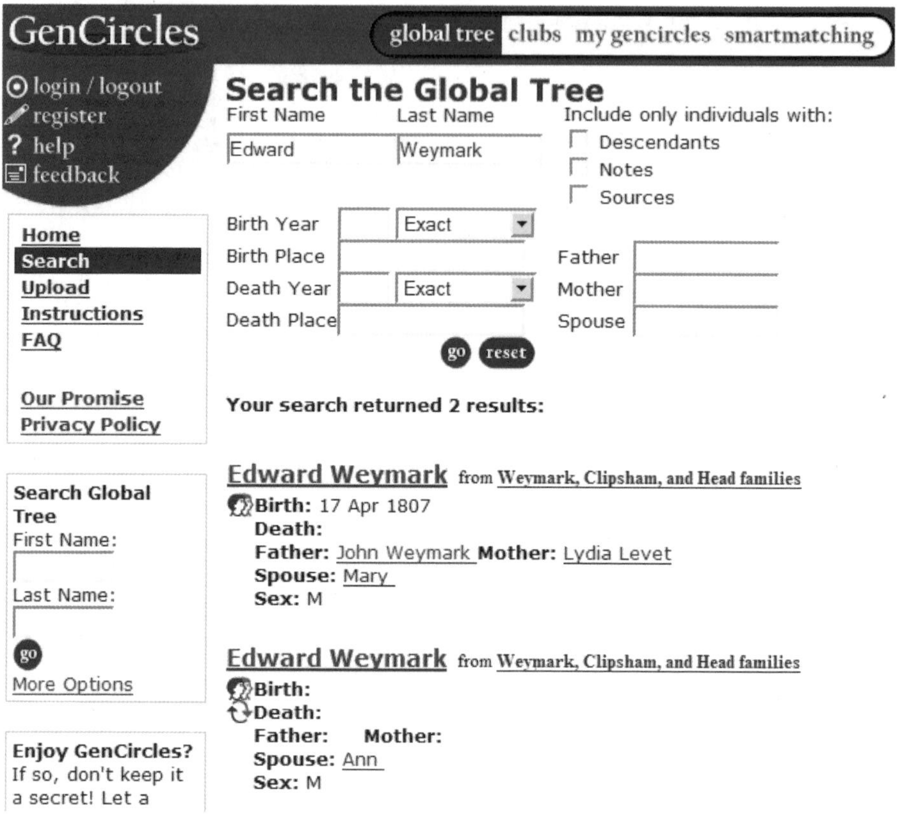

GenCircles

global tree | clubs | my gencircles | smartmatching

⊙ login / logout
✎ register
? help
▣ feedback

Home
Search
Upload
Instructions
FAQ

Our Promise
Privacy Policy

Search Global
Tree
First Name:

Last Name:

go
More Options

Enjoy GenCircles?
If so, don't keep it
a secret! Let a

Search the Global Tree

First Name	Last Name	Include only individuals with:
Edward	Weymark	☐ Descendants
		☐ Notes
		☐ Sources

Birth Year	Exact ▾		
Birth Place		Father	
Death Year	Exact ▾	Mother	
Death Place		Spouse	

go **reset**

Your search returned 2 results:

Edward Weymark from Weymark, Clipsham, and Head families
Birth: 17 Apr 1807
Death:
Father: John Weymark **Mother:** Lydia Levet
Spouse: Mary
Sex: M

Edward Weymark from Weymark, Clipsham, and Head families
Birth:
Death:
Father: **Mother:**
Spouse: Ann
Sex: M

Figure 10.6 Search results on GenCircles

material in order to subscribe. Once you have done this you can have a free 60-day trial subscription, while a regular subscription is $12/£8 per year, which allows you to do unlimited searches. Details of how to subscribe are given at <www.genserv.com/gs/gsh2sub.htm>. A more limited trial (one surname search for any one e-mail address) is available under the 'Sample Search' option. There is also a demo version on a more limited database 'designed for non-members to sample the full range of searching and reporting capabilities available' at <demo.genserv.com>.

World Family Tree is a subscription database (also available on CD-ROM) at <familytreemaker.genealogy.com/wfttop.html> with about 125 million individuals in around 200,000 pedigrees. There is a free search facility, but you need to subscribe in order to view any matching pedigrees. The site has been criticised for charging for access to freely submitted pedigrees, and the charges ($19.99 per month, $79.99 per year) are quite high if you are only going to use the site occasionally. However, you can use the site as an index to the CD-ROMs, which means you can buy only those which hold material of interest to you, or look for them in a library.

OneGreatFamily at <**www.onegreatfamily.com**> was launched in the summer of 2000 and now claims over 150,000 users sharing over 42 million ancestors. It represents a more sophisticated approach to on-line pedigrees. Rather than just seeing itself as a repository for a copy of your data, it acts as a substitute for a traditional genealogy program. Like GenCircles, it has facilities for matching your own data with other trees on the site. Subscriptions are $14.95, $49.95 and $74.95 for one, six and twelve months respectively, and there is also a seven-day free trial. To view pedigrees on the site you need to download the Genealogy Browser, which is a plug-in for your web browser. Figure 10.7 shows part of Elvis Presley's family tree in the Genealogy Browser, one of the examples on the site which you can try out. To find out more, it is worth reading Dick Eastman's account of using the site, originally published in his newsletter, but also reproduced on the OneGreatFamily site at <**www.onegreatfamily. com/static-tpls/pr-eastman06-21-00.htm**>.

Half-way between the free and the subscription services is GenesConnected at <**www.genesconnected.co.uk**>. This site, launched in November 2002, is an offshoot from the very successful FriendsReunited. It is a mix of a free and a subscription service. You do not have to subscribe in order to enter or upload your pedigree, nor to carry out searches on the database. But contact details are not given on the site itself – you need to be a subscriber, in which case you can get GenesConnected to send mail to other submitters. An added advantage of this, for some people, is that it offers some measure of privacy protection. The subscription is a very modest £5 per year. Currently GenesConnected claims to have around half a million users and over five million names. This may be quite a small figure compared to the other sites discussed here, but the UK focus of GenesConnected makes this difference much less

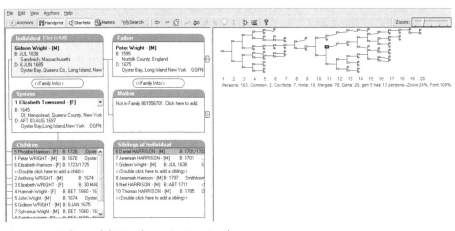

Figure 10.7 Pedigree of Elvis Presley on OneGreatFamily

significant than you might at first think. An important consideration, too, is that the connection with FriendsReunited (around nine million registrations) suggests there may be many submissions from people who do not regard themselves as serious family historians and who are unlikely to use any of the other resources discussed in this chapter.

GENDEX

GENDEX at <www.gendex.com> is rather different from the sites mentioned so far, in that it does not store pedigrees at all, but acts as a central registry for pedigrees on personal web sites. It currently holds details of over 52 million individuals from around 20,000 web sites. GENDEX was developed by Gene Stark as a feature of his GED2HTML program, one of the most widely used programs for converting a GEDCOM file into an on-line pedigree (GEDCOM files are explained on p. 239). But it is also used by many other pieces of software that can create family trees for the Web. Anyone who creates a set of web pages using software with GENDEX facilities can have the individuals on their web site automatically added to the index at GENDEX.

The search facilities on GENDEX are not particularly sophisticated but allow you reasonably easily to home in on the names you are looking for – they are stored on permanent index pages, not in a searchable database. Each entry has name, dates of birth and death, with links to information about the submitter and his or her web site and a direct link to their data on the named individual.

GENDEX can be used free of charge, but also operates a pay-per-view system for registered users (1,000 hit credits per $10 payment), which gives access to more sophisticated searching facilities, and customisation of search results.

Limitations

One point to bear in mind is that the majority of the individuals in these databases were born in the US, so in spite of the amount of material you should not be surprised if you do not find matches for your UK ancestors in them. However, as many American pedigrees have some roots in the British Isles, it is still well worth checking them. Also, as more British genealogists submit their family trees to such sites, they become more useful for British genealogy.

The material on these sites consists entirely of submissions from individual genealogists. The completeness and accuracy of information is therefore highly variable, though some sites do basic checks in order to detect obvious errors, such as a death date earlier than a birth date. It is therefore best to regard these databases as a way of contacting people with similar interests, rather than as direct resources of data. It would be very unwise to incorporate such material directly into your own genealogy database without thorough checking. In some cases this will be simple – the example in Figure 10.4 gives a christening date and parish, which should be easy to check; in others the information may be of little value, perhaps just a year and a country. Of course, it may be that the person who has submitted the information has a substantial collection of supporting material, particularly as some genealogists are wary of putting *all* their information on-line. And the advantage of these databases over the surname resources discussed earlier in this chapter is that they provide information about individuals and families, not just about surnames. This should make it fairly easy to establish whether the submitter is interested in the same family as you, something that may be particularly important for a common surname.

Rights

If you are intending to submit your own pedigree to one of these databases, there is one important issue you need to be aware of. On some sites, when you upload material to a database you grant the site ownership of your pedigree or unlimited rights to use the material as they see fit. This is not necessarily as unreasonable as it might sound. With FamilySearch your data file will be permanently archived in the LDS Church's Granite Mountain Records Vault, ensuring preservation, and it is unrealistic to expect an archive to keep track of the legal ownership of thousands if not millions of files over many decades. Also, FamilySearch makes the data freely accessible on-line and its CD-ROMs are sold more or less at cost. On the other hand, it is perhaps understandable that some people baulk at allowing the fully commercial exploitation of their data without royalty by some sites, when they are already paying a subscription.

It is therefore important to check the terms and conditions of any pedigree database before you submit your own material. Of the sites mentioned here, RootsWeb, GenCircles, GenesConnected, and GenServ make no claim on material submitted, and you retain complete rights over your GEDCOM including editorial control.

Privacy

Another issue in placing your pedigree on-line is the privacy of living individuals. This is nothing to do with data protection, as is often thought – much of your information comes from public sources and there can be no legal bar in the UK to publishing it on-line, or indeed in any other medium, as long as it is accurate. The real issue is that many people are under-standably distressed if they find their personal details published on-line by someone else. Because of this all the on-line pedigree databases have a policy on publishing information about living individuals. Here are some typical policies:

- RootsWeb has facilities which make it possible for you to remove living people entirely, or clean their entries of specific pieces of information, but it does not check your efforts.

- GenesConnected and OneGreatFamily have conditions that you do not include living individuals without their permission, but they do not check or modify the submitted data.
- World Family Tree removes all details of living people apart from name, gender and family links.
- GenCircles uses a number of techniques for identifying living individuals and then ensures that they are not displayed, though the submitter can still see the information.

If you're going to submit to a site that doesn't have its own privacy protection mechanism, you will need to remove living individuals or at least their details. Many genealogy software programs have facilities for doing this, and there are a number of tools for purging GEDCOM files of sensitive information (see the 'Software & Computers' page on Cyndi's List at <**www.cyndislist.com/software.htm#Privacy**>).

Locating people

The surname lists and databases already discussed will put you in touch with other genealogists who have made their researches – or at least their research interests – public, but you can also use the internet to locate long-lost relatives or their descendants, or simply people with a particular surname.

Phone numbers and addresses

The UK phone directories are on-line at <**www.bt.com/directory-enquiries/dq_home.jsp**> and this will give you an address, postcode and phone number. 192.com at <**www.192.com**> provides more extensive searching, including electoral rolls. This is a commercial service, though the initial free registration allows you to conduct 10 searches. A list of UK dialling codes can be found at <**www.brainstorm.co.uk/uk_std_code_search.htm**>.

The internet is particularly useful for foreign phone numbers, since only a small number of major reference libraries in the UK have a full set of international directories. Yahoo has many links to national phone directories. One way to locate these is to go directly to the relevant reference page for the country, e.g. for Ireland <**dir.yahoo.com/Regional/Countries/Ireland/Reference/**> will provide links to various reference resources including phone books.

Infospace has world-wide telephone listings available from <**www.infospace.com**>. Infobel's 'Telephone Directories' pages at <**www.infobel.com/teldir/**> has links to Yellow Pages, White Pages, Business Directories, Email Addresses and Fax Listings from 184 countries. International dialling codes are at <**kropla.com/dialcode.htm**>.

E-mail addresses

Finding e-mail addresses is not straightforward. For a start, there is no single authoritative directory of e-mail addresses in the way that the phone book is for phone numbers. There are simply too many e-mail addresses and they are changing all the time. Also, there is no single place to register them. However, there are a number of directories of e-mail addresses on the Web.

Yahoo has a 'People Search' at <people.yahoo.com> with a UK/Ireland version at <ukie.people.yahoo.com>. The Yahoo directory has links to many sites providing general or specific e-mail address searches at <uk.dir.yahoo.com/Reference/Phone_Numbers_and_Addresses/Email_Ad resses/>. One of the best-known e-mail directories is Bigfoot at <www.bigfoot.com>. Cyndi's List has a 'Finding People' page at <www. cyndislist.com/finding.htm>.

One point to bear in mind is that it is easy for these databases to add an e-mail address by extracting it from a message sent to a mailing list or newsgroup, or if it is provided on a web page. However, it is quite impossible for a database to know when the address ceases to be valid (perhaps because the person concerned has changed their internet provider), so the databases are full of old, no longer valid e-mail addresses as well as current ones. For example, Yahoo People includes an old e-mail address of mine which ceased to be valid in 1995. Except for fairly unusual names, you will find multiple entries, and since e-mail addresses often give no clue to the geographical location of the person it may be hard to identify the one you are looking for. Also, people posting messages to newsgroups often give fake e-mail addresses to prevent spam (i.e. unsolicited bulk mail), though these should be easy to spot if you are familiar with the way e-mail addresses are constructed. All in all, these sites are much less useful than they might seem at first sight.

Another way to find an e-mail address is simply to use a standard search engine to look for the relevant name, but success will depend on the person concerned having a web page, and the search could be time consuming.

If you want to make it easy for people to find your e-mail address some of the services mentioned above (Yahoo People and Internet Address Finder, for example), allow you to submit your details. Alternatively, you could create a web page with your contact details and submit its URL to a few of the major search engines (see Chapter 17).

Adoption and child migration

While the resources discussed so far can be useful for tracing people when you know their names they may be of little use in the case of adoption or child migration, and you may need to go to sites specifically devoted to these issues.

The FamilyRecords portal has brief information on UK adoption records at <www.familyrecords.gov.uk/topics/adoption.htm> and more detailed information, including details of the Adoption Contact Register, is available on the ONS site at <www.statistics.gov.uk/nsbase/registration/adoptions.asp>. The FFHS has a leaflet 'Tracing The Birth Parents Of Adopted Persons In England And Wales' (relevant to the period since 1927) at <www.ffhs.org.uk/General/Help/Adopted.htm>.

The Salvation Army offers a Family Tracing Service. The home page for this is at <www.salvationarmy.org.uk/en/Departments/FamilyTracing/Home.htm> and there is an FAQ at <www.salvationarmy.org.uk/en/Departments/FamilyTracing/FAQs.htm>. Searching in Ireland has a page for Irish-born adoptees at <www.netreach.net/~steed/search.html>. The newsgroup alt.adoption is for all issues relating to adoption.

The UK Birth Adoption Register at <www.ukbirth-adoptionregister.com> is a site for adoptees and birth parents to register their interest in making contact. A one-off registration fee of £10 is required to place your details in the database. LookUpUK at <www.lookupuk.com> is a general site for tracing missing persons and those separated by adoption, with a number of message boards and other resources. Adoptee's UK [*sic!*] at <adopteesuk.homestead.com> has adoption-related links, and message boards for those looking to make contact.

Cyndi's List has a page devoted to adoption resources at <www.cyndislist.com/adoption.htm>, and John Fuller has an extensive list of mailing lists relating to adoption at <www.rootsweb.com/~jfuller/gen_mail_adoption.html>.

The Department of Health has information on child emigration at <www.doh.gov.uk/childmigrants/> and links to organisations that provide information and support for child migrants. The National Archives of Australia has information on child migration records at <www.naa.gov.au/Publications/fact_sheets/FS124.html>. The 'Young Immigrants to Canada' page on Marjorie Kohli's site <www.ist.uwaterloo.ca/~marj/genealogy/homeadd.html> has information and links relating to child emigration to Canada up to 1939.

11 Social Groups

Earlier chapters have covered the major sources of primary genealogical data on-line which, because they are common to all our forebears, are of use to every family historian. However, our ancestors did much more than be born and buried, or be discovered living in a certain place by the census enumerator, and there is great variety when it comes to questions of occupation, religious persuasion and geographical mobility. The aim of this chapter is to cover some of the more important of these social groupings. Unlike the sites mentioned in the earlier chapters, the material discussed here is mostly general historical information, but there are still a number of sites which include data extracts for particular groups of people. Each of these topics is a large subject in itself, so this chapter can only hint at the range of on-line resources available.

Churches and clergy

Records relating to parish registers are covered in Chapter 7. However, most of the available material relates to the Anglican Church, though FamilySearch does include some Catholic and Nonconformist registers. Beyond the major sources mentioned in Chapter 7 you should not expect to find much parish register material on-line. Nonetheless, there is some useful information on the Web about churches and religious denominations.

John Fuller has a page for mailing lists relating to individual churches and denominations at <www.rootsweb.com/~jfuller/gen_mail_religions. html>.

Anglican churches
The official web sites for the national Anglican churches of the UK are:

- Church of England <www.cofe.anglican.org>
- Church in Wales <www.churchinwales.org.uk>
- Church of Ireland <www.ireland.anglican.org>
- Church of Scotland <www.churchofscotland.org.uk>
- Scottish Episcopal Church <scotland.anglican.org>.

You can expect these to provide information about individual parishes, usually organised by diocese or accessible via a search facility such as the C of E's Church-Search site at <www.church-search.com>.

A useful web directory of Christian sites is Praize.com at <www.praize. com>. This offers a directory page for each Christian denomination at <www.praize.com/engine/Denominations/>. Church Net at <www. churchnet.org.uk> offers similar links, just for the UK, though they are mostly to the web sites of individual congregations, at <www.churchnet. org.uk/cgi-bin/directory.cgi?sectionid=354>.

Lambeth Palace Library has a very comprehensive leaflet 'Biographical sources for Anglican clergy' at <www.lambethpalacelibrary.org/holdings/ Guides/clergyman.html>. A resource to look out for is the Clergy of the Church of England Database. This project, based at King's College, London, aims to construct and publish on-line a database of all the Church's clergy from 1540 to 1835. It is due to be completed in 2004 and information will be found at <www.kcl.ac.uk/humanities/cch/cce/ cce.htm>. Meanwhile the Institute of Historical Research already has an on-line version of the *Fasti Ecclesiae Anglicanae*, which gives basic biographical information on the 'higher clergy' up to 1837 at <www.history.ac.uk/fasti/>.

There is a CHURCHMEN-UK mailing list for those with clerical ancestors. Subscription details are at <lists.rootsweb.com/index/other/ Occupations/CHURCHMEN-UK.html>.

Many individuals have placed pictures of local churches on-line, and these are discussed under 'Photographs' in Chapter 14, p. 184.

Roman Catholic Church

The official web sites for the Roman Catholic Church in the UK are:

- England and Wales <www.catholic-ew.org.uk>
- Scotland <www.catholic-scotland.org.uk>.

The National Archives has a leaflet on 'Catholic Recusants' at <catalogue.pro.gov.uk/Leaflets/ri2173.htm>, which gives a guide to the relevant official records. The Catholic Record Society at <www.catholic-history.org.uk/crs/> is the main publishing body for Catholic records, while the Catholic Central Library has a guide to its collections at <www.catholic-library.org.uk>. The Catholic Archives Society has a web site at <www.catholic-history.org.uk/catharch/>.

Information about the Catholic Family History Society will be found at <www.catholic-history.org.uk/cfhs/>, and the Catholic History site at <www.catholic-history.org.uk> also hosts three regional Catholic FHS web sites.

The Local Catholic Church History and Genealogy Research Guide and Worldwide Directory at <home.att.net/~Local_Catholic/> is a comprehensive research guide to Catholic records. It has details of individual churches and links to on-line information, with very thorough pages for the UK and Ireland. The Fianna web site has a guide to Roman Catholic records in Ireland at <www.rootsweb.com/~fianna/county/parishes.html> taken from Brian Mitchell's *A Guide to Irish Parish Registers*.

Cyndi's List has over 200 links to Catholic resources at <www.cyndislist.com/catholic.htm>.

Nonconformist churches

The Spartacus Internet Encyclopaedia has a brief history of the most important religious groups at <www.spartacus.schoolnet.co.uk/religion. htm>, with links to details of individual reformers and reform movements. Cyndi's List has individual pages devoted to Baptist, Huguenot, Methodist, Presbyterian and Quaker materials, and links to many other relevant resources on the 'Religion and Churches' page at <www. cyndislist.com/religion.htm>. Many of the denominational mailing lists at <www.rootsweb.com/~jfuller/gen_mail_religions.html> are for dissenting groups. (Huguenot immigration is covered on p. 151.)

For details of the records, consult the FamilyRecords portal's factsheet on 'Nonconformist Registers' at <www.familyrecords.gov.uk/frc/pdfs/ nonconformist_registers.pdf>. For Scotland and Ireland, look at Sherry Irvine's article 'Protestant Nonconformity in Scotland' at <www. genuki.org.uk/big/sct/noncon1.html>, and Fianna's guide to 'Baptist, Methodist, Presbyterian and Quaker Records in Ireland' at <www. rootsweb.com/~fianna/county/churches.html>.

GenDocs has lists of London churches for a number of nonconformist denominations on its 'Victorian London Churches' page at <www. gendocs.demon.co.uk/churches.html>.

Societies which are relevant for those with nonconformist ancestors are:

- The Quaker Family History Society <www.qfhs.co.uk>, which has details of Quaker records and their location, with a page for each county
- The Baptist Historical Society at <www.baptisthistory.org.uk>, which has no general genealogical material but does have information on Baptist ministers.

There are a number of libraries which specialise in nonconformist material. The John Rylands University Library in Manchester has a strong nonconformist collection, particularly for the Methodist Church. A description of the main resources will be found at <rylibweb.man.ac.uk/ data2/spcoll/intchris.html> and the home page of the Methodist Archives and Research Centre is at <rylibweb.man.ac.uk/data1/dg/text/method. html>.

Dr Williams's Library, the main repository of English and Welsh nonconformist registers, is not on-line, though there is brief information at

<www1.rhbnc.ac.uk/hellenic-institute/Drwilliams%27s.html>. The ARCHON Directory at <www.hmc.gov.uk/archon/archondirectory.htm> (see p. 92) has an entry for the Library – follow the link to the 'England' page and you will find it listed under D. The ARCHON entry for the Library has links to the materials from the Library catalogued in the National Register of Archives, including papers relating to around 200, mainly nonconformist, clergymen.

The official Quaker web site has information about the collections in the library at Friends House at <www.quaker.org.uk/library/>, with details of genealogical sources at <www.quaker.org.uk/library/guides/libgenea.html>.

Occupations

Occupational records have on the whole not formed part of the official state records discussed in Chapter 4, so they do not feature strongly in the major on-line data collections. The National Archives' 'Pathways to the Past' (see p. 6) includes material on occupations, under the title 'People at Work', at <www.pro.gov.uk/pathways/FamilyHistory/gallery2/>, with pages devoted to apprentices, the police, customs and excise officers, coastguards and the legal profession. The National Archives has leaflets on the following occupations and professions for which there are state records:

- Royal Warrant Holders and Household Servants
- Attorneys and Solicitors
- Tax and Revenue Collectors
- Metropolitan Police
- Royal Irish Constabulary
- Teachers
- Nurses
- Railway Staff.

All are linked from the Leaflets home page at <www.pro.gov.uk/leaflets/Riindex.asp>.

Genuki has an 'Occupations' page at <www.genuki.org.uk/big/eng/Occupations.html> with a number of links for particular occupations, and links to all the National Archives' leaflets mentioned. Cyndi's List has a page of resources relating to occupations at <www.cyndislist.com/occupatn.htm> and many other pages which have information on occupations related to particular topics – for example the Prisons page at <www.cyndislist.com/prisons.htm> includes links to Police sites.

The largest set of occupational records on-line is the apprenticeship material on the English Origins site at <www.englishorigins.com>: the London City Apprenticeship Abstracts 1531–1850 (100,000 records with

300,000 names, already on-line) and the Apprentices of Great Britain 1710–1774 (600,000 records, to be available by the end of 2003). The site has additional information about apprenticeship records, and a list of City Livery Companies, at <www.englishorigins.com/help/lonapps-details.aspx>. More information about the Livery Companies will be found on the Corporation of London site at <www.cityoflondon.gov.uk/leisure_heritage/livery/>.

The Modern Records Centre at the University of Warwick holds records relating to 'labour history, industrial relations and industrial politics'. While it has not put any records on-line, the main genealogy page at <cal.csv.warwick.ac.uk/services/library/mrc/mrcgene.shtml> has links to genealogical guides for the following occupations:

- Bookbinders
- Brushmakers
- Bus and Cab Workers
- Carpenters
- Carvers
- Compositors
- Gilders
- House Decorators
- Ironfounders
- Joiners
- Miners
- Painters
- Picture-frame makers
- Plasterers
- Printing workers
- Quarrymen
- Railwaymen
- Seamen
- Steam Engine Makers
- Stonemasons
- Tramway Workers.

There are many sites devoted to individual occupations, sometimes with just historical information, sometimes with a database of names. Examples of the latter are the Database of Sugar Bakers and Sugar Refiners at <www.mawer.clara.net/intro.html> and the Biographical Database of British Chemists at <www5.open.ac.uk/Arts/chemists/>. The Coalmining History Resource Centre at <www.cmhrc.pwp.blueyonder.co.uk> has lists of mines at various dates, reports from an 1842 Royal Commission on child labour in the mines, and a database of mining deaths with 90,000 names. The Institute of Historical Research has pages with names of Royal Office Holders in Modern Britain at <ihr.sas.ac.uk/office/> ('modern' here meaning 'post-medieval').

There are an increasing number of mailing lists devoted to occupations. These are listed at <www.rootsweb.com/~jfuller/gen_mail_occ.html> and those most relevant to UK family historians are:

- BLACKSMITHING
- CIRCUS-FOLK
- COALMINERS
- DOCTORS-NURSES-MIDWIVES
- ENG-CANAL-PEOPLE
- ENG-PUBS-INNS
- Itinerantroots
- MUSIC-OCCUPATIONS
- ORGAN-BUILDERS
- PAPER-MILLS-MAKERS
- POLICE-UK
- RAILWAY-UK
- SCOTTISH-MINING
- THEATRE-UK
- TOWNCRIERS-UK
- UK-WATCHMAKERS
- VIOLIN-MAKERS
- WOODWORKERS.

Many of these are hosted by RootsWeb, where details and archives will be found, linked from <lists.rootsweb.com/index/other/Occupations/>. There is also a general OCCUPATIONS list.

Resources relating to the merchant seamen are discussed along with those for the Royal Navy, on p. 136. Trade directories are an important source of occupational information, and these are discussed on p. 89. A number of resources for clergymen are mentioned earlier in this chapter.

Occupational terms

Brief explanations of terms for past occupations are provided in John Hitchcock's 'Ranks, Professions, Occupations and Trades' page at <www.gendocs.demon.co.uk/trades.html> and John Lacombe's 'A List of Occupations' at <cpcug.org/user/jlacombe/terms.html>. These are very similar and cover about 1,600 occupational terms. The 'Dictionary of Ancient Occupations and Trades, Ranks, Offices, and Titles' at <freepages. genealogy.rootsweb.com/~dav4is/Sources/Occupations.html> is a smaller collection of around 600 terms.

For the period before parish registers Olive Tree's list of 'Medieval And Obsolete English Trade And Professional Terms' at <olivetreegenealogy. com/misc/occupations.shtml#med> may be useful, especially since it includes medieval Latin terms for many occupations, and some older English spellings.

The most comprehensive listing of occupational terms, with something like 30,000 entries and descriptions, is the Open University's *Dictionary of Occupational Terms*. However, this is available only on CD-ROM and is not on-line.

Crime and punishment

The official records of crime are those of the courts and the prison system, and these will be found in the National Archives, which has a number of leaflets devoted to the subject, including:

- Outlawry in Medieval and Early Modern England
- Criminal Trials, Old Bailey and the Central Criminal Court
- Criminal Trials at the Assizes
- Convicts and Prisoners 1100–1986.

All of these are on-line at <**www.pro.gov.uk/leaflets/Riindex.asp**>. The National Archives also has material on 'Ancestors and the Law' in its 'Pathways to the Past' section (see p. 6).

Cyndi's List has a page devoted to 'Prisons, Prisoners & Outlaws' at <**www.cyndislist.com/prisons.htm**>. Genuki lists relevant resources under the headings Court Proceedings and Correctional Institutions on national and county pages.

A major on-line resource is the Proceedings of the Old Bailey site at <**www.oldbaileyonline.org**>, which went live in March 2003. The site contains transcriptions and scanned images free of charge. When complete in Spring 2004 there will be details of 100,000 trials from 1670 to 1834, and the initial offering covers December 1714 to December 1759. Sophisticated search facilities allow trials to be selected by keyword, name, place, crime, verdict and punishment, or you can browse the trials by date. The text of trials also contains the names of jurors, which can be found via the name search, so the site is not only of interest to those with criminal ancestors.

In addition to the records themselves, the site has extensive background material about particular communities, which will be of general interest:

- Black Communities of London
- Homosexuality
- Gypsies and Travellers
- Irish in London
- Jewish Communities.

Additional background includes material on the various types of verdict and punishment.

Other crime records on-line include Jeff Alvey's page on 'Newgate

THE
PROCEEDINGS
OF THE
OLD BAILEY

Homepage

Search the
Proceedings

About the
Proceedings

Historical
Background

For Schools

About this
Project

Contact
Details

Sitemap

The University of
Sheffield

UH University of
Hertfordshire

A · H · R · B

THE PROCEEDINGS OF THE OLD BAILEY LONDON
1674 TO 1834

A fully searchable online edition of the largest body of texts detailing the lives of non-elite
people ever published, containing accounts of over 100,000 criminal trials held at London's
central criminal court.

Now available: 22,000 trials, from December 1714 to December 1759. Project Timetable.

ON THIS DAY IN 1742...
A group of excise officers rode down some night watchmen in the street, and one of
the watchmen was shot and killed. Read more...

SEARCH THE PROCEEDINGS
By Keyword · Name · Place · Crime, Verdict and Punishment · Advanced Search ·
Browse by Date · Statistics · Search the Associated Records

ABOUT THE PROCEEDINGS
Publishing History of the Proceedings · Associated Records · Advertisements · Notable
Trials

HISTORICAL BACKGROUND
Crime, Justice and Punishment · London and its Hinterland · The Old Bailey Courthouse · Community Histories ·
Gender in the Proceedings · Glossary · Bibliography

Figure 11.1 Proceedings of the Old Bailey at <www.oldbaileyonline.org>

Prison' at <www.fred.net/jefalvey/newgate.html> which has a list of
names taken from an 1896 book on the subject. The same site lists some of
the executions in England from 1606 at <www.fred.net/jefalvey/execute.
html>.

For information on prisons, the Rossbret Prisons Website at
<www.institutions.org.uk/prisons/> is an essential resource. This has a list
of prisons organised by county with historical information and details of
the relevant records. There is a PRISONS-UK mailing list, details of which
will be found at <lists.rootsweb.com/index/intl/UK/PRISONS-UK.html>.
Records relating to crime and punishment in Scotland are held by the NAS
(see p. 101), which has a fact sheet 'Crime and Criminals' at <www.
nas.gov.uk/miniframe/fact_sheet/crime.pdf>.

There are many resources on-line relating to convict transportation to
the colonies, and these are discussed under Colonies and Migration on
p. 141 ff.

The armed forces

There are two official sites for information on the armed forces and their
records: the National Archives and the Ministry of Defence (MoD). The
National Archives provides an extensive series of leaflets to help you
understand how the records are organised and how to locate and

understand them. These can be found at <www.pro.gov.uk/leaflets/
Riindex.asp>. The 'Pathways to the Past' pages have a section devoted to
the army and navy at <www.pro.gov.uk/pathways/FamilyHistory/
gallery3/>.

The MoD site at <www.mod.uk>, while mainly devoted to the present-
day forces, has detailed pages on the location of recent service records, and
provides many contact addresses. Each branch of the services has its own
web site within the MoD's internet domain: <www.royal-navy.mod.uk>,
<www.army.mod.uk> and <www.raf.mod.uk>. Beyond these central
bodies, there are the individual regiments, ships, squadrons and other
units, many of which have their own web pages with historical
information. The easiest way to find these is from the site for the relevant
arm of the services, which has links to its constituent bodies.

The MoD site does not offer information about individuals, and at
present the only major collection of on-line data relating to service
personnel is the Debt of Honour Register at <www.cwgc.org>, discussed in
Chapter 8 (p. 83), which lists the Commonwealth war dead from the two
world wars. However, there are other small collections of data at some of
the sites for individual branches of the services. The National Archives has
not announced any project to make military records available on-line, but
they are among those recommended as potential digitisation projects to
prospective commercial partners – see <www.pro.gov.uk/corporate/
licensed/recommendations.htm>. The *London Gazette* (see p. 86) contains
details of appointments in the armed forces, and the text search facility on
the site at <www.gazettes-online.co.uk> can be used to do a name search.

The Scots at War site at <www.scotsatwar.org.uk> concentrates mainly
on the 20th century. It has a Commemorative Roll of Honour with service
and biographical information on Scottish servicemen, and detailed
genealogical help pages which will be of interest to anyone with
Commonwealth military ancestors.

Genuki has pages devoted to Military Records at <www.genuki.org.uk/
big/MilitaryRecords.html> and Military History at <www.genuki.org.uk/
big/MilitaryHistory.html>. Cyndi's List has a page devoted to UK Military
at <www.cyndislist.com/miluk.htm>, which covers all branches of the
services, while her 'Military Resources Worldwide' page at <www.
cyndislist.com/milres.htm> has more general material.

If you need to identify medals, a good starting point is MedalNet at
<www.medal.net> which is devoted to Commonwealth medals. There are
also sites devoted to the holders of gallantry medals, particularly the
Victoria Cross, for which lists of recipients can be found at <www.chapter-
one.com/vc/> and <www2.prestel.co.uk/stewart/vcross.htm>. Stephen
Stratford has information on gallantry medals, with photographs at
<www.stephen-stratford.co.uk/gallantry.htm>. There are also photo-
graphs of British medals at <faculty.winthrop.edu/haynese/medals/
britain.html>. The Gazettes Online web site, described in more detail on

p. 86, has a facility to search the on-line issues for awards of medals at <www.gazettes-online.co.uk/honours.asp>.

The National Archives has two main leaflets on military medals and their records:

- Campaign Medals, and other Service Medals at **<catalogue.pro.gov.uk/Leaflets/ri2296.htm>**
- Gallantry Medals **<catalogue.pro.gov.uk/Leaflets/ri2297.htm>**.

The Imperial War Museum at **<www.iwm.org.uk>** has a family history section at **<www.iwm.org.uk/lambeth/famhist.htm>**, and links to many military museums, while the MoD has a comprehensive listing of British military museums at **<www.army.mod.uk/ceremonialandheritage/museums_main.htm>**.

There are quite a few sites devoted to particular wars or battles, such the pages on the Battle of Culloden **<www.electricscotland.com/history/culloden/>**. Some are devoted to a war as a whole, such as the Trenches on the Web site at **<www.worldwar1.com>**, which is subtitled 'An Internet History of The Great War'. Others are devoted to a particular aspect – for example, The Second Battle of the Marne at **<perso.club-internet.fr/batmarn2/menuseng.htm>** offers information about all the British divisions involved in this engagement and what they did.

There are also a number of mailing lists devoted to particular wars, including:

- NAPOLEONIC
- CRIMEAN-WAR
- BOER-WAR
- GREATWAR
- WORLDWAR2
- KOREAN-WAR.

WW20-ROOTS-L is devoted to 'genealogy in all 20th century wars'. All these lists are hosted by RootsWeb and details for these will be found at **<lists.rootsweb.com/index/other/Military/>**.

The Royal Navy and Merchant Navy[8]

The official Royal Navy site at **<www.royal-navy.mod.uk>** has separate sections for ships, the Fleet Air Arm, submarines, the Royal Marines and naval establishments. Historical information is in a section called 'RN profile' at **<www.royal-navy.mod.uk/static/pages/168.html>**.

Although the merchant navy is not an arm of the state, it has long been

---

[8] A more detailed look at resources for seafaring ancestors will be found in my article in issue 11 of *Ancestors* (December 2002/January 2003).

subject to government regulation and many maritime ancestors will have served in both the Royal Navy and the merchant fleet.

The most important gateway to British maritime resources on the Web is the National Maritime Museum's Port site at **<www.port.nmm.ac.uk>**. In addition to a search facility, there is an option to browse by subject or historical period. The site offers a detailed description of each resource it links to. The focus of this gateway is not primarily genealogical, but a search for 'genealogy' turns up almost 200 resources. The site includes a range of research leaflets for all aspects of ships and the sea, including a number on tracing people in the Royal Navy and merchant marine. In addition, the Research Guides on uniforms and medals may be useful. Leaflets are listed at **<www.port.nmm.ac.uk/research/research.html>**.

Another site with many links, though again it is not specifically genealogical, is Peter McCracken's Maritime History on the Internet site at **<ils.unc.edu/maritime/mhiweb/webhome.shtml>**. There is a useful

latest additions | suggest a resource | feedback | help on searching

02 April 2003

Events

Research

Journal of
Maritime
Research

Caird Library

About PORT

Welcome to PORT
The premier portal of high-quality maritime resources on the internet

[   ] [Search database]

Tip: you can search for any one of several terms; **voyages OR exploration**

⦿ Show Descriptions   ◯ Titles Only
An advanced search form is also available.

Browse subject category

Art	Government & Law	Navigation
Adventures & Sport	Health & Safety	Reference Works
Biography	Hydraulic Engineering	Transport & Trade
Careers	International Relations & Migration	Travel & Exploration
Education		Underwater Archaeology
Environment	Military Affairs & Naval Forces	Water Craft Engineering
Fishing		Museums

Browse historical period

Ancient History	16th Century	19th Century
Middle Ages (500–1500)	17th Century	20th Century
	18th Century	21st Century

Figure 11.2 The National Maritime Museum's PORT gateway at <www.port.nmm.ac.uk>

collection of links to other official naval sites at <www.royal-navy.mod.uk/static/pages/2090.html>.

Genuki has a page of merchant marine links at <**www.genuki.org.uk/big/MerchantMarine.html**>, while the Royal Navy is included in its Military Records and Military History pages mentioned above.

The MARINERS mailing list is for all those whose ancestors pursued maritime occupations. The list has its own web site at <**www.mariners-l.co.uk**> with sections devoted to individual countries, as well as more general topics such as wars at sea, and shipping companies. The site also has a guide to ranks in both the Royal and merchant navy at <**www. mariners-l.co.uk/GenBosun'sLocker.html**>.

In addition to the NMM's site at <**www.nmm.ac.uk**>, the Royal Navy site has links to this and UK naval museums on its links page at <**www.royal-navy.mod.uk/static/pages/2090.html**>, while almost 300 maritime museums are listed at <**www.cus.cam.ac.uk/~mhe1000/ marmus.htm**>.

Records

Since the majority of the records are held by the National Archives, one of the best places to find out about them is the collection of on-line leaflets at <**www.pro.gov.uk/leaflets/Riindex.asp**>, where the relevant materials are grouped under Royal Navy and Merchant Navy. Information about the records of merchant seamen will also be found in 'Pathways to the Past' at <**www.pro.gov.uk/pathways/FamilyHistory/gallery3/seaman.htm**>.

The Royal Navy site has details on obtaining service records for those who joined the Navy from 1924 onwards at <**www.royal-navy.mod.uk/ static/pages/1034.html**> (earlier records are at the National Archives).

For a more discursive guide to naval records, Fawne Stratford-Devai's articles on the Global Gazette site are recommended, 'British Military Records Part 2: The Royal Navy' at <**globalgenealogy.com/globalgazette/ gazfd/gazfd48.htm**> and 'Maritime Records & Resources', in two parts, at   <**globalgenealogy.com/globalgazette/gazfd/gazfd50.htm**>   and <**globalgenealogy.com/globalgazette/gazfd/gazfd52.htm**>. Among other things, these articles have very useful lists of some of the main groups of records (mainly from the National Archives) which have been microfilmed by the LDS Church can therefore be consulted at Family History Centres.

Other guides to tracing seafaring ancestors include Bob Sanders' site at <**www.angelfire.com/de/BobSanders/Site.html**>, which has an extensive collection of material on 'Tracing British Seamen & their ships', including not only naval occupations but also Fishermen, Customs & Excise Officers and Coastguards. Len Barnett has what he calls 'a realistic guide to what is available to those looking into merchant mariners' careers' at <**www. barnettresearch.freeserve.co.uk/main.htm**>.

Apart from the Commonwealth War Graves Commission's Debt of Honour Register at <**www.cwgc.org**>, almost all on-line data transcriptions relating to seamen will be found on the web sites of individuals. For example, Bob Sanders has an index to O'Byrne's *Royal Navy Biography* of 1849 with details of Royal Navy officers, linked from <www.angelfire.com/de/BobSanders/Site.html>, as well as many other small data collections. Warships.net has crew listings for a number of naval vessels lost during the world wars, as well as a list of submariners awarded the Victoria Cross at <www.warships.net/royalnavy/men/>. Finding such material with a search engine will be easier if you already know the name of a ship or a port.

Genuki has a listing of those who served at Trafalgar at <www.genuki.org.uk/big/eng/Trafalgar/> compiled by the NZ Society of Genealogists. The Age of Nelson at <www.unepassion.be> has a complete Navy List for the period of the Napoleonic Wars. It also has a project to trace the descendants of those who fought at Trafalgar, as well as its own Trafalgar Roll.

Ships

There are a number of sites relating to the ships rather than the seamen who served on them, and these can be useful for background. For example, Gilbert Provost has transcribed details of vessels from the Lloyd's Register of British and Foreign Shipping from 1764 up to 2001 at <www.webruler.com/gprovost/Lloyd's.htm>. Michael P. Palmer maintains the Palmer List of Merchant Vessels at <www.geocities.com/mppraetorius/>, which has descriptions of hundreds of merchant vessels, compiled from a variety of sources. Both sites provide names of masters and owners as well as information on the ships themselves. Steve Johnson provides a 'photographic A to Z of British Naval warships, submarines, and auxiliaries from 1880 to 1950' at <freepages.misc.rootsweb.com/~cyberheritage/>.

If you suspect that an ancestor was on a naval vessel, either in port or at sea, on census night in 1901, you should find Jeffery Knaggs' index to the location of Royal Navy ships at <homepage.ntlworld.com/jeffery.knaggs/RNShips.html> of interest. Bob Sanders has a similar list of Ships in UK Ports for the 1881 census at <www.angelfire.com/de/BobSanders/81Intro.html>.

The Army

In addition to the detailed information about army records in the National Archives' leaflets mentioned above, there is basic information about locating records in the National Archives for individual soldiers at <www.pro.gov.uk/research/easysearch/Army.htm>. Genuki has a page devoted to British Military History at <www.genuki.org.uk/big/MilitaryHistory.html>, and an article by Jay Hall on 'British Military Records for the 18th and 19th Centuries' at <www.genuki.org.uk/big/MilitaryRecords.html>. The FFHS provides some basic information in the on-line version of its leaflet 'In search of your Soldier Ancestors' at <**www.ffhs.org.uk/General/Help/Soldier.htm**>; and there is a useful article by Fawne Stratford-Devai devoted to 'British Military Records Part 1: The Army' in *The Global Gazette* at <**globalgenealogy.com/globalgazette/ gazfd/gazfd44.htm**>.

While the National Archives does not have individual army records on-line, the on-line catalogue PROCAT (see p. 96) includes the names of individual soldiers from documents in class WO 97, which comprises discharge papers for the period 1760–1854.

The crucial piece of information about any ancestor in the army is the regiment or unit he served in. A useful area of the army site at the MoD is that devoted to the organisational structure of the army at <**www. army.mod.uk/unitsandorgs/**>, which has links to the web pages for the individual regiments, as well as to the special units and the Territorial Army. On the page for each regiment is a brief history and a list of its main engagements.

However, over the centuries, regiments have not been very stable in either composition or naming and you are likely to need historical information about the particular period when an ancestor was in uniform. Apart from the official material on the MoD site, the essential resource for regimental history is T. F. Mills' Land Forces of Britain, the Empire and Commonwealth site at <**www.regiments.org**>. The site not only provides detailed background information on the regimental system at <**regiments.org/milhist/uk/forces/bargts.htm**>, but also lists the regiments in the army in particular years since the 18th century. For an overview of regimental name changes and amalgamations, see Cathy Day's listing of 'Lineages of all British Army Infantry Regiments' at <**members. ozemail.com.au/~clday/regiments.htm**>.

The Scots at War site has a list of Scottish regiments at <**www. scotsatwar.org.uk/army/regiments/**> with pages devoted to each one.

Many individuals have put up pages on individual regiments, sometimes in relation to a particular war or engagement. There is no single comprehensive listing of these, but you should be able to find them by entering the name of the regiment in a search engine.

There is a britregiments mailing list, details of which will be found at <**groups.yahoo.com/group/britregiments/**>. Note that this is a military rather than genealogical discussion forum.

If you need to identify a cap badge, you could have a look at <**www.egframes.co.uk/indexbadge.htm**>, which is a commercial site offering badges for sale but has photographs of current badges and a searchable database of regiments. If you want to know what uniform an ancestor wore, or are trying to identify a photograph, the illustrations from two booklets by Arthur H. Bowling on the uniforms of British Infantry Regiments 1660–1914 and Scottish Regiments 1660–1914 are on-line at <**geocities.com/Pentagon/Barracks/3050/buframe.html**>.

Otherwise, you will need to browse through some of the on-line photographic collections, such as Photographs of Soldiers of the British Army 1840 to 1920 at <**web.archive.org/web/20011031231036/pobox. upenn.edu/~fbl/phtobrit.html**>.

In addition to the data in the Debt of Honour Register (see p. 83), the Officers Died site at <redcoat.future.easyspace.com> lists officers killed in a whole range of wars from the Peninsular Wars in 1808 to Kosovo in 1999, compiled from various books, casualty lists, medal rolls, newspapers, and memorials. Britains Small Wars at <**www.britains-smallwars.com**> covers the period from 1945 up to the present and has extensive information about each war, including in many cases lists of casualties.

For army museums, the MoD has a comprehensive listing on its web site at <**www.army.mod.uk/ceremonialandheritage/museums_main.htm**>,   which can be viewed alphabetically or by special interest covered, though of course many of the museums themselves do not yet have a web presence. The National Army Museum in Chelsea has a web site at <**www.national-army-museum.ac.uk**>. A list of Scottish military museums is provided on the Scottish Military Historical Society's web site at <**www.btinternet. com/~james.mckay/disp_018.htm**>. Regimental museums can be found via the regiment's page on the Army web site.

The Royal Air Force

The official RAF site is at <**www.raf.mod.uk**>, with a list of units and stations at <**www.raf.mod.uk/stations/**>. The 'Histories' section at <**www. raf.mod.uk/history/histories.html**> offers historical material on individual squadrons and stations, with images of squadron badges and details of battle honours and aircraft. If you have an ancestor who took part in the Battle of Britain, you will want to look at the operational diaries at <**www.raf.mod.uk/bob1940/bobhome.html**>. The 'Links' page at <**www. raf.mod.uk/links/**> has links to the web sites of individual squadrons and stations. The MoD site has (non-electronic) contact details for RAF Personnel records at <**www.mod.uk/contacts/raf_records.htm**>.

The RAF Museum has a web site at <**www.rafmuseum.org.uk**>, and the pages for the museum's Department of Research & Information Services at Hendon has information on archive and library material at <**www. rafmuseum.org.uk/hendon/research/**>.

There do not seem to be any genealogical mailing lists specifically for the RAF, though the general lists for 20th century wars mentioned on p. 134 above will cover RAF interests.

Colonies and migration

Former British colonies are genealogically important for British and Irish family history for three reasons: they have been the destination of emigrants from the British Isles (both voluntary and otherwise), the source of much immigration, and a place of residence and work for many British soldiers, merchants and others. There have, of course, been other sources of immigration and these are discussed towards the end of this section.

There is not space here to deal with internet resources relating to the individual countries, or to overseas records unrelated to immigration or emigration, but good places to start are Cyndi's List at <www.cyndislist. com>, which has individual pages for all the countries or regions, and the GenWeb site for the country at <worldgenweb.org> (see p. 24).

Genuki has links relating to both emigration and immigration at <www.genuki.org.uk/big/Emigration.html>. Resources relating to child migration are covered in 'Adoption and child migration' on p. 125.

For the official British records of emigration, the National Archives' 'Emigration' leaflet is the definitive on-line guide at <catalogue.pro.gov.uk/ Leaflets/ri2272.htm>. For convict transportation, there are leaflets relating to North America and the West Indies at <catalogue.pro.gov.uk/Leaflets/ ri2234.htm>, and to Australia at <catalogue.pro.gov.uk/Leaflets/ri2235.htm>.

Key general records for emigration from the British Isles are passenger lists, and there are a number of sites with information about surviving passenger lists, or with data transcribed from them. Cyndi's List has a 'Ships and Passenger Lists' page at <www.cyndislist.com/ships.htm>. Among other information, this has links to many passenger lists and lists of ship arrivals.

The Immigrant Ships Transcribers Guild at <istg.rootsweb.com> has transcribed over 5,000 passenger lists and is adding more all the time. These can be searched by date, by port of departure, port of arrival, passenger name or captain's name. In addition to its own material, the Guild's 'Compass' web site at <istg.rootsweb.com/newcompass/ pcindex.html> has an enormous collection of links to passenger-list sites on-line. For Irish emigration, the ScotlandsClans site has many links at <www.scotlandsclans.com/irshiplists.htm>. There are a number of mailing lists for immigrant ships, but the most general is TheShipsList, which has its own web site at <www.theshipslist.com>. Details of other lists relating to emigration and immigration will be found at <www.rootsweb.com/ ~jfuller/gen_mail_emi.html>.

The National Archives has information about official records in leaflets devoted to 'Immigration' at <catalogue.pro.gov.uk/Leaflets/ri2156.htm> and 'Naturalisation' at <catalogue.pro.gov.uk/Leaflets/ri2257.htm>.

Probably the most important site for information on immigration to the British Isles is Moving Here at <www.movinghere.org.uk>. This covers Caribbean, Irish, South Asian and Jewish immigration to England over the past two centuries and the subsequent history of the immigrant communities. The site has a catalogue of resources as well as general historical material and individual historical testimony. There is specifically genealogical information in the 'Tracing Your Roots gallery' at <www.movinghere.org.uk/galleries/roots/>.

Another good general site is The Channel 4 Guide to Genealogy, which has material on tracing an ancestor who was an immigrant at <www.channel4.com/history/microsites/U/untold/resources/geno/geno3.html> covering Jewish, African-American, West Indian, African, and Asian immigration.

A good resource for all ethnic groups is The Open Directory (see p. 29) at <www.dmoz.org> which has pages for over 50 ethnic groups at <dmoz.org/Society/Ethnicity/>. The links collected here are primarily to historical and cultural material, however, and you should not expect to find any genealogical resources that cannot be found on Cyndi's List. For more specifically British resources, it is worth going to <dmoz.org/Regional/Europe/United_Kingdom/Society_and_Culture/Ethnicity/> which links to pages for 11 immigrant communities.

There is a Museum of Immigration at Spitalfields in London which has a web site at <www.19princeletstreet.org.uk>. The British Empire & Commonwealth Museum in Bristol has a web site at <www.empiremuseum.co.uk> with information on the museum and its collections.

Figure 11.3 MovingHere at <www.movinghere.org.uk>

North America

The American colonies were the first dumping ground for convicts, and the National Archives' leaflet 'Transportation to America and the West Indies, 1615–1776' at <catalogue.pro.gov.uk/Leaflets/ri2234.htm> gives details of the records. More general information about colonies on the other side of the Atlantic will be found in 'The American and West Indian Colonies Before 1782' at <catalogue.pro.gov.uk/Leaflets/ri2105.htm>. For post-colonial emigration to the US, see 'Emigrants to North America After 1776' at <catalogue.pro.gov.uk/Leaflets/ri2107.htm>. The US National Archives and Records Administration has information on 'Immigration and Naturalization Records' at <www.archives.gov/research_room/genealogy/research_topics/immigration_and_naturalization.html>

For other links relating to emigration to North America, the best starting point is the 'Immigration and Naturalization' page on Cyndi's List at <www.cyndislist.com/immigrat.htm>.

US sites of course have a wealth of data relating to immigrants. Ancestry.com, for example, has databases of Immigrants to New England 1620–33, Irish Quaker Immigration into Pennsylvania, New England Founders, New England Immigrants, 1700–75, New England Irish Pioneers and Scots-Irish in Virginia (most of these databases require a subscription to Ancestry). Ancestry.com is discussed more fully on p. 40. For the late 19th and early 20th centuries, Ellis Island On-line (the American Family Immigration History Center) at <www.ellisislandrecords.org> has a searchable database of passengers who entered America through Ellis Island between 1892 and 1924.

There are many sites devoted to individual groups of settlers, for example the *Mayflower* Passenger List at <members.aol.com/calebj/passenger.html>. The immigration page on Cyndi's List is the easiest way to find such sites. The 'Immigration And Ships Passenger Lists Research Guide' at <home.att.net/~arnielang/shipgide.html> offers help and guidance on researching ancestors who emigrated to the USA.

There is less material on-line for Canada. Marjorie Kohli's Immigrants to Canada site at <www.ist.uwaterloo.ca/~marj/genealogy/thevoyage.html> has an extensive collection of material, and links to many related resources. The National Archives of Canada has information on 'Immigration Records' at <www.archives.ca/02/02020204_e.html>, covering both border entry and passenger lists. There is a pilot on-line database for the passenger list records for the years 1925–35. The inGeneas site at <www.inGeneas.com> also has a database of passenger lists and immigration records; the National Archives of Canada Miscellaneous Immigration Index is free; the index to other material can be searched free, but there is a charge for record transcriptions.

African and Caribbean[9]

The best starting points for researching Black British ancestry are the material on the BBC and Channel 4 web sites. The Channel 4 Guide to Genealogy has already been mentioned (see p. 6 and p. 141) and includes material on African, West Indian and African-Americans genealogy. The BBC web site offers an introduction to Caribbean family history by Kathy Chater at <www.bbc.co.uk/history/your_history/family/caribb_family_1.shtml>, which gives some historical background and discusses the relevant records.

CaribbeanGenWeb at <www.rootsweb.com/~caribgw/> has areas devoted to all the islands of the Caribbean. Though there are considerable differences in scope, as each island site has its own maintainer, all have message boards to make contact with other researchers, and many have substantial collections of links. You should also find information on civil registration, parish registers and other records. Another useful collection of genealogy links for the Caribbean will be found on the Candoo site at <www.candoo.com/genresources/>, including lists of relevant microfilms in the LDS Church's Family History Centres.

An important site to be launched in the near future is the Database of London's Black and Asian History. This project of the London Metropolitan Archives (LMA) is creating an on-line database of Black and Asian Londoners between 1536 and 1840, with names and area of residence based on information from church registers, family papers in the LMA and material from the British Library and the India Office. It will also cover migration to the capital among these groups, and identify links between these and overseas communities. Information about the project will be found at <www.bl.uk/collections/britasian/britasialondon.html> and the LMA Web site at <www.cityoflondon.gov.uk/leisure_heritage/libraries_archives_museums_galleries/lma/> will presumably be providing a link when the database goes live.

For anyone with Caribbean ancestry, the Caribbean Surnames Index (CARSURDEX) at <www.candoo.com/surnames/> will be an essential resource. It has over 3,000 surname interests with surname, island and an e-mail contact address, and there is an on-line form for submitting your own surnames.

There is a newsgroup for discussion of Caribbean ancestry, soc.genealogy.west-indies, which is gatewayed with the CARIBBEAN mailing list (see <lists.rootsweb.com/index/other/Newsgroup_Gateways/CARIBBEAN.html>). Details of other West Indies mailing lists will be found at <www.rootsweb.com/~jfuller/gen_mail_country-wes.html>. The GEN-AFRICAN-L mailing list, gatewayed with the soc.genealogy.african newsgroup, also covers the genealogy of Africa and the African diaspora.

---

[9] For additional material on this topic, see my article on the subject in issue 10 of *Ancestors* (October/November 2002).

There are also genealogical mailing lists for individual African countries – see <www.rootsweb.com/~jfuller/gen_mail_african.html>.

While there is still relatively little specifically genealogical material on-line for those with Black British ancestry, there has recently been a huge increase in the amount of general historical information on-line relating to Black immigration.

Both the BBC and Channel 4 sites include such material. Resources relating to the BBC's *Windrush* season, broadcast in 1998, at <www.bbc.co.uk/history/society_culture/multicultural/windrush_01.shtml> include a factfile and oral testimony from those who came to Britain on the *Windrush*. This is part of the 'multiculture' area of the BBC's site which has a range of material relating to Black History and the British Empire. Channel 4's Black and Asian History Map at <www.channel4.com/history/microsites/B/blackhistorymap/> provides a large number of links to sites with biographical and historical information on Black and Asian immigrants to Britain. There is a timeline to provide an overview, a map which allows you to select links for particular parts of the UK, and a search facility.

Figure 11.4 The BBC Multicultural History page

CASBAH is a project which aims to identify and map national research resources in the UK library and archives sectors, that are relevant to Caribbean studies and the history of Black and Asian peoples in Britain. The CASBAH web site at <www.casbah.ac.uk>, while aimed primarily at academic researchers, is useful to anyone researching Black History in Britain because it provides links to around 120 other relevant web sites, particularly libraries with relevant collections.

Share the Dream has a timeline of Black Londoners from the Romans to the present day in The Shaping of Black London at <www.thechronicle. demon.co.uk/tomsite/capsule.htm>.

A number of off-line organisations have useful web sites, for example the Archives & Museum of Black Heritage at <www.aambh.org.uk> and the Black and Asian Studies Association at <www.basauk.com>.

The Open Directory's African-British page at <dmoz.org/Society/ Ethnicity/African/African-British/> is a good starting point for Web resources relating to African and Afro-Caribbean immigration into Britain, though the listing does not specialise in genealogical sources.

Black Search at <www.blacksearch.co.uk> is a UK-based Web directory of Black web sites around the world. It has a genealogy page, which can be found by following the 'History and Culture' link from the home page. There are also headings in this section for Africa, African American, Black British, and Caribbean.

For convict transportation to the West Indies, see the National Archives' leaflets mentioned under 'North America', above.

India

A number of the resources mentioned in the previous section cover Asian immigration to Britain as well as Black immigration. The Channel 4 Guide to Genealogy has material on tracing Indian and other Asian ancestry at <www.channel4.com/history/microsites/U/untold/resources/geno/geno3e. html>.

The British Library has a whole set of pages devoted to 'Sources relating to Asians from the Indian Subcontinent' at <www.bl.uk/collections/ britasian/britasia.html>, including an outline of Asian immigration and contemporary material from various walks of life (Figure 11.5).

The BL site is also useful for ancestors from the British Isles who lived or worked in India, as it includes the India Office web site. This has pages for family historians at <www.bl.uk/collections/oiocfamilyhistory/family. html>, with information on the various types of genealogical source.

Another good starting point for genealogical research into British India is Cathy Day's Family History In India site at <members.ozemail.com.au/ ~clday/>, which provides a comprehensive guide for 'people tracing their British, European and Anglo-Indian family history in India, Burma, Pakistan and Bangladesh'. It has extensive material relating to the British army in India and many small data extracts. The Families in British

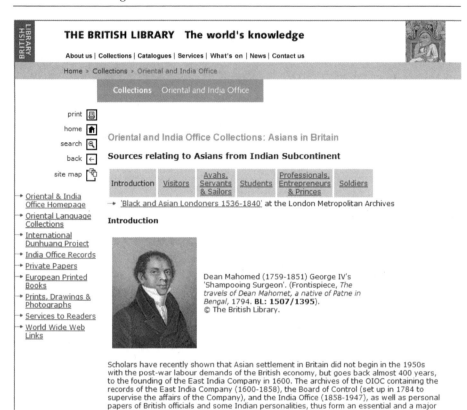

Figure 11.5 'Asians in Britain' on the British Library site

India Society has a web site at **<fibis.org>**.

If your ancestors had some connection with the East India Company, you will find relevant links on some of the maritime resources discussed on p. 136, in addition to the India Office material mentioned above.

There are currently two genealogical mailing lists relevant to the Indian sub-continent, BANGLADESH and INDIA. Details will be found at **<lists.rootsweb.com/index/intl/BGD/BANGLADESH.html>** and **<lists.rootsweb.com/index/intl/IND/INDIA.html>** respectively. RootsWeb hosts genealogical mailing lists for a number of other Asian countries, listed at **<lists.rootsweb.com/index/>**.

Australasia

There are extensive materials on-line relating both to convict transportation to Australia, and to later free emigration to Australia and New Zealand. Good starting points are the Australia and New Zealand pages on Cyndi's List at **<www.cyndislist.com/austnz.htm>** and **<www.cyndislist.com/newzealand.htm>** respectively. Another worthwhile site is the Australian Family History Compendium, which has a list of on-line sources at <**www.cohsoft.com.au/afhc/netrecs.html**>. For information on the official records held by the British state, see the National Archives' on-line leaflets.

Convict lists for the first, second and third fleets will be found on Patricia Downes' site at <**www.pcug.org.au/~pdownes/**>. The National Archives of Ireland has an on-line database of Transportation Records 1788–1868 at <**www.nationalarchives.ie/search01.html**> (see Figure 11.6). In addition to the passenger-list sites mentioned above, links to on-line passenger lists for Australasia will be found at <**www.users.on.net/ proformat/auspass.html**>.

Australian government agencies have much information relating to convict and free settlers on-line. The National Archives of Australia web site at <**www.naa.gov.au**> has a family history section, which includes material on immigration at <**www.naa.gov.au/The_Collection/ Family_History/immigrants.html**>. The Victoria Public Record Office has an on-line database of Immigration to Victoria 1852–1889 at <**proarchives.imagineering.com.au**>. The Archives Office of Tasmania, at <**www.archives.tas.gov.au**>, has a Colonial Tasmanian Family Link Database, with about 500,000 entries, and an Index to Naturalisation Applications for 1835–1905. New South Wales has all 19th-century civil registration indexes on-line at <**www.bdm.nsw.gov.au/histind.html**> and Indexes to Assisted Immigrants, 1839–96 at <**www.records.nsw.gov.au/ indexes/immigration/introduction.htm**>, though the full records are not

---

The National Archives of Ireland

Search results

Found 1 record matching **O'Brian**. Printing first 1 of 1 records.

The document reference in each entry below is the National Archives of Ireland reference to the original document in the archives The microfilm reference number refers to the set of microfilms presented to Australia in 1988.

Record 1 of 1

```
SURNAME: O'BRIAN              OTHER NAMES: MARGARET
    AGE:  25        SEX: F        ALIAS:

PLACE OF TRIAL: Co. Antrim          TRIAL DATE: 21/10/1839
PLACE OF IMPRISONMENT:              DOCUMENT DATE:

        CRIME DESCRIPTION: Larceny
        SENTENCE: Transportation 7 yrs
        SHIP:

PETITIONER:                    RELATIONSHIP:

DOCUMENT REFERENCES:  TR 3, p 193
MICROFILM REFERENCES:
COMMENTS:
```

Figure 11.6 An entry from the National Archives of Ireland's Transportation Records

on-line. Comprehensive links to Australian archives are on the Archives of Australia site at <**www.archivenet.gov.au**>.

Archives New Zealand has a web site at <**www.archives.govt.nz**> with a genealogy page at <**www.archives.govt.nz/holdings/research/genealogical/ genealogical_sources_frame.html**>. The Registrar General's site at <**www.bdm.govt.nz**> has information on births, deaths and marriages but no on-line data.

There are dozens of mailing lists for Australian and New Zealand genealogy, all listed at <**www.rootsweb.com/~jfuller/gen_mail_country- aus.html**> and <**www.rootsweb.com/~jfuller/gen_mail_country-nez.html**>. Those of most general interest are: AUS-CONVICTS, AUS-IMMIGRATION- SHIPS, AUS-IRISH, AUS-MILITARY, AUSTRALIA, convicts-australia, NEW-ZEALAND, TRANSCRIPTIONS-AUS and TRANSCRIPTIONS- NZ. But there are also lists for individual states, regions and even towns. The newsgroup soc.genealogy.australia+nz is gatewayed with the GENANZ mailing list.

Jews

There are many sites devoted to Jewish genealogy, though not many are specifically concerned with British Jewry. A general history of Jews in Britain is provided in Shira Schoenberg's Virtual Jewish History Tour, which has a page devoted to England at <**www.us-israel.org/jsource/vjw/ England.html**>. The JewishGen site at <**www.jewishgen.org**> is a very comprehensive site with a number of resources relevant to Jewish ancestry in the British Isles. These include an article on researching Jewish ancestry at <**www.jewishgen.org/infofiles/ukgen.txt**>, and the London Jews Database <**www.jewishgen.org/databases/londweb.htm**>, which has about 9,000 names, compiled principally from London trade directories. The Jewish genealogical magazine *Avotaynu* has a 'Five-minute Guide to Jewish Genealogical Research' at <**www.avotaynu.com/jewish_genealogy. htm**>. The National Archives has a leaflet 'Anglo Jewish History: Sources in the National Archives, 18th–20th Centuries' on-line at <**catalogue. pro.gov.uk/Leaflets/ri2183.htm**>. As usual, Cyndi's List has a good collection of links at <**www.cyndislist.com/jewish.htm**>.

The Jewish Genealogical Society of Great Britain's web site, at <**www.jgsgb.org.uk**>, has a substantial collection of links to Jewish material in Britain and worldwide. It also has a number of data files available for downloading at <**www.jgsgb.org.uk/downl2.shtml**>. *Avotaynu* has a Consolidated Jewish Surname Index at <**www.avotaynu. com/csi/csi-home.html**> with over half a million names. There is a varied collection of material relating to London Jews on Jeffrey Maynard's site at <**www.jeffreymaynard.com**>. The Channel 4 Guide to Genealogy has material on tracing Jewish ancestry at <**www.channel4.com/history/ microsites/U/untold/resources/geno/geno3a.html**>.

The JewishGen Family Finder (JGFF) at <**www.jewishgen.org/jgff/**> is a 'database of ancestral towns and surnames currently being researched by Jewish genealogists worldwide', with around 80,000 surnames submitted by 60,000 Jewish genealogists.

The newsgroup soc.genealogy.jewish is devoted to Jewish genealogy. This group is gatewayed with the JEWISHGEN mailing list and John Fuller lists another three dozen mailing lists for Jewish genealogy at <www.rootsweb.com/~jfuller/gen_mail_jewish.html>. Most are specific to particular geographical areas, and JEWISHGEN and JEWISH-ROOTS are the only general interest lists. The BRITISH-JEWRY list – details at <lists.rootsweb.com/index/other/Ethnic-Jewish/BRITISH-JEWRY.html> – is the only one specifically relevant to the UK.

Huguenots

Cyndi's List has links to Huguenot resources at <www.cyndislist.com/huguenot.htm>, while for historical background there is a Huguenot timeline at <www.kopower.com/~jimchstn/timeline.htm>. Some basic information on the Huguenots will be found on Olive Tree Genealogy at <olivetreegenealogy.com/hug/overview.shtml>.

There are two main mailing lists: HUGUENOTS-WALLOONS-EUROPE and a general Huguenot mailing list, both hosted at RootsWeb (subscription details at <lists.rootsweb.com/index/other/Religion/>). The former has its own web site at <www.island.net/~andreav/> with a good collection of links and its own surnames list. There is also a less busy HUGUENOT-WALLOON list – see <lists.rootsweb.com/index/other/Miscellaneous/HUGUENOT-WALLOON.html>.

The Huguenot Surnames Index at <www.aftc.com.au/Huguenot/Huguenot.html> will enable you to make contact with others researching particular Huguenot families.

The Huguenot Society of Great Britain & Ireland has a web site at <www.huguenotsociety.org.uk>. Information about the Huguenot Library, housed at University College London, will be found at <www.ucl.ac.uk/Library/huguenot.htm>, and information on the French Protestant Church of London is on the Institute of Historical Research site at <ihr.sas.ac.uk/ihr/associnstits/huguenots.mnu.html>.

Gypsies

There are two starting points on the Web for British gypsy ancestry. The Romany & Traveller Family History Society site at <website.lineone.net/~rtfhs/>, apart from society information (including a list of contents for recent issues of its magazine), has a page on 'Was Your Ancestor a Gypsy?'. This lists typical gypsy surnames, forenames and occupations. The site also has a good collection of links to other gypsy material on the Web.

The Gypsy Collections at the University of Liverpool site at <sca.lib.liv.ac.uk/collections/gypsy/intro.htm> has information about, and photographs of, British gypsy families as well as a collection of links to other gypsy sites.

Directories of gypsy material can be found in the Open Directory at <dmoz.org/Society/Ethnicity/Romani/> and there is more specifically genealogical material on Cyndi's List at <www.cyndislist.com/peoples. htm#Gypsies> on a page entitled 'Unique Peoples & Cultures'.

In June 2001, Kent County Council received Lottery funding for a digitisation project which is to include 'a traveller archive for the largest ethnic community in Kent' with a range of sources, manuscript, oral and photographic. Although due to go live by the end of 2002, there was no further information about the project's progress by summer 2003. However, BBC Kent has a Romany Voices site at <www.bbc.co.uk/kent/voices/>, which also has useful links to other Gypsy web sites.

There is a UK-ROMANI mailing list for British gypsy family history, details of which will be found at <lists.rootsweb.com/index/intl/UK/UK-ROMANI.html>.

Royal and notable families

The Web has a wide range of resources relating to the genealogy of royal houses and the nobility, as well as to famous people and families. For initial orientation, Genuki's page on 'Kings and Queens of England and Scotland (and some of the people around them)' at <www.genuki.org.uk/big/royalty/> provides a list of Monarchs since the Conquest, Kings of England, Kings of Scotland, Queens and a selection of the most notable Queens, Kings, Archbishops, Bishops, Dukes, Earls, Knights, Lords, Eminent Men, Popes and Princes. There is also a detailed table of the Archbishops of Canterbury and York, and the Bishops of London, Durham, St David's and Armagh, from AD 200 to the present day at <www.genuki.org.uk/big/eng/History/Archbishops.html>.

Cyndi's List has a page with over 200 links relating to 'Royalty and Nobility' at <www.cyndislist.com/royalty.htm>.

The best place for genealogical information on English royalty is Brian Tompsett's Directory of Royal Genealogical Data at <www.dcs.hull.ac.uk/public/genealogy/royal/catalog.html>, which contains 'the genealogy of the British royal family and those linked to it via blood or marriage relationships'. The site provides much information on other royal families, and includes details of all English peerages at <www.dcs.hull.ac.uk/public/genealogy/royal/peerage.html>. It can be searched by name, by date, or by title. Another massive database devoted to European nobility will be found on the WW-Person site at <www8.informatik.uni-erlangen.de/html/ww-person.html>.

The official web site of the royal family is at <www.royal.gov.uk> which, among other things, offers family trees of the royal houses from the ninth-century Kingdom of Wessex to the present day in PDF format linked from <www.royal.gov.uk/output/Page5.asp>. Royal and noble titles for many languages and countries are explained in the 'Glossary of European Noble, Princely, Royal, and Imperial Titles' at <www.heraldica.org/topics/odegard/titlefaq.htm>.

Burke's Peerage and Gentry at <www.burkes-peerage.net> is a subscription site providing access to on-line data from the published books, including

- *Burke's Peerage & Baronetage*
- *Burke's Landed Gentry Scotland*
- *Burke's Landed Gentry Ireland*
- *Burke's Landed Gentry England & Wales*

and a number of other works. The site also provides a number of free resources including articles and reference material. Genuki has part of *The English Peerage* (1790) on-line at <www.genuki.org.uk/big/eng/History/Barons/>, with information on a number of barons and viscounts of the period.

Alongside royalty and nobility, you can almost certainly find information on the Web on any other genealogically notable group of people. Thus there are sites devoted to the sons of Noah (<www.geocities.com/Tokyo/4241/geneadm2.html>), the *Mayflower* pilgrims (<www.mayflowerhistory.com/Passengers/passengers.php >) and even the *Bounty* mutineers (<www.lareau.org/genweb.html>).

Mark Humphrys has a site devoted to the Royal Descents of Famous People at <www.compapp.dcu.ie/~humphrys/FamTree/Royal/famous.descents.html>, while Ulf Berggren provides genealogical information on many notable people from Winston Churchill to Donald Duck (really!) at <www.stacken.kth.se/~ulfb/genealogy.html>. The ancestry of the US presidents will be found on a number of sites, and <www.dcs.hull.ac.uk/public/genealogy/presidents/presidents.html> provides a tree for each of them.

The Bolles Collection has the index and epitome for the 1903 edition of the *Dictionary of National Biography* on-line, containing brief biographies of over 30,000 notable individuals – follow the link to the DNB from <www.perseus.tufts.edu/cache/perscoll_Bolles.html>. The easiest way to locate a particular individual is to use the search facility on this main page.

There are number of relevant mailing lists including:

- GEN-ROYAL <lists.rootsweb.com/index/other/Miscellaneous/GEN-ROYAL.html>
- BRITISH-NOBILITY <lists.rootsweb.com/index/intl/UK/BRITISH-NOBILITY.html>
- PLANTAGENET <lists.rootsweb.com/index/intl/UK/PLANTAGENET.html>

● SCT-ROYAL <lists.rootsweb.com/index/intl/SCT/SCTROYAL.html>.

Lists for further countries will be found at <**www.rootsweb.com/~jfuller/
gen_mail_nobility.html**>. Yahoo has many discussion groups for royal and
noble genealogy, listed at <**dir.groups.yahoo.com/dir/Family___Home/
Genealogy/Royal_Genealogies**> (note the *three* underscores).

Clans

Information on Scottish clans will be found among the surname resources
discussed in Chapter 10, but there are also some general sites devoted to
clans. The Scottish Tourist Board offers some general information about
clans from its 'History' page at <**www.visitscotland.com/aboutscotland/
history/**>, while ScotlandsClans at <**www.scotlandsclans.com**> has links to
sites for individual clans, as well as a message board and a mailing list.
Another mailing list is CLANS, details of which can be found at
<**lists.rootsweb.com/index/intl/SCT/CLANS.html**>, and RootsWeb has
many mailing lists for individual clans, listed at <**lists.rootsweb.
com/index/intl/SCT/**>. However, none of these seem to be particularly
thriving. There is a newsgroup, alt.scottish.clans. The Gathering of the
Clans site at <**www.tartans.com**> has pages devoted to individual clans
(with a brief history, badge, motto, tartan, etc.) and a 'Clan Finder' which
matches surnames to clans.

Heraldry

Heraldry is intimately connected with royal and noble families, and there
is quite a lot of material relating to it on the Web. The authoritative source
of information about heraldry in England and Wales is the web site of the
College of Arms at <**www.college-of-arms.gov.uk**>. Its FAQ page deals
with frequently asked questions about coats of arms. The SoG has a leaflet
on 'The Right to Arms' at <**www.sog.org.uk/leaflets/arms.html**>. For
Scotland, the Lord Lyon King of Arms is the chief herald, and information
on the Lyon Court will be found at <**www.heraldry-scotland.co.uk/
Lyoncourt.htm**>. Information on heraldry in Ireland will be found on the
National Library of Ireland's web site at <**www.nli.ie/fr_offi2.htm**>.

The Heraldry on the Internet site at <**www.digiserve.com/heraldry/**> is
a specialist site with a substantial collection of links to other on-line
heraldry resources, and Cyndi's List has a page of heraldry links at
<**www.cyndislist.com/heraldry.htm**>. The British Heraldry site at
<**www.heraldica.org/topics/britain/**> has a number of articles on heraldry.
The Heraldry Society will be found at <**www.theheraldrysociety.com**>,
while the Heraldry Society of Scotland has a site at <**www.heraldry-
scotland.co.uk**>.

For the meaning of terms used in heraldry, an on-line version of
Pimbley's 1905 *Dictionary of Heraldry* is at <**www.digiserve.com/
heraldry/pimbley.htm**>, while there is an on-line version of James Parker's

A Glossary of Terms used in Heraldry (1894) at <www002.upp.so-net.ne.jp/saitou/parker/>. Burke's Peerage has a 'Guide to Heraldic Terms' at <www.burkespeerage.net/sites/common/sitepages/heindex.asp>. Heraldic terms will also be found in the 'Knighthood, Chivalry & Tournament Glossary of Terms' at <www.chronique.com/Library/Glossaries/glossary-KCT/glssindx.htm>.

12 Geography

Maps and gazetteers are essential reference tools for family historians and while the internet cannot offer the wealth of maps available in reference libraries and record offices, let alone the British Library Map Library (web site at <www.bl.uk/collections/maps.html>), there are nonetheless many useful resources on-line. Good starting points for on-line maps and gazetteers are the 'Maps, Gazetteers & Geographical Information' page on Cyndi's List <www.cyndislist.com/maps.htm> and the Genuki county pages.

Gazetteers

The definitive gazetteer for the present-day UK is that provided by the Ordnance Survey (OS) at <www.ordnancesurvey.co.uk/products_new/Landranger/index.cfm> which has a database of all places listed on the Landranger series of maps. The search results list all relevant places, the current county or unitary authority, with grid reference, latitude and longitude. Each entry has a link to a diagrammatic map of the area in which the chosen place is located, which in turn links to a 600 x 536 pixel graphic of the whole Landranger map. This is not large enough to see any detail, but sufficient to get an idea of the geography of the area. (See 'Present-day maps', below, for more information about the maps on the OS site.)

Genuki has two gazetteers. The first can be found at <www.genuki.org.uk/big/eng/Gazetteers.html>. This page provides a search form for a gazetteer which will tell you the county and OS grid reference of a place, and also provides a list of other places within a chosen distance. If there is a Genuki page for the parish a link is provided, and there will also be a link to the relevant Genuki county. See Figure 12.1.

A more specialised facility is Genuki's Parish Locator at <www.genuki.org.uk/big/parloc/search.html>. Rather than listing places, this lists churches and register offices (Figure 12.2). Genuki also has a database of places mentioned in the 1891 census at <www.genuki.org.uk/big/census_place.html> (England, Wales and Isle of Man only).

Three university geography departments have useful gazetteers. Queen Mary and Westfield College, London, has an on-line gazetteer at <www.geog.qmw.ac.uk/gbhgis/gaz/start.html> based on the parishes in the 1911

UK & Ireland Genealogy   ⬆ Lancashire   📖 GENUKI Contents   📗 Help

Search for	Distance
SD190690	5	Miles ▾ [New Search]

Further searches by placename, or OS Grid Reference

Places within 5 miles of Barrow-In-Furness , OS Gridref SD190690

SD190690 Barrow-in-Furness, Lancashire which encompasses the area containing:

> SD190690 Hindpool ; Barrow-In-Furness
> ~ 1 miles NW SD180700 North Scale
> ~ 2 miles W SD170690 North Walney

~ 2 miles SSW SD180670 Walney, Lancashire which encompasses the area containing:

> ~ 1 miles SW SD180680 Vickerstown
> ~ 2 miles SSW SD180670 Water Garth Nook
> ~ 2 miles S SD190660 Biggar
> ~ 4 miles S SD200630 South End

~ 4 miles ENE SD243708 Dendron, Lancashire
~ 4 miles ESE SD240660 Rampside, Lancashire
~ 4 miles NE SD230740 Dalton-in-Furness, Lancashire which encompasses the area containing:

> ~ 1 miles E SD200690 Salthouse
> ~ 2 miles N SD190710 Ormsgill

Figure 12.1 The Genuki Gazetteer

UK & Ireland Genealogy   📄 GENUKI Contents   ⇦⇨ Nearby churches   📘 Help

Parishes/churches within 5 miles of SD190690

Gridref/Place	Dedication	Distance	Year	Denomination
SD190690		5	Miles ▾	- Any - ▾	[New Search]

Miles

~0.0   St Mary (*Roman Catholic*), Duke St, Barrow in Furness, Lancashire

~0.0   St Patrick (*Roman Catholic*), Barrow-in-Furness, Lancashire

~1.4 SSW St Mary the Virgin (*Church of England*), Walney, Lancashire

~3.2 ENE St Mathew (*Church of England*), Dendron, Lancashire

~4.0 NE   Our Lady of the Rosary (*Roman Catholic*), Dalton-in-Furness, Lancashire

~4.0 NE   St Mary (*Church of England*), Dalton-in-Furness, Lancashire

Figure 12.2 The Genuki Parish Locator

census. The University of Edinburgh has a project to provide an on-line gazetteer of Scotland, details of which can be found at <**www.geo.ed.ac.uk/scotgaz/**>. An interesting feature of the search on this site is that you can specify what sort of thing you are looking for, from Airport, Archaeological Site, Bank or Shoal, down to Waterfall and Whirlpool. It also provides a Scottish geographical glossary – follow the 'Glossary' link at <**www.geo.ed.ac.uk/scotgaz/scotland.html**>. The Great Britain Historical Database Online at the University of Portsmouth provides an excellent, though experimental and incomplete, Gazetteer of Placenames in England and Wales at <**alpha4.iso.port.ac.uk:8001/geog/owa/gbd_gazx.find_place**>.

The National Archives in Ireland has a searchable index of documents in its OS collection at <**www.nationalarchives.ie/cgi-bin/naigenform02? index=OS**>, which includes lists of towns and parishes, and thus effectively acts as a gazetteer. For Northern Ireland, PRONI has a collection of geographical indexes at <**www.proni.gov.uk/geogindx/geogindx.htm**>, which links to lists of Counties, Baronies, Poor Law Unions, Dioceses, Parishes, and Townlands. Sean Ruad has a searchable database of townlands, parishes and baronies at <**www.seanruad.com**>.

Other on-line gazetteers include the Gazetteer of British Place Names maintained by the Association of British Counties at <**www.gazetteer.co.uk**>, and county record offices may also provide resources for their local area. For example, Greater Manchester County Record Office has a 'Greater Manchester Gazetteer' at <**www.gmcro.co.uk/guides/gazette/gazframe.htm**>.

Going beyond the UK, probably the most important single gazetteer site on the Web is the Getty Thesaurus of Geographic Names Browser at <**www.getty.edu/research/tools/vocabulary/tgn/**>, which covers the whole world. Even for the UK this is useful, since it includes geographical, and some historical information (see Figure 12.3).

Present-day maps

The OS web site at <**www.ordsvy.gov.uk**> is the obvious starting point for any information about present-day mapping of the British Isles. The OS runs another site called Get-a-map at <**www.getamap.co.uk**>, which allows you to call up a map centred on a particular place. You can search by place name, postcode, or OS grid reference. Alternatively, you can just click on the map of the UK and gradually zoom in to your chosen area. The maps are free for personal use (including limited use on personal web sites). There is also an option to go to the 19th-century OS maps discussed in 'Historical maps', below.

There are three main commercial sites that provide free UK maps. The Streetmap site at <**www.streetmap.co.uk**> allows searches by street, postcode, place name, OS grid, Landranger grid, latitude/longitude, or telephone code. Multimap at <**uk.multimap.com**> offers similar facilities:

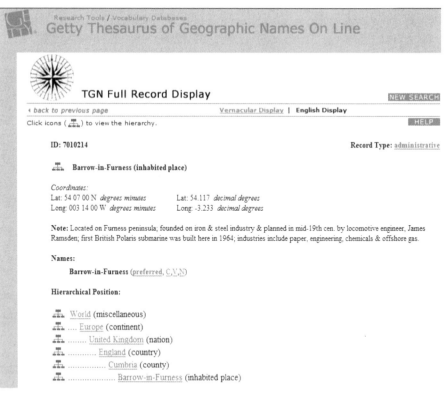

Figure 12.3 The Getty Thesaurus of Geographic Names

the initial search option offers place or postcode, while the advanced search includes building and street. Yahoo Maps at <**uk.maps.yahoo.com**> offers a rather more abstract style of map, intended primarily for driving. But it has the advantage of including a range of house numbers for each stretch of road at the higher zoom levels.

Genuki has instructions on 'How to find a present day house, street or place in the U.K. (or to find only the Post Code)' by using the Royal Mail site or the Multimap site at <**www.genuki.org.uk/big/ModernLocations. html**>.

Both Streetmap and Multimap provide aerial photographs, often at quite a high level of detail, for cities and some other parts of the country. Those on Streetmap are displayed larger and are linked directly from the map display. Obviously these photographs are of limited use for some purposes – for example, identifying streets by name – but can be useful for features like field boundaries (which are marked on the 6 inch OS maps but are not shown on the present-day maps available on-line). With Streetmap and Multimap, availability of an aerial photograph is indicated by an icon on each map page.

Historical maps

There are quite a lot of historical maps available on the Web, though many that are of interest to historians have insufficient local detail to be of use to genealogists. In general, the best places to look for links to on-line maps of counties or towns are Genuki's county pages, though it is also worth looking at county record office web sites. The Guildhall Library, for instance, has an extensive collection of maps and views of London on-line at <collage.nhil.com>.

However, the single most useful map resource for the genealogist is Landmark's complete collection of 19th-century 6 inch OS maps at <www.old-maps.co.uk>. The maps date from 1846 to 1899 and cover the whole of England, Wales and Scotland at 1:10,560 scale.

You can locate towns and villages by place name, address, postcode, or OS grid reference; alternatively a gazetteer gives a list of places in each pre-1974 county. This takes you to a map centred on the place in question and there are five levels of zoom. You cannot go directly to an adjacent map, but clicking on any part of a map will recentre it on that point, which means that the edge of one map can become the centre of the next. The map area on the screen is approximately 500 x 270 pixels and the resolution is sufficient for you to see the main details and read the larger

Figure 12.4 Old-maps: the 1888 OS map of Cambridge

pieces of text. There is an option to print from this screen, and you can also download the map image from the print preview page. There are links to a modern map and an aerial photograph of the selected area.

However, once you have located the place you are interested in, the most useful option is probably the 'Enlarged Image'. This gives a much larger image – each one is 2,666 x 1,786 pixels in size, and so represents a 36 x 24 inch paper map. At this size, you cannot view the whole map on screen at once, and have to scroll around. There is no facility for zooming or scrolling to an adjacent area. At this higher resolution, all the detail on the maps is clearly visible, though some of the smaller text can be hard to read, and one or two of the original maps used for scanning seem to have been rather faint. Alternatively you can download the image and use a graphics program to zoom in or print out either the whole image or part of it. The file sizes vary, with those for densely populated areas up to 400k while more rural areas will be under 100k.

The 19th century OS maps are the basis of the definitive parish maps, *Historic Parishes of England & Wales*, available on CD (details at <www.ex.ac.uk/geography/research/boundaries.html>). The reason for mentioning them here is that the authors, Roger Kain and Richard Oliver, allow the maps to be published on-line, and you will find a number of them available on Genuki parish pages, such as Brian Randell's pages for Devon parishes at <www.cs.ncl.ac.uk/genuki/DEV/indexpars.html> and my own for Sussex at <homepages.gold.ac.uk/genuki/SSX/parishes.html>.

Another set of national maps, which is complete for England, Wales and Ireland, with a small selection for Scotland, are those from the 1885 Boundary Commission, available on the London Ancestor site at <www.londonancestor.com/maps/maps.htm>. The maps, with a scale of 4 inches to 1 mile, are available in two sizes. Each county or borough page shows a small version at around 100k in size, with a link to a much larger scan, with a file size typically between 1Mb and 2Mb and around 3,000 pixels square, but the quality of the scans makes these well worth downloading.

Tom Courtney has digitally photographed the complete set of Samuel Lewis' county maps from the 1830s and has put them on his personal web site at <homepage.ntlworld.com/tomals/>. YourMapsOnline at <www.yourmapsonline.org.uk> is a fairly new site, launched in March 2003, which allows individuals to upload scans or digital photographs of old maps and engravings. It is associated with the gbr-maps-online mailing list (see <www.british-genealogy.com/mailman/listinfo/gbr-maps-online>), which provides a general forum for discussing and publicising on-line maps of the British Isles.

There are some significant on-line map collections for Scotland. Charting the Nation at <www.chartingthenation.lib.ed.ac.uk> is maintained by the University of Edinburgh and covers maps of Scotland for the period 1550–1740. The National Library of Scotland has around 800 maps on-line dating from the 16th to the 20th century at <www.nls.uk/digitallibrary/map/early/>, as well as Timothy Pont's 16th-century maps of Scotland at <www.nls.uk/pont/> and 18th-century military maps at <www.nls.uk/digitallibrary/map/military/>.

The University of Wisconsin-Madison has some historical maps of Ireland, including a Poor Law map, at <history.wisc.edu/archdeacon/famine/>.

Another source for historical maps on-line may be the sites of commercial map-dealers. For example, Heritage Publishing at <www.chycor.co.uk/heritage-publishing/index.htm> has scans of some of John Speed's 1610 maps of the British counties. It is well worth using a search engine to locate sites which have the phrase 'antique maps' and the town or county of your choice.

A more general resource on historical maps will be found on the Institute of Historical Research web site at <ihr.sas.ac.uk/maps/>. This is a gateway for Map History, which includes a collection of links to web map resources for Europe at <ihr.sas.ac.uk/maps/webimages.html#europe>.

It is not possible here to give detailed coverage of historical maps of individual counties and areas – these are best found by looking at the relevant Genuki county page or by visiting the Genmaps site at <freepages.genealogy.rootsweb.com/~genmaps/>, which has an extensive collection of historical maps and links to many others, organised by county. But perhaps it is worth mentioning Charles Booth's famous 1889

• contact   • news • collections • info for users • catalogues ⊙ digital library • professional info • search

digital library

National Library of Scotland

Military Maps of Scotland

Title:	A plan of the Battle of Culloden and the adjacent country, shewing the incampment of the English army at Nairn and the march of the Highlanders in order to attack them by night.
Name:	Finlayson, John?]
Description:	1 map : col. ; 564 x 748 mm.
Original Survey:	1746?
Date on Map:	1746?
Placename:	Culloden
Parish:	Inverness, Croy, Daviot and Dunlichity
County:	Inverness-shire
Shelfmark:	EMS.s.156

Zoom into map: (small) (medium) (large) (help)

Return to Index   Copyright   Enquiries & Copies

All images © National Library of Scotland

Figure 12.5 A plan of the Battle of Culloden from the NLS map collection

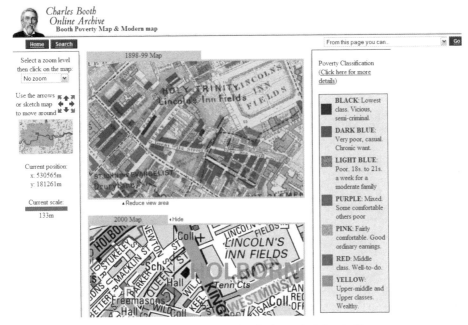

Figure 12.6 Charles Booth's Map of London Poverty at the Charles Booth Online Archive

Map of London Poverty on the LSE's Charles Booth site at <booth.lse. ac.uk>, which shows Booth's original map against a modern one (Figure 12.6).

Map collections

For guides to map collections, the British Cartographic Society's 'A Directory of UK Map Collections' at <www.cartography.org.uk/Pages/ Publicat/Ukdir/UKDirect.html> is a very comprehensive starting point.

The catalogues of the archives and libraries mentioned in Chapter 9 include their map holdings. The National Archives has a leaflet 'Maps in the Public Record Office' at <catalogue.pro.gov.uk/Leaflets/ri2179.htm>, while PRONI's map holdings are described at <www.proni.gov.uk/ records/maps.htm>.

The national libraries all have significant map collections which are described on their web sites:

- The British Library <www.bl.uk/collections/maps.html>
- The National Library of Scotland <www.nls.uk/collections/maps/>
- The National Library of Wales <www.llgc.org.uk/dm/dm0067.htm>
- The National Library of Ireland <www.nli.ie/co_maps.htm>.

Streets and street names

The Streetmap, Multimap and Yahoo Maps sites mentioned above show street names for the present day. If you are looking for a street that no longer exists, or has been renamed, you will find that many of the historical maps available on the Web are at too large a scale to indicate street names. However, for major cities, especially London, you may well be able to locate a particular street on-line. The best starting point for a particular city will be the relevant Genuki county page.

The Bolles Collection London Map Browser at <**www.perseus.tufts. edu/cgi-bin/city-view.pl**> has digitised copies of two dozen maps of London from the 17th to the 19th century. There is an optional overlay of the modern street pattern and the ability to identify streets and major buildings by location or name (see Figure 12.7). Once you have chosen a particular grid square to view, you can then select different maps to see how the area looked at different periods.

GenDocs has a 'Victorian London A–Z Street Index' at <**www.gendocs. demon.co.uk/lon-str.html**>, which gives the registration districts for over 60,000 streets. The 'Lost London Street Index' at <**members.aol.com/ WHall95037/london.html**> lists over 3,500 streets that have undergone a name change or have disappeared altogether over the last 200 years, giving locations on the modern A–Z.

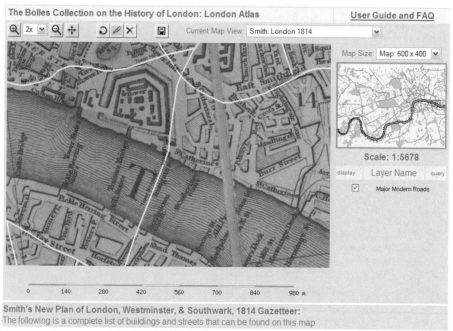

Figure 12.7 The Bolles Collection: an 1814 map of London, with an overlay of the modern street plan (showing the later position of Tower Bridge)

The counties

All towns and villages in the British Isles have a place in the administrative geography of the constituent counties, and this has not necessarily remained constant over the last few hundred years. Genuki provides a general overview of Administrative Regions and, as well as pages for the individual counties, has material on 'Local Government Changes in the United Kingdom' at <**www.genuki.org.uk/big/Regions/UKchanges.html**> with detailed tables for England, Wales, Scotland and Northern Ireland. The situation in the Republic of Ireland is more straightforward as the pre-independence counties remain. The Association of British Counties has maps of the old counties as well as the new counties and unitary authorities at <**www.abcounties.co.uk/newgaz/**>. It is also well worth looking at their 'Additional notes for historians and genealogists' at <**www.abcounties. co.uk/newgaz/cen.htm**>, which explains the difference between the historic counties, the 'registration counties' used by the GRO, and the 19th and 20th century administrative counties and county boroughs.

Genuki has maps of the counties of England, Wales and Scotland at <**www.genuki.org.uk/big/Britain.html**> and of Ireland at <**www.genuki. org.uk/big/Ireland.html**>. Each Genuki county page also has a description of the county, usually drawn from a 19th-century directory or similar source.

If you are from outside the UK and are not familiar with the counties and other administrative divisions you will find Jim Fisher's page 'British Counties, Parishes, etc. for Genealogists' at <**homepages.nildram.co.uk/ ~jimella/counties.htm**> useful.

Where counties have changed their boundaries over the years, the individual Genuki county pages will provide relevant details. The creation of Greater London and demise of Middlesex in 1965 is dealt with at <**homepages.gold.ac.uk/genuki/LND/parishes.html**>, which lists the changes that gave rise to the metropolitan boroughs in 1888, and to the current London boroughs. The major reorganisation of 1974 saw the creation of new counties and boroughs. The Department of the Environment, Transport and the Regions has comprehensive information on the current structure of local government, and proposed changes, under the heading 'Local Government Reorganisation in England' at <**www. local.doe.gov.uk/struct/reorg.htm**>.

Genealogists almost always refer to pre-1974 counties and any genealogical material on the internet is likely to reflect that. This is why there are no pages on Genuki for Tyne and Wear or the present-day Welsh counties. But non-genealogical sites will tend to locate places in their current counties – a number of the sites with photographs discussed in Chapter 14 do this, for example.

Counties are often referred to by three-letter abbreviations, the Chapman County Codes, e.g. SFK for Suffolk. A list of these can be found on Genuki at <**www.genuki.org.uk/big/Regions/Codes.html**>.

13 History

While genealogists are concerned mainly with individual ancestors, both their lives and the documents that record them cannot be understood without a broader historical appreciation of the times in which they lived. The same can be said of the historical documents essential to genealogical research. The aim of this chapter is to look at some of the general historical material on the internet that is likely to be of use to family historians.

Local and social history

Local history

For introductory material on local history the Local History page on the BBC History site at <**www.bbc.co.uk/history/lj/locallj/index.shtml**> is a good starting point. As well as describing what is involved in local history, it looks at how to approach the history of a factory, a landscape and a village, by way of example. Archives in Focus has a section devoted to the question 'What is Local History?' at <**www.hmc.gov.uk/focus/ your_history/localintro.htm**> with material on archival sources, where to go for information and a page of useful links.

If you just want guidance on where to find information and sources, then the 'Getting Started' page on the *Local History Magazine* web site will prove useful, while Archives in Focus has a bibliography and other information to get you started.

Local History Magazine has a collection of links at <**www.local- history.co.uk/links/**>, and its 'Useful links to historical sites' page will point you to the web sites of local history societies, university departments and individuals who are publishing local history material on the Web.

Victoria County History

It would be unrealistic to expect much of the printed material on local history to be available on-line, but the *Victoria County History* has a lottery-funded project to create an on-line edition. Information about the project will be found at <**www.englandpast.net/online.html**>. This is still in the early stages – there are 12 county web sites with varying amounts of material. To see which are on-line, and which other counties will be coming on-line in the near future, go to <**www.englandpast.net/ counties.html**>.

In addition to the official material, Chris Phillips, who runs the very useful Medieval English Genealogy site at <**www.medievalgenealogy. org.uk**>, has compiled an index to place names mentioned in the titles of topographical articles in the published volumes of the VCH. This can be found at <**www.medievalgenealogy.org.uk/vch/index.shtml**>.

Individual places

There is an increasing amount of material on-line for individual cities, towns and villages. County record offices are among those exploiting the Web to publish on-line resources for local history, and good examples of this can be seen in the Powys Heritage Online site at <**history.powys. org.uk**> or the Knowsley (Lancs) Local History site at <**history.knowsley. gov.uk**>. The City of Liverpool has an on-line project at <**www. liverpool2007.org.uk**> as a 'gateway to Liverpool's historical past', and I think we can expect many more such initiatives in future.

The Genuki county and parish pages provide links to local material for individual places and often include descriptive extracts from historical directories. See page 89 for more information about on-line directories.

For Scotland, the *Statistical Accounts of Scotland* at <**edina.ac.uk/ statacc/**> are a major source. These accounts, dating from the 1790s and 1830s, are descriptive rather than financial, and offer 'a rich record of a wide variety of topics: wealth, class and poverty; climate, agriculture, fishing and wildlife; population, schools, and the moral health of the people'. The site has images of every page of the original printed volumes, and there is an index by county and parish to take you straight to the place of interest.

David Hawgood's book *One-Place Genealogy* is designed to help genealogists find studies about the places where their ancestors lived. The entire text of the book is on-line at <**www.hawgood.co.uk/opg/**>, with a list of studies by county at <**www.hawgood.co.uk/opg/counties.htm**> which is kept up-to-date. There is a ONE-PLACE-STUDY mailing list for those involved in studying a single parish or group of parishes, details of which can be found at <**lists.rootsweb.com/index/other/Miscellaneous/ ONE-PLACE-STUDY.html**>.

Curious Fox at <**www.curiousfox.com**> is a relatively new site providing message boards for local history and genealogy. While most mailing lists are county based, this is different in that it is based on a gazetteer of 50,000 UK towns and villages, each with its own page. You can search for the settlement name, generate lists of nearby villages and hamlets, and link to the exact location on Multimap and Old-maps. You can also search by family name. The site calls itself 'semi commercial': you can use it free of charge, but a subscription of £5 provides additional facilities, including an automatic e-mail when someone adds a message relating to a town or village you have stored as a place of interest. Without a subscription you can only contact subscribers.

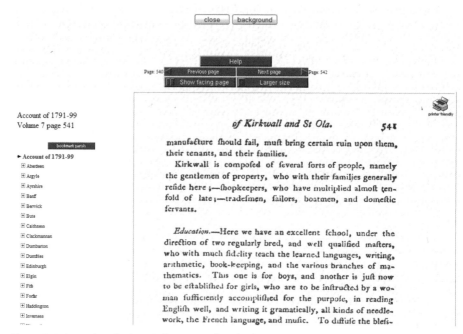

Figure 13.1 A page from the *Statistical Accounts of Scotland*

For information on the origin of place names, *The Oxford Dictionary of English Place Names* can be consulted on-line at <**www.xrefer.com/ search.jsp**>. The home page does not have a direct link to the dictionary, but you must select 'Place Names' from the 'Select a Topic' field and enter the name you're searching for.

Social history

Although the Web provides material on any aspect of social history you care to name, from slavery to education, it is difficult to know what you can expect to find on a given topic in terms of quality and coverage. In view of the large number of possible subjects which come under 'social history', and the very general application of these headings (education, poverty, etc.), using a search engine to locate them can be quite time-consuming. However, if you know any terms that refer only to historical material (1840 Education Act, Poor Law, etc.) this may make searching easier. Also, local history sites are likely to include some material on social history and local museums, and may provide useful links to non-local material.

For more recent local and social history, local newspapers are an important source, and these are discussed on p. 86.

Where aspects of social history are bound up with the state, you can expect to find some guidance on official sites. The National Archives, for example, has leaflets on Education, Enclosures, Lunacy and Lunatic Asylums, Outlawry, and the Poor Law, among other subjects. Records relating to crime and punishment are discussed on pp. 133f.

A comprehensive guide to social history sites is beyond the scope of this book, but the following examples may give a taste of some of the resources on the internet.

Professor George P. Landow's Victorian Web includes an overview of Victorian Social History at **<65.107.211.206/history/sochistov.html>**, with a considerable amount of contemporary documentation. This site, incidentally, was one of the first to use the Web to make linked historical materials available.

The Workhouses site at **<www.workhouses.org.uk>** provides a comprehensive introduction to the workhouse and the laws relating to it, along with lists of workhouses in England, Wales and Scotland, and a guide to workhouse records (see Figure 13.2). The Rossbret Institutions site at **<www.institutions.org.uk>** has information not only on workhouses but on a wide range of institutions, including Asylums, Almshouses, Prisons, Dispensaries, Hospitals, Reformatories, and Orphanages.

GenDocs has a list of 'Workhouses, Hospitals, Lunatic Asylums, Prisons, Barracks, Orphan Asylums, Convents, and other Principal Charitable Institutions' in London in 1861 at **<www.gendocs.demon.co.uk/ institute.html>**.

The Powys Heritage Online project mentioned above has sections devoted to crime and punishment, education and schools, religion in Wales, and care of the poor, at **<history.powys.org.uk/history/intro/ themes.html>**, which make use of original documents and photographs.

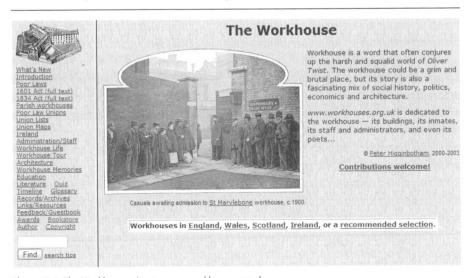

Figure 13.2 The Workhouses site at <www.workhouses.org.uk>

Scots Life, part of the Scots Origins site at <www.origins.net/ScotsLife/>, has articles on aspects of Scottish social history.

Finally, the Spartacus Educational site at <www.spartacus.schoolnet.co.uk> is a model of what can be done with historical material on the Web. It has information on many topics in social history since the mid-18th century, such as child labour, the railways, the textile industry and female emancipation. The site contains both general information and historical documents. The pages devoted to the textile industry, for example, at <www.spartacus.schoolnet.co.uk/Textiles.htm>, contain general information on the machinery, the various occupations within the industry and the nature of daily life in the textile factory, but also include biographical material on individual inventors, entrepreneurs and factory workers, the latter taken from interviews before a House of Commons Committee in 1832.

There are many examples of small data extracts for local areas. They include:

- Tithe Titles for Kelsall, Cheshire at <www.the-dicksons.org/Kelsall/kelsall/tithespg.htm>.
- Tithe Book of Bolton with Goldthorpe, 1839 at <www.genuki.org.uk/big/eng/YKS/WRY/Boltonupondearne/TitheBook/>.
- The English Surnames Survey has a number of local datasets at <www.le.ac.uk/elh/pot/intro/intro3a.html>, including Lay Subsidy transcriptions for Lincolnshire (1332) and Rutland (1296/7), and some of Poll Tax databases.

The best way to find such material is via the Genuki county and parish pages.

Societies

There are at least as many groups devoted to local history as there are family history societies, though of course not all of them have web sites. A comprehensive listing for all parts of the UK and Ireland is provided by *Local History* magazine in the Local History Directory at <www.local-history.co.uk/Groups/>. This gives contact details including e-mail addresses and web sites where available. But you should note that many of the entries in this listing have not been updated recently, and it is probably not a reliable guide to which societies have *no* Web presence. Knowing the name of a society, however, it is a simple matter to use a search engine to see if it has its own site. The British Association for Local History has a select list of links to local history society web sites at <www.balh.co.uk/links.htm>.

Mailing lists

Most of the genealogical mailing lists for counties, areas, and individual places are useful for local history queries, and there are some lists which specifically include local history in their remit. For example, the sussexpast group on Yahoo Groups at <groups.yahoo.com/group/sussexpast/> describes its interests as 'Discussions and questions/answers on archaeology, local history, museums and architecture in Sussex.' HAMPSHIRE-LIFE, which has its own web site at <freepages.genealogy.rootsweb.com/~villages/>, is for discussion not only of genealogy but also 'history of towns and villages; folklore; songs, poetry and sonnets; and nostalgic pictures'.

LOCAL-HISTORY is a general mailing list for the British Isles, which is hosted by JISCmail, the national academic mailing list service. You can see the archive of past messages for the list at <www.jiscmail.ac.uk/lists/local-history.html> and there are also instructions on how to subscribe. RootsWeb is host to a list for Wales – details at <lists.rootsweb.com/index/intl/WLS/WALES-LOCAL-HISTORY.html>.

Names

Origins

A regular topic on mailing lists and newsgroups is the origin of surnames. When talking about surnames, though, the term 'origin' has two distinct meanings: how the name came about linguistically (its etymology); and where it originated geographically (its home). Unfortunately there is little reliable information on the Web relating to the first of these. The definitive sources for British surname etymologies are the modern printed surname dictionaries, which are not available on-line. If you are lucky you may find a surname site that quotes and gives references for the relevant dictionary entries for your particular surname, but in the absence of source references you should treat etymological information on genealogy web sites as unreliable. Even where sources are given, you should be cautious – some of the older surname dictionaries are the work of amateurs rather than scholars.

The most reliable site I am aware of is the Surname Origins Index at <freepages.genealogy.rootsweb.com/~haslam/surnames/soi.html>. This has a growing number of surname etymologies, and for many it gives references to reputable surname dictionaries. Another good site for surname etymology, though with less detailed information, is that of the Family Chronicle, whose Surname Origin List at <www.familychronicle.com/british.htm> has material on the origins of many British surnames. It also provides a classification of names as patronymic, geographical, occupational, or nickname.

There are two mailing lists devoted to discussion of surname etymology. SURNAME-ORIGINS-L is a US-based list devoted to the etymology and distribution of surnames, and details can be found at <members.tripod.com/~Genealogy_Infocenter/surname-origins.html>. The English Surname List (ESL) is a forum for discussion of the etymology, history and significance of surnames in England. It has a web site at <**www. jiscmail.ac.uk/lists/esl.html**> with an archive of past messages and a web form for joining the list.

Cyndi's List has a page devoted to surnames in general at <**www. cyndislist.com/surn-gen.htm**>.

Variants

There is no definitive on-line source to help you to decide whether surname X is in fact a variant of surname Y, or what variant spellings you can expect for a surname. However, if a name has been registered with the Guild of One-Name Studies, the Guild's on-line register at <**www.one-name.org/register.shtml**> may give some indication of major variants, and it will be worth contacting the person who has registered it. Posting a query about variants on one of the many surname mailing lists and query boards (see Chapter 15) would also be a sensible step.

The Thesaurus of British Surnames is a project to develop an on-line thesaurus of British surname variants. The ToBS web site at <**www. tobs.org.uk**> does not have details of individual variants as yet but has a number of resources relating to the issues of surname matching, including papers on the problems of identifying surname variants. There are a number of computerised surname matching schemes. The most widely used, though it has severe shortcomings, is Soundex, information on which will be found in many places on-line. The ToBS web site has links to some of these at <**www.tobs.org.uk/links/online.html**>.

Distribution

Looking at the geographical distribution in a major database such as FamilySearch at <**www.familysearch.org**> can sometimes be helpful, though you should be cautious about drawing etymological inferences from distributional information in this sort of database.[10]

Harry Wykes has a site devoted to Surname Distribution Analysis at <**www.wykes.org/dist/**>, which produces distribution maps for individual surnames. To use the site, you need to have the 1881 census on CD-ROM, and you can then extract and upload the data for a surname, from which the site will create a distribution map, which you can then download (Figure 13.3).

Philip Dance's Modern British Surnames site at <**homepages. newnet.co.uk/dance/webpjd/**> is designed as a guide to the resources for the study of surname frequency and distribution. The site also includes discussion of the various approaches to surname origins, and has interesting statistical material. A site covering local names is Graham Thomas' Gloucestershire Names and their Occurrence at <**www. grahamthomas.com/glocnames.html**>.

---

[10] See my article 'What surname distribution can't tell us', on-line at <**www.spub. co.uk/surnames.pdf**>.

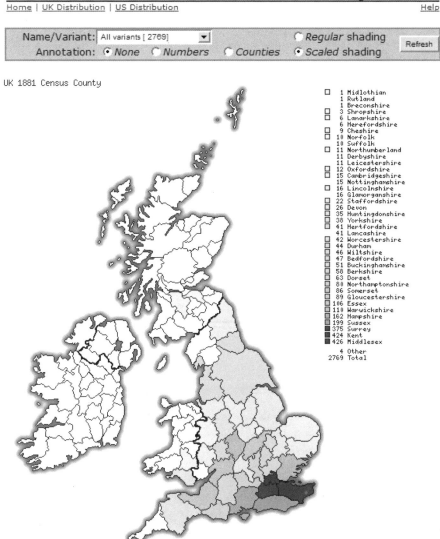

Figure 13.3 Distribution of the surname Woodham(s) as displayed by UK Surname Distribution Analysis

Forenames

Behind the Name at <www.behindthename.com> is a very comprehensive site devoted to the etymology and history of first names. In addition to English and Irish names it has details for a number of other countries and regions, as well as a listing of Biblical names.

About.com has a page of links for 'Naming Patterns for Countries & Cultures' at <**genealogy.about.com/cs/namingpractices/**>, which includes links for British and Irish names, as well as many others. A search for 'naming patterns' in a search engine will reveal many other sites devoted to this topic. Anne Johnston has a useful list of diminutives for common Christian names at <**www.nireland.com/anne.johnston/Diminutives. htm**>. The web site for the OLD-ENGLISH mailing list (see p. 177 below) has a listing of Latin equivalents of common forenames at <**homepages. rootsweb.com/~oel/latingivennames.html**>.

For present-day forename frequencies, the authoritative sources are government sites. The National Statistics site at <**www.statistics.gov.uk**> has a number of reports on the current and historical frequency of first names. If you enter 'name' in the search box on the home page, you will get a list of relevant documents. GROS has a paper on 'Popular Forenames in Scotland, 1900–2000' at <**www.gro-scotland.gov.uk/grosweb/ grosweb.nsf/pages/name00**>.

Eponym has a good collection of links to sites with material on English, Scottish, Welsh and Irish first names at <**www.eponym.org/britisles.html**>, including a number of sites with frequencies for older periods. (But note that this page has not been checked for some time, and you should expect some broken links.)

Image Partners has a forename thesaurus which attempts to match variant forename spellings at <**www.imagepartners.co.uk/Thesaurus/ Forenames.aspx**>.

Understanding old documents

If the queries on genealogy mailing lists are anything to go by, one of the main things genealogists need help with is making sense of old documents, whether it is a census entry or a 16th-century will. In some cases it's just a matter of deciphering the handwriting, in others it is understanding the meaning of obsolete words, and in older documents the two problems often occur together. While the internet hardly provides a substitute for the specialist books on these subjects, there are quite a few resources on-line to help with these problems.

Handwriting

As the mistakes in census transcriptions show, even fairly modern handwriting can often be problematic to read, and once you get back beyond the 19th century the difficulties become ever greater. Few genealogists bother to go on palaeography courses, but there are some outstanding on-line resources to help you.

The English Faculty at Cambridge University has an on-line course on English Handwriting 1500-1700 at <**www.english.cam.ac.uk/ceres/ehoc/**> with high quality scans of original documents. There are extensive examples of every individual letter in a variety of hands as well as examples of the many abbreviations found in documents of this period. A series of graded exercises gives you an opportunity to try your own skills at transcribing original manuscripts.

The Scottish Archive Network site has materials on Scottish handwriting for the same period at <www.scan.org.uk/researchrtools/handwriting/scottishhandwriting.htm>, which will be useful not only to those needing to read Scottish records. These pages are to form the basis of a more extensive Palaeography web site – see <www.scan.org.uk/researchrtools/handwriting/whatsnew.htm> for information.

Dave Postles of the University of Leicester has materials relating to an MA in Palaeography on-line at <freespace.virgin.net/dave.postles/palindex.html>. The site has two areas, one devoted to medieval and the other to early modern palaeography.

Andrew Booth's Two Torches at Keighley site has downloadable TrueType fonts of 16th- and 17th-century handwriting at <www.booth1.demon.co.uk>, with a page in Adobe Acrobat format showing the different forms for all the characters at <www.booth1.demon.co.uk/Characters.pdf>. The documents reproduced on the site provide a good test of reading skills.

Dianne Tillotson has a site devoted to all aspects of Medieval Writing at <medievalwriting.50megs.com/writing.htm>, and the material on abbreviations at <medievalwriting.50megs.com/scripts/abbreviation/abbreviation1.htm> looks as if it will be useful when complete.

Dates and calendars

There are a number of useful resources on the Web to help you make sense of the dates and calendars used in older genealogical sources.

There are two particular types of dating which are generally unfamiliar to modern readers. The first is the dating of documents, particularly legal ones, by regnal years, i.e. the number of years since the accession of the reigning monarch (so 1 January 2003 is 1 January 50 Eliz. II). The Regnal Year Calculator at <www.albion.edu/english/calendar/regnal.htm> will convert regnal years for the period from the Norman Conquest to George I. There is a useful table of regnal years up to Queen Victoria at <www.amostcuriousmurder.com/kingdateFS.htm>.

Saints' days are also frequently encountered in early documents, and the On-line Calendar of Saints' Days at <members.tripod.com/~gunhouse/calendar/home.htm> should enable you to decode these. The Catholic Encyclopedia's 'Dates And Dating' page at <www.newadvent.org/cathen/04636c.htm> is also useful.

In September 1752 Britain switched from the old Julian calendar to the Gregorian. For information on this change see Mike Spathaky's article 'Old Style And New Style Dates And The Change To The Gregorian Calendar' at <www.genfair.com/dates.htm>. Steven Gibbs has a conversion routine for the Julian and Gregorian calendars at

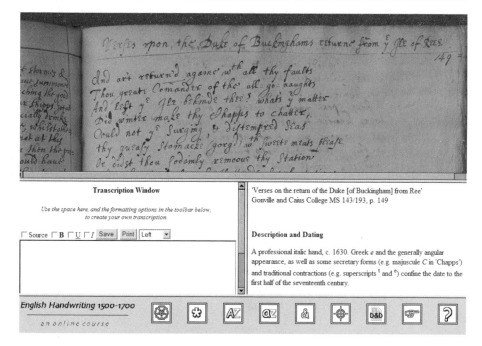

Figure 13.4 English Handwriting 1500–1700, an on-line course

<www.guernsey.net/~sgibbs/roman.html>, which may be useful if you are consulting records from countries which switched either earlier (most of Europe) or later (Russia) than the UK. Calendopaedia, the Encyclopaedia of Calendars at <www.geocities.com/calendopaedia/> has extensive information on calendars including information on the dates lost in the switch from the Julian to the Gregorian calendar for all the individual countries in Europe at <www.geocities.com/calendopaedia/gregory.htm>.

To find out what day a particular date fell on, consult Genuki's Perpetual Calendar at <www.genuki.org.uk/big/easter/>, which also gives the dates of Easter. The years 1550 to 2049 are covered.

Chris Phillips provides a comprehensive guide to chronology and dating at <www.medievalgenealogy.org.uk/guide/chron.shtml>, as part of a site devoted to medieval genealogy, while the Ultimate Calendar Webpage at <www.ecben.net/calendar.shtml> has over 250 links to on-line resources for all contemporary and historical calendars.

Latin

For medieval genealogy and for legal records up to the 1730s, you will often encounter texts written in Latin. Even in English texts Latin phrases or, worse, abbreviations for them are not uncommon. Latin has also, of course, been much used for inscriptions.

General help in reading Latin documents will be found at <italiangenealogy.tardio.com> – follow the relevant link on the home page – while there are Latin dictionaries at **<humanum.arts.cuhk.edu.hk/ Lexis/Latin/>** and **<www.nd.edu/~archives/latgramm.htm>**. The latter also provides a grammar and links to other useful resources. Be warned, however, that these cover classical Latin and not the Latin of medieval and early modern Britain. Lynn H. Nelson's 'Latin Word List' at **<kufacts.cc.ukans.edu/ftp/pub/history/latin_language/latwords.html>** seems to be based on the Vulgate and will therefore be of use for Christian Latin terms. There is a list of 'Hard Little Words: Prepositions, Adverbs, Conjunctions (With Some Definitions of Medieval Usage)' at **<www. georgetown.edu/faculty/irvinem/classics203/resources/latin.lex >**.

Frank Arduini has a useful list of 'Some Latin Genealogy Terms And Their English Equivalents' on his site at **<www.arduini.net/tools/ latin.htm>**.

These sites do not include feudal land-tenure terms, and will not be sufficient to enable you to translate a medieval charter, but they can certainly help with Latin words and phrases embedded in English prose.

Latin abbreviations are often used, particularly in set phrases, and the FAQ for the soc.genealogy.medieval newsgroup has a list of some of those commonly found in genealogical documents at **<users.erols.com/wrei/ faqs/medieval.html#GN13>**.

Eva Holmes has three articles on translating Latin at **<www. suite101.com/welcome.cfm/italian_genealogy>**.

There is a LATIN-WORDS mailing list, which is for 'anyone with a genealogical or historical interest in deciphering and interpreting written documents in Latin from earliest to most recent 20th century times, and discussing old Latin words, phrases, names, abbreviations and antique jargon'. Subscription details will be found at **<www.rootsweb.com/ ~jfuller/gen_mail_trans.html>** and the list archive is at **<archiver. rootsweb.com/th/index/LATIN-WORDS>**.

Technical terms

Genealogists encounter technical terms from many specialist areas, and have the additional difficulty that it may not be apparent whether a term is just specialised or in fact obsolete. The definitive resource for such questions remains the Oxford English Dictionary, but this is available on-line at <www.oed.com> only via a very hefty subscription (£350 as of summer 2003), which makes the CD-ROM version a better buy.

Other places to turn when you encounter this sort of problem include the rather inappropriately named OLD-ENGLISH mailing list, which is for 'anyone who is deciphering old English documents to discuss inter-pretations of handwriting and word meanings' or the OLD-WORDS mailing list 'for the discussion of old words, phrases, names, abbreviations, and antique jargon useful to genealogy'. Details of how to subscribe to these lists are at <www.rootsweb.com/~jfuller/gen_mail_trans.html>. You can also browse or search the archives for them at <archiver.rootsweb. com/th/index/OLD-ENGLISH> and <archiver.rootsweb.com/th/index/ OLD-WORDS > respectively. Bear in mind that the contributors to the lists have widely varying expertise, and you will need to evaluate carefully any advice you receive. However, the companion web site for the OLD-ENGLISH list at <homepages.rootsweb.com/~oel/> has an excellent collection of material, as well as some useful links at <homepages. rootsweb.com/~oel/links.html>.

A wide-ranging glossary of Scottish terms will be found on The Wedderburn Pages at <pro.wanadoo.fr/euroleader/wedderburn/glossary. htm>, including both archaic and modern terms.

Old terms for occupations are discussed on p. 132.

Legal

Even where they are not written in Latin many early modern texts, particularly those relating to property, contain technical legal terms that are likely to mean little to the non-specialist, but which may be crucial to the understanding of an ancestor's property holdings or transactions. A useful list of 'Legal Terms in Land Records' will be found at <users. rcn.com/deeds/legal.htm>, while the equivalent but distinct terminology for Scotland is explained on the Customs & Excise site at <www. hmce.gov.uk/forms/notices/742-3.htm>. These are both guides to present-day usage, but in view of the archaic nature of landholding records this should not be a hindrance. A more specifically historical glossary is provided on the Scottish Archive Network site at <www.scan.org.uk/ researchrtools/glossary.htm>, and legal terms are included in The Wedderburn Pages mentioned above. The Manorial Society of Great Britain has a glossary of manorial terms at <www.msgb.co.uk/glossary.html>.

Medical

Death certificates of the last century, and earlier references to cause of death, often include terms that are unfamiliar. Some can be found in one of the on-line dictionaries of contemporary medicine, such as MedTerms at <www.medterms.com> or the University of Newcastle's On-line Medical Dictionary at <cancerweb.ncl.ac.uk/omd/>. But for comprehensive coverage of archaic medical terms, Paul Smith's Archaic Medical Terms site at <www.paul_smith.doctors.org.uk/ArchaicMedicalTerms.htm> is the best place to go. Cyndi's List has a 'Medical & Medicine' page at <www.cyndislist.com/medical.htm>.

Measurements

Leicester University's palaeography course materials, mentioned on p. 174, include a number of useful lists covering terms likely to be found in old legal documents: land measurement terms, the Latin equivalents of English coinage, and Roman numerals. See the Medieval Palaeography pages at <freespace.virgin.net/dave.postles/medfram.html>.

Steven Gibbs' site, mentioned on p. 175, has facilities for converting to and from Roman numerals at <www.guernsey.net/~sgibbs/roman.html>.

Details of old units of measurement (though not areal measurements) can be found at <www.shaunf.dircon.co.uk/shaun/metrology/english.html>, while both linear and areal measures are covered by <www.johnowensmith.co.uk/histdate/measures.htm>. There is a comprehensive Dictionary of Measures at <www.unc.edu/~rowlett/units/> which includes a useful article on 'English Customary Measures' at <www.unc.edu/~rowlett/units/custom.html>. Cyndi's List has a page devoted to 'Weights and Measures' at <www.cyndislist.com/weights.htm>.

Medieval

There are a number of general guides to medieval terms, including NetSERF's Hypertext Medieval Glossary at <netserf.cua.edu/glossary/home.htm>, and The Glossary Of Medieval Terms at <cal.bemidji.msus.edu/History/mcmanus/ma_gloss.html>. Resources for the terminology of heraldry are discussed on p. 154.

Value of money

A very frequent question on genealogy mailing lists is the present-day equivalent of sums of money in wills, tax rolls and the like. There is a very detailed analysis of the historical value of sterling in a House of Commons Research Paper 'Inflation: the Value of the Pound 1750–1998', which is available on-line in PDF format at <www.parliament.uk/commons/lib/research/rp99/rp99-020.pdf>. For a longer time span, there are two tables covering the period from the 13th century to the present day at <www.johnowensmith.co.uk/histdate/moneyval.htm>.

Alan Stanier's 'Relative Value of Sums of Money' page at <privatewww.essex.ac.uk/~alan/family/N-Money.html> has statistics for the wages of various types of worker, mainly craftsmen and labourers, but also domestic servants and professionals.

The Economic History Services' site has a page on 'The Purchasing power of the pound' at <eh.net/ehresources/howmuch/poundq.php>, which enables you to find the modern equivalent of an amount in pounds, shillings and pence in a particular year. This is part of a 'How much is that?' section at <eh.net/hmit/> which also has information on UK and US inflation rates since the 1660s and the pound–dollar conversion rate for the last 200 years. If you are too young to remember the pre-decimal system of pounds, shillings and pence, then 'What's A Guinea?' at <www.deadline.demon.co.uk/wilkie/coins.htm> will enlighten you.

The Scottish Archive Network (see p. 92) provides a Scots Currency Converter at <www.scan.org.uk/researchrtools/scots_currency.htm>.

1859 - 1861

Average Yearly Wages paid to Domestics

Source: *Beeton, 1859-61*

THE FOLLOWING TABLE OF THE AVERAGE YEARLY WAGES paid to domestics, with the various members of the household placed in the order in which they are usually ranked, will serve as a guide to regulate the expenditure of an establishment:-

	When not found in Livery.	When found in Livery.
The House Steward	£40 to £80	-.
The Valet	25 to 50	£20 to £30
The Butler	25 to 50	-
The Cook	20 to 40	-
The Gardener	20 to 40	-
The Footman	20 to 40	15 to 25
The Under Butler	15 to 30	15 to 25
The Coachman	-	20 to 35
The Groom	15 to 30	12 to 20
The Under Footman	-	12 to 20
The Page or Footboy	8 to 18	6 to 14
The Stableboy	6 to 12	-

Figure 13.5 Wages for domestic servants <privatewww.essex.ac.uk/~alan/family/N-Money.html>.

For the most recent period, the Retail Price Index is the official source, and its home is the Office for National Statistics, whose page on inflation indices at <www.statistics.gov.uk/rpi/> has links to an Adobe Acrobat file with data going back to the birth of the RPI in June 1947.

An excellent collection of links to sites with information on the historical value of the pound and other currencies is Roy Davies' 'Current value of Old Money' page at <www.ex.ac.uk/~RDavies/arian/current/howmuch.html>, which includes an extensive list of printed sources.

14 Photographs

Among the many reasons for the success of the Web is the ease with which it can be used to make images available to a wide audience. The questions of cost and commercial viability that face the printed photograph do not really apply on the Web – apart from the labour involved, it costs effectively nothing to publish a photograph on-line. The widespread availability of inexpensive scanners and the popularity of the digital camera mean that more and more people have the equipment to create digital images. No archive is in a position to publish a significant fraction of its photographic holdings in print, but on-line image archives are mushrooming. Also, there is no significant difference between putting colour and black and white photographs on-line, whereas the printing of colour photographs is an expensive business.

Photographs are, of course, primary historical sources. But you are not particularly likely to come across a picture of your great-great-grandmother on the Web (unless she was, say, Queen Victoria), so for the genealogist on-line photographs mainly provide historical and geographical background to a family history, rather than primary source material.

The Web is also a good source of information for dealing with your own family photographs, with sites devoted to dating, preservation, restoration, and scanning.

Cyndi's List has a page with links for 'Photographs and Memories' at <www.cyndislist.com/photos.htm>, covering all aspects of photography and family history. Information on using search engines to locate images on-line is covered in Chapter 16 on p. 226. Present-day aerial photographs tend to be provided by mapping sites and are covered in Chapter 12, p. 158.

National collections

For photographs of historic buildings, there are two national sites. The National Monuments Register's (NMR) Images of England site at <www.imagesofengland.org.uk> is intended to be 'an internet home for England's listed buildings' with good-quality photographs and descriptions of every listed building in the country. So far around 70,000 of the 370,000 listed properties are included on the site. You can do a quick search without further ado (retrieving a maximum of 50 images), while the free registration gives you access to more sophisticated standard and advanced searches. Search facilities include search by county or town, building type, period, or person (an architect or other individual associated with a building). Thumbnail images link to full size images with a description.

ViewFinder is run by English Heritage at <**viewfinder.english-heritage.org.uk**>. This aims to make part of the NMR's image archive available on-line. Whereas Images of England contains contemporary photographs, the ViewFinder images are all older. At present, the site has material relating to two themes, 'England at Work', illustrating England's industrial heritage (5,000 images), and the work of Henry W. Taunt, an important Oxford photographer of the late 19th and early 20th century (13,800 images).

Local collections

Record offices and libraries have substantial collections of photographic material, and this is increasingly being made available on-line.

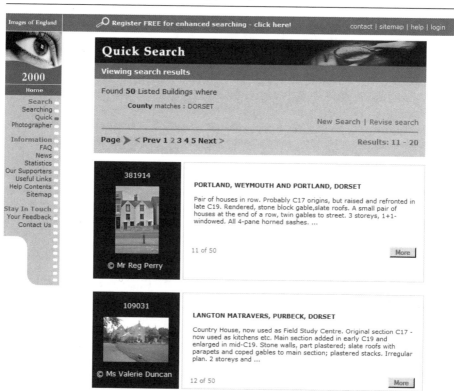

Figure 14.1 Images of England at <www.imagesofengland.org.uk>

For London, there is PhotoLondon at <**www.photolondon.org.uk**>, designed to highlight and promote historic photographs of London in the capital's libraries, museums and archives, with links to the collections of the Guildhall Library, the London Metropolitan Archives, Westminster City Archives, the Museum of London and the National Monuments Record. The Guildhall Library's contribution to this, Collage at <**collage.nhil.com**>, has around 20,000 images of London. As well as maps, plans and photographs of places, there is a large collection relating to trades and industries, including the City livery companies.

Glasgow's Mitchell Library, which houses the City Archives, offers the 'Virtual Mitchell Collection' at <**www.mitchelllibrary.org/vm/**> – note the three l's in the URL – which is a selection from the images in the collection covering 'street scenes and buildings, but also scenes of past working lives and of social life in the city'. Searches can be made by street name or subject.

West Sussex Record Office has an on-line database at <**www2. westsussex.gov.uk/RO/DB/pick.asp**> with details of 31,000 photographs held in the Record Office, of which around 2,000 are available on-line. According to the home page, 'as resources permit, more images will be added to the database and eventually there will be 150,000 entries consisting of photographs, prints and drawings'. The database provides references so that scans of photographs can be requested if the image is not already on-line.

It is always worth checking a relevant record office web site for photographic collections. Even if there is little or no material on the Web, you can expect to find information about their holdings – for example, the

Museum of London   *photo*London

Children playing on the beach near
Tower Bridge,
c.1934
Cyril Arapoff

Queen Street Place Looking South
Towards Southwark Bridge,
11 May 1941
Arthur Cross & Fred Tibbs

Quayside Crane in the Royal Victoria
Dock Damaged in the Silvertown
Explosion, 2 February
1917
John H. Avery

View of the Houses of Parliament and
Westminster Bridge from the stairs at
County Hall.
George Davison Reid

Suffragette Demonstration,
May 1909
Christina Broom

Piccadilly Circus,
c1890
Charles A. Wilson

Westminster Abbey and the Palace of
Westminster under construction,
c.1857
Roger Fenton

'The "Crawlers"', c1877
John Thomson

Figure 14.2 Photographs from the Museum of London's collection on PhotoLondon

Greater Manchester CRO has details of its Documentary Photography Archive at <www.gmcro.co.uk/dpa.htm>. Photographs are also likely to be an important part of any official local history site (see p. 166).

Personal sites

Alongside these efforts by public bodies, there are many images published on the Web by individuals. In particular, there are many present-day photographs of parish churches, for example:

- Richard's Church Album at <www.thirdman.ukhq.co.uk> has photographs of around 1000 churches in all parts of England.
- The Old Scottish Borders Photo Archive at <www.ettrickgraphics. co.uk/bordersindex.htm>.
- Bedfordshire Church photographs at <met.open.ac.uk/group/kaq/beds/ church.htm>.
- Guy Etchells' Worldwide Cemetery Page at <gye.future.easyspace.com> also has a collection of links to UK church photographs.

The best way to find such sites is to go to the relevant Genuki county page.

Commercial photographs

The commercial picture libraries have not been slow to exploit the Web as a means of providing a catalogue for prospective purchasers of their material or services. The reasons that these resources are useful to non-professional users is that access to the on-line catalogues and databases is usually free, though the image size and quality is likely to be reduced.

For example, PastPix <www.pastpix.com> is a subscription service with over 20,000 historical photographs, mainly from the UK, but the collection can be searched free of charge. There is a whole range of photographs of places and occupations.

Perhaps the most important commercial site with old photographs for the UK is the Francis Frith Collection at <www.francisfrith.com/uk/>. Frith was a Victorian photographer whose company photographed over 7,000 towns and villages in all parts of the British Isles, from 1860 until the company closed in 1969. The entire stock was bought by a new company, which now sells prints. While the aim of the web site is to act as a sales medium, it has reasonable size thumbnails (under 300x200 pixels) of all the pictures in the collection, which can be located by search or via a listing for each (present-day) county without the need to make a purchase. The images are also available electronically on CD-ROM.

Frith's photographs and many other commercial photographs of towns and villages were issued as postcards, which means that postcard sites may have material of interest. For example, Data Wales has a number of early

20th century postcards of various parts of Wales at <www.data-wales.co.uk/postcard.htm>; there is a collection of Isle of Wight postcards at <members.lycos.co.uk/bartie/>; Eddie Prowse has an on-line collection of postcards of Weymouth and Portland at <www.eprowse.fsnet.co.uk>.

In one sense, professional photographers are just another occupational group. But their role in creating a unique part of the recent historical record makes them of interest not just to their descendants. Information about their working lives can be important in dating family photographs, or even suggesting the location of a family holiday. The 'Photographs and Memories' page on Cyndi's List at <www.cyndislist.com/photos.htm> lists a number of sites with dates and places for British professional photographers.

UK-PHOTOGRAPHERS is a mailing list for the discussion and sharing of information regarding the dating of photographs produced by professional photographers in England and Wales between 1850 and 1950. Information on subscribing will be found at <lists.rootsweb.com/index/other/Occupations/UK-PHOTOGRAPHERS.html>, which has a link to the archive of past messages.

Portraits

While most of the on-line historic photographs are of places, there are some photographs of individuals. The military is particularly well represented. For example, the Military Images site at <www.capefam. freeserve.co.uk/militaryimages.htm> has several thousand images of military personnel, though unfortunately most are unidentified. Fred Larimore's site devoted to Nineteenth Century British And Indian Armies And Their Soldiers, now defunct but archived at <web.archive.org/web/20011019045240/pobox.upenn.edu/~fbl/>, has a large collection of photographs for the period 1840 to 1920. Other sites with military photographs are mentioned on p. 139.

School photographs will also be found on-line. It's worth checking the web site for a relevant school and web sites devoted to local information (official or unofficial) as they often put historical material on-line. For a simple example, see Kennethmont School's page at <www.kinnethmont. co.uk/k-school.htm> which offers a selection of group photos from 1912 onwards. Jeff Maynard has a more extensive collection for Harrow County School with form and sports team photos going back to the 1920s at <www.jeffreymaynard.com/Harrow_County/photographs.htm>.

As well as these individual efforts, there are on-line photo archives to which you can contribute scans of your own material. Perhaps the best known is DeadFred at <www.deadfred.com>, which has 27,000 records for 8,000 surnames, but the 'Photographs and Memories' page on Cyndi's List at <www.cyndislist.com/photos.htm> has many more.

Dating, preservation, restoration

The Web can also be useful in connection with your own photographs, if you need to date them or if you need advice on preservation or restoration. For help with the dating of old photographs, look at the BBC's History web site, which has articles on Victorian Studio Photographs at <www.bbc.co.uk/history/your_history/family/victorian_photo1.shtml>. Andrew J. Morris' site 19th Century Photography at <www.ajmorris.com/ roots/photo/photo.htm> is a more detailed account of the various types of photographic process and technique.

If you are interested in preserving and restoring old photographs, Colin Robinson has information about the care and conservation of old photographs at <www.photomedia.u-net.com/care.html>, while David L. Mishkin's article on 'Restoring Damaged Photographs' at <www. genealogy.com/10_restr.html> covers the various approaches to restoration. If you want to scan photographs and restore them digitally, it is worth looking at Scantips <www.scantips.com>, which not only has extensive advice about scanning in general but also includes a page on 'Restoration of genealogical photos' at <www.scantips.com/restore.html>. The Internet Eye has tutorials on this topic linked from <the-internet-eye.com/HOWTO/>. These sites offer advice both on the obvious topic of repairing damage and on correcting tonal problems with faded originals. Sites devoted to digital restoration assume you are using Adobe Photoshop, but the general principles transfer to other major graphics editing packages.

A general source of help with old photographs is the RootsWeb mailing list VINTAGE-PHOTOS, which is devoted to 'the discussion and sharing of information regarding vintage photos including, but not restricted to, proper storage, preservation, restoration, ageing and dating, restoration software, photo types and materials used, restoration assistance, and scanning options'. Information on how to join the list will be found at <lists.rootsweb.com/index/other/Miscellaneous/VINTAGE-PHOTOS. html>, which also provides links to the list's archives. The GenPhoto list at Yahoo Groups is a photographic mailing list for family historians. Its coverage includes identifying old photographs, and using digital photo-graphy and scanning to share and preserve family photos. You can read archived messages and join the group at <groups.yahoo.com/group/ genphoto/>. There are a number of newsgroups devoted to photography (rec.photo and others in the same hierarchy), but none specifically relating to old photographs.

15 Discussion Forums

One of the most useful aspects of the internet for anyone researching their family history is that it is very easy to 'meet' other genealogists on-line to discuss matters of common interest, to exchange information and to find help and advice. The specific issues of locating other people with interests in the same surnames and families are dealt with in Chapter 10.

Mailing lists

Electronic mailing lists provide a way for groups of people to conduct on-line discussions via e-mail. They are simply a logical extension of your electronic address book – instead of each member of a group having to keep track of the e-mail addresses of everyone else, this list of e-mail addresses is managed by a computer called a 'list server'. This allows people to add themselves to the list, or remove themselves from it, without having to contact all the other members.

You join a list by sending an e-mail message to a list server. Thereafter you receive a copy of every message sent to the list by other list members; likewise, any message you send to the list gets circulated to all the other subscribers.

What lists are there?
The first genealogical mailing list, ROOTS-L, goes back to a period long before the internet was available to the general public – its first message was posted in December 1987. There may now be as many as 40,000 English-language mailing lists devoted to genealogy.

A large proportion of the genealogy lists are hosted by RootsWeb (over 26,000), and details of these will be found at **<lists.rootsweb.com>**. Another site that hosts many genealogy lists is Yahoo Groups at **<groups.yahoo.com>**. Most of the groups hosted here are listed under the Family & Home | Genealogy category, though there are many others for particular countries and areas, which can be found by using the search facility.

In spite of the large number of lists, it is a simple matter to find those which might be of interest to you. John Fuller and Chris Gaunt's Genealogy Resources on the Internet site has a comprehensive listing of genealogy mailing lists at **<www.rootsweb.com/~jfuller/gen_mail.html>**, subdivided into the following categories:

- Countries Other Than USA
- USA
- Surnames
- Adoption
- African-Ancestored
- Cemeteries/Monuments/ Obituaries
- Computing/Internet Resources
- Emigration/Migration Ships and Trails
- Family History, Folklore, and Artifacts
- Genealogical Material/Services
- General Information/Discussion
- Jewish
- LDS
- Native American
- Newspapers
- Nobility/Heads of State/Heraldry
- Occupations
- Religions/Churches (other than Jewish/LDS)
- Societies
- Software
- Translations and Word Origins
- Vital Records (census, BDM)
- Wars/Military
- Uncategorised

The 'uncategorised' lists include a number devoted to topics of general interest, such as the GEN-MEDIEVAL and SHIPWRECK lists.

The mailing lists most likely to be of use to UK and Irish family historians are the county-based lists (including some which cover a group of adjacent counties), and these can be most easily found on Genuki's mailing list page at <www.genuki.org.uk/indexes/MailingLists.html> and on John Fuller's site at <www.rootsweb.com/~jfuller/gen_mail_country-unk.html>.

For the past few years almost all of these county lists have been hosted by RootsWeb, and can also be found via <lists.rootsweb.com/index/> (they are mostly listed on the pages for England, Scotland, Wales, and Ireland rather than on the general UK page). In March 2003, however, Rod Neep started a county mailing list system on his British-Genealogy site at <www.british-genealogy.com/lists/>. This means that for most counties there are two mailing lists. It is too early to say what the relationship between the two lists will be – how many people will join both, will one group predominate? Unfortunately, one thing seems guaranteed to cause confusion: in some cases the two lists have exactly the same name. However, their *addresses* will always be different, e.g. the RootsWeb Durham list is ENG-DURHAM@rootsweb.com, while the equivalent British-Genealogy list is at eng-durham@british-genealogy.com.

As well as the lists for each county as a whole, there are an increasing number of lists devoted to areas within a county, or even to particular towns and villages. Hampshire, for example, is covered not only by two general lists, HAMPSHIRE and ENG-HAMPSHIRE, but also by local lists for Kingsclere, Portsmouth & Gosport, Romsey, Southampton, the Isle of Wight, and the New Forest.

Alongside such geographically based lists, there are many general lists covering particular topics in relation either to the entirety of the British Isles, or to some constituent of it. Examples of these are lists like AUS-CONVICTS, BRITREGIMENTS, RAILWAY-UK and UK-1901-CENSUS, and others are mentioned in Chapters 12 and 13.

Incidentally, the advantage of the Genuki listing is that it includes lists which, although of interest to UK genealogists, are not categorised under the UK by John Fuller or RootsWeb – notably war-related lists such as AMERICAN-REVOLUTION, BOER-WAR or WARBRIDES.

Of course Genuki and John Fuller only have details of lists relating to genealogy. If you want to find mailing lists on other topics, there is unfortunately no definitive catalogue – in fact such a thing would be impossible to compile and maintain. However, the International Federation of Library Associations and Institutions provides some useful links on its 'Internet Mailing Lists Guides and Resources' page at **<www.ifla.org/I/training/ listserv/lists.htm>**. Also, since many mailing lists have either a web site of their own or at least a listing somewhere on the Web, a search engine can be used to locate them.

John Fuller has a regular electronic newsletter called NEW-GENLIST, which carries announcements of new lists added to his sites. Subscription details will be found at **<www.rootsweb.com/~jfuller/gen_mail_ computing.html>**.

List archives

Many genealogy mailing lists, including almost all the lists hosted by RootsWeb, have an archive of past messages. The RootsWeb list archives can be found at **<archiver.rootsweb.com>**. Not all list archives are open to non-members of the relevant list, but where a list has open membership it is not very common to find that the archive is closed. The archives of the county lists at **<www.british-genealogy.com>**, however, are only open to list members.

The archives have several uses. First, they allow you to get an idea of the discussion topics that come up on the list and judge whether it would be worth your while joining. In particular, an archive will give you some idea of the level of traffic on the list, i.e. how many messages a day are posted. Also, they provide a basis for searching, whether by the list server's own search facility, or by a general search engine such as those discussed in Chapter 16. This means that you can take advantage of information posted to a mailing list without even joining it, though of course you will need to join to post your own messages.

Joining a list

In order to join a list you need to send an e-mail message to the list server, the computer that manages the list, instructing it to add you to the list of subscribers. The text of the e-mail message must contain nothing but the correct command.

Although the basic principles for joining a list are more or less universal, there are a small number of different list systems and each has its own particular features.

Many lists are run on 'listserv' systems (listserv is the name of the software that manages the lists). To join one of these you need to send a message to listserv@*the-name-of-the-list-server*, and the text of the e-mail message should start with the word **SUB** (short for 'subscribe'), followed by the name of the list and then your first and last names. So to join WW20-ROOTS-L, a list for the discussion of genealogy in all 20th-century wars, you would send the following message (supposing your name was John Smith):

```
To:  listserv@listserv.indiana.edu
SUB WW20-ROOTS-L John Smith
```

You need to specify the list name because this particular list server could be managing many different lists.

On systems such as RootsWeb, however, there may be a separate subscription e-mail address for each list. This is typically formed by adding the word *request* to the list name. So to join the GENBRIT-L list, for example, you send your joining command to GENBRIT-L-request@rootsweb.com and the text of the message itself only needs to say *subscribe*:

```
To:  GENBRIT-L-request@rootsweb.com
subscribe
```

Yahoo Groups uses a similar system – to join the yorkshiregentopics group, you would need to send the following message:

```
To:  yorkshiregentopics-subscribe@yahoogroups.com
```

You should not need to worry about which subscription format to use: any site with details of mailing lists, such as Genealogy Resources on the Internet, should give explicit instructions on how to join the lists mentioned. As you can see from Figure 15.1, on Yahoo Groups the home page for each group gives subscription instructions.

Because these messages are processed by a computer, you should send *only* the commands – there is no point in sending a message to an automatic system saying, 'Hello, my name is … and I would like to join the list, please'. Also, it is a good idea to remove any signature at the end of your e-mail message, so that the list server does not attempt to treat it as a set of commands.

Incidentally, do not be worried by the word 'subscription'. It does not mean you are committing yourself to paying for anything, it just means that your name is being added to the list of members.

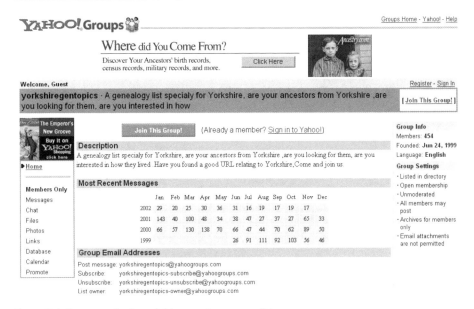

Figure 15.1 Home page for the yorkshiregentopics group on Yahoo

If you have more than one e-mail address you need to make sure that you send your joining message from the one you want messages sent to. Most mailing lists will reject an e-mail message from an address it does not have in its subscriber list. If you want to be able to use more than one e-mail address to post messages to a list, you will need to ask the list administrator to add additional addresses for you.

Some lists have web pages with an on-line form for joining. In this case you simply type your e-mail address in the box. There is a similar system for the mailing lists at Yahoo Groups, though here you have to register (free) before you can join any of its lists. Once you have signed in, you can click on the subscribe button for any list and it will bring up a page such as the one in Figure 15.2 for the yorkshiregentopics list, where you can select your subscription options and join the list.

When you join a list you will normally get a welcome message. You should make sure you keep this, as it will give you important information about the list and the e-mail addresses to use. There are few things more embarrassing on-line than having to send a message to everyone on a mailing list asking how to unsubscribe because you have lost the welcome message which contains the instructions.

There are some circumstances in which you will not be able to join a list by one of the methods discussed here: some lists are 'closed', which means that they are not open to all comers. This is typically the case for mailing lists run by societies for their own members. In this case, instead of sending

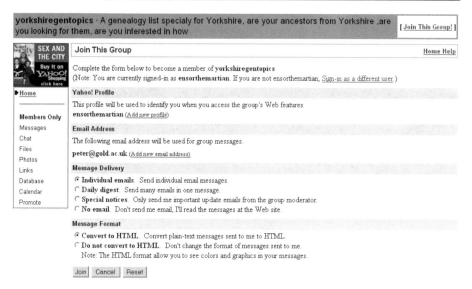

Figure 15.2 Subscribing to a list on Yahoo Groups

an e-mail to the list server you will probably need to contact the person who manages the list, providing your society membership number, so that he or she can check that you are entitled to join the list and then add you.

Closed mailing lists are also often used for the management of genealogical projects. In such cases those involved in the project are usually added to a list as soon as they join the project and no outsiders are admitted. Closed lists can also allow geographically remote committee members of a society to keep in touch, as with the trustees of Genuki, who conduct all affairs via a closed mailing list.

Subscription options

Many mailing lists have two ways in which you can receive messages. The standard way is what is called 'mail mode', where every individual message to the list is forwarded to you as soon as it is received. However, some older e-mail systems were not able to cope with the potentially very large number of incoming messages, so lists also offered a 'digest mode'. In this a bunch of messages to the list are combined into a single larger message, thus reducing the number of messages arriving in the subscriber's mailbox. Even though few of us nowadays are likely to be affected by this sort of technical limitation, some people do not like to receive the dozens of mail messages per day that can come from a busy list, and prefer to receive the messages as a digest.

However, there are also disadvantages to this. For a start, you need to look through each digest to see the subjects of the messages it contains, whereas individual messages with subject lines of no interest to you can quickly be deleted unread. Also, if you want to reply to a message contained within a digest your e-mail software will automatically include the subject line of the *digest*, not just the subject of the individual message within the digest you are replying to. The result is that other list members will not be able to tell from this subject line which earlier message you are responding to. If your e-mail software automatically quotes the original message in reply, then you will need to delete almost all of the quoted digest if you are not to irritate other list members with an unnecessarily long message, most of which will be irrelevant (see Netiquette, p. 208).

There are a number of different ways of arranging to receive a list in digest form. With the lists on RootsWeb there is a different subscription address, containing -D- instead of -L-, so subscription messages for the digest form of GENBRIT list go to GENBRIT-D-request@rootsweb.com. On listserv systems, once you have joined a list you should send a message with the text 'set LISTNAME digest' to change to digest mode, and 'set LISTNAME nodigest' to switch back to mail mode. On lists with

Address	What it's for
The list server	Automatic control of your subscription to the lists. Messages sent to this address are not read by a human, and can only consist of specific commands.
The list itself	This is the address to be used for contributions to the discussion. Anything sent to this address is copied to all the list members. A common beginner's mistake is to send a message meant for the list server to the list address, and hundreds or even thousands of people receive your 'unsubscribe' message.
The list owner/administrator	This is for contacting the person in charge of the list. For most lists, it should only be needed if there is some problem with the list server (e.g. it won't respond to your messages) or something the automated server can't deal with that requires human intervention (e.g. abusive messages). For closed lists, you will probably need to use this address rather than the list server address in order to subscribe.

Table 15.1 Mailing List Addresses

a Web subscription form, you may be able to choose between mail and digest on the form, as you can see in Figure 15.2.

Text formatting

E-mail software generally allows you to send messages in a number of different formats, and normally you do not need to worry about exactly how your mail software is formatting them. When you start sending messages to mailing lists, however, you may find that this is an issue you need to consider. The reason for this is that some mailing lists will not accept certain types of formatting, and even if they do, some recipients of your formatted messages may have difficulties.

The standard format for an e-mail message is plain text. This can be handled by any list server and any e-mail software. However, most modern e-mail software will let you send formatted text with particular fonts and font sizes, colour, italics and so on, i.e. something much more like what you produce with your word processor, and some software even uses this as the default. The way it does this is to include an e-mail attachment containing the message in RTF format (created and used by word processors) or HTML format (used for web pages).

You may feel that this is exactly how you want your e-mail messages to look. But if someone is using e-mail software that can't make sense of this format they may have trouble with your message. They may even receive what looks like a blank message with an attachment, and many people are, rightly, wary of opening an attachment which could contain a virus, particularly if it's attached to a suspicious-looking blank message. The only way they will be able to read your message is by saving the attachment as a file and then opening it with the relevant piece of software, and no one will thank you for sending a message requiring all that extra work. Indeed, people using text-based e-mail on some systems, such as UNIX, may not even have access to software for reading such files.

Also, messages with formatting are inevitably larger than plain text messages, so people have to spend more time on-line to download them, which, while trivial for an individual message, could be significant for someone who is a member of a few busy lists. All things considered, there is really no good reason for using formatted text in mailing-list messages.

Different lists and list systems deal with this problem in a variety of ways. As you can see from Figure 15.2, Yahoo Groups allows you to choose whether you receive messages from the list as HMTL or as plain text. RootsWeb does not permit the use of HTML or RTF formatting at all, and will not allow messages with formatted text to get through.

If you need to find out how to turn off the formatting features of your e-mail software, RootsWeb has a useful page on 'How to Turn Off HTML or RTF in Various E-mail Software Programs' at <**helpdesk.rootsweb.com/ help/html-off.html**>. The page shows you how to do this for all the most popular e-mail software, but even if it does not include the software you use, it should give you an idea of what to look for in your own e-mail package.

The only formatting feature that can be really useful in an e-mail message is the ability to highlight words to be stressed, and the traditional way of doing this in a plain text message is to put *asterisks* round the relevant word. One thing *not* to do, in genealogy mailing lists anyway, is put words in upper case – this is traditionally reserved for indicating surnames.

Filtering

If you do not want to subscribe to mailing lists in digest mode, you can still avoid cluttering up your inbox with incoming messages from mailing lists. Most modern e-mail software has a facility for *filtering* messages, i.e. for moving them automatically from your incoming mailbox to another mailbox when it spots certain pieces of text in the header of the message. You will need to consult the on-line help for your e-mail software in order to see exactly how to do it, but Figure 15.3 shows a filter in Eudora which will move all mail received from the GENBRIT mailing list into a dedicated mailbox called genbrit (in Eudora, filters are created via the **Tools | Filters** menu). This does not reduce the number of messages you

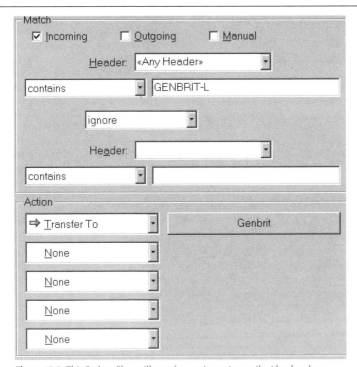

Figure 15.3 This Eudora filter will transfer any incoming mail with a header including the text 'GENBRIT-L' to a dedicated mailbox

receive, but it keeps your list mail separate from your personal mail and you can look at it when it suits you. Since GENBRIT can give rise to as many as 100 messages a day, this is the only practicable way to deal with the volume.

Other uses of mailing lists

Although in general mailing lists allow all members to send messages, and messages are forwarded to all members, there are two types of list that work differently.

Some lists are not used for discussion at all, but only for announcements. Typically, this sort of list is used by an organisation to publish an e-mail newsletter. It differs from a normal list in that you will not be able to send messages, only receive the announcements. The electronic newsletters mentioned in Chapter 18 (p. 264) are in fact mailing lists of this type.

Normally, mailing lists allow only members of the list to send messages to it, and messages from non-members are rejected. But there are a few lists that accept messages from non-members, for example to allow people to submit information to a project. In a case like this you will not be able to join the list yourself but will be able to send messages to it. Genuki uses a system like this for users to report errors or submit additional information, which is automatically circulated via a mailing list to all Genuki county maintainers. In fact, from the non-members' point of view this is just a special e-mail address, and the fact that it is actually a list is not even apparent.

Newsgroups

While mailing lists are very useful, they do have some disadvantages. Join a big mailing list or a few smaller ones and the number of e-mails you get in a day will rise drastically. Particularly if you have a slow internet connection, you may feel you do not want to spend ages downloading messages when a good proportion of them may not be relevant to your interests. Even if you have broadband or faster internet connection, you may not want to be swamped.

An alternative type of forum for discussion and questions is the newsgroup. Newsgroups work in a completely different way from mailing lists, and have the great advantage that you do not have to join anything and you do not end up receiving messages which do not relate to your interests.

Whereas a mailing list is like an on-line club – you really need to be a member to get the best from it – newsgroups are more like electronic notice-boards, where anyone can post a message and everyone can read it. What is good about newsgroups is that you can dip in and out of them as you like. However, there is also the disadvantage that you may miss something useful, since it is up to you to remember to check for new messages – they do not automatically come to you.

News servers

Unlike mailing lists, which are simply a particular way of using e-mail, news is actually a quite separate internet facility which requires special software and which depends on a network of computers around the world called 'news servers'. The way it works is that when you post a message to a newsgroup, the message is uploaded to your local news server, which passes your message on to all the neighbouring news servers. These in turn pass it on until your message has reached every news server on the internet. Within a day, anyone with access to a news server will be able to read your message. One of the advantages of this way of doing things is that the news service as a whole never breaks down, though it might be locally unavailable. This is quite different from a mailing list, whose operation is completely suspended if the particular server that hosts it is out of action, as happens, for example, when RootsWeb from time to time closes down its servers for maintenance over a weekend.

Most subscription ISPs provide a news server for their subscribers, though a free provider may not. If your ISP does not provide a news server, you will need to use one of the Web-based news archives discussed below.

Newsreading software

In order to look at newsgroups you need a piece of software called a newsreader, or you need to use a web browser or e-mail package that has newsreading facilities. There are several shareware newsreaders and a number of freeware ones available. Forté's Free Agent is a popular freeware newsreader for Windows, while Newswatcher is a freeware Macintosh newsreader. These can be downloaded from <**easynet.tucows. com/news95.html**> and <**easynet.mac.tucows.com/email_news_default. html**> respectively. (These pages also list a variety of other shareware and freeware packages.)

Some web browsers and e-mail software include news reading facilities – check the on-line help for a mention of newsgroups.

Newsgroup hierarchies

Newsgroups are organised in a particular way, which you need to understand in order to use them. With mailing lists, each one is guaranteed to have a unique name because each is hosted on a particular list server, and the people managing the list server make sure that names are distinct (as well as giving some indication of the topic the list is devoted to). Newsgroups are a single global system and they are named in such a way that you can easily see what topic a newsgroup covers; groups devoted to related topics have similar names. Newsgroup names are built up of two or more parts, separated by a dot. The first part of the name indicates the general subject area and each additional part indicates a narrower subject area. Each subject area, or subdivision of one, is called a 'hierarchy'.

Most of the genealogy newsgroups are in the *soc.* hierarchy, which is for social and cultural topics. Their names start soc.genealogy (as opposed to soc.history, soc.culture, etc.), followed by a specific genealogical subject area, for example soc.genealogy.computing or soc.genealogy.ireland. There are many other hierarchies, but the oldest and most important are *alt*, *comp*, *news*, *misc*, *rec*, and *sci* (see Figure 15.4, the home page for Google's news archive at **<groups.google.com>**).

Genealogy newsgroups

There are a number of groups dedicated to the genealogy of particular countries, regions or ethnic groups:

- soc.genealogy.african
- soc.genealogy.australia+nz
- soc.genealogy.benelux
- soc.genealogy.britain
- soc.genealogy.french

| Web | Images | **Groups** | Directory | News-New! |

                                  Google Search   • Advanced Groups Search
                                                      • Preferences
                                                      • Groups Help

Post and read comments in Usenet discussion forums.

alt. Any conceivable topic.   **news.** Info about Usenet News...

biz. Business products, services, reviews...   **rec.** Games, hobbies, sports...

comp. Hardware, software, consumer info...   **sci.** Applied science, social science...

humanities. Fine art, literature, philosophy...   **soc.** Social issues, culture...

misc. Employment, health, and much more...   **talk.** Current issues and debates...

                                              Browse complete list of groups...

Advertise with Us - Search Solutions - Services & Tools - Jobs, Press, & Help

@2002 Google - Searching 700,000,000 messages

Figure 15.4 Google's news service at <groups.google.com>

- soc.genealogy.german
- soc.genealogy.hispanic
- soc.genealogy.ireland
- soc.genealogy.italian
- soc.genealogy.jewish
- soc.genealogy.nordic
- soc.genealogy.slavic
- soc.genealogy.west-indies
- alt.scottish.clans
- wales.genealogy
- wales.genealogy.general

These are the best groups for discussion (in English) of genealogical sources and issues relating to the individual countries, etc.

There are a few non-geographical groups devoted to general genealogical topics:

- alt.genealogy
- soc.genealogy.computing (for anything relating to genealogy software and electronic data)
- soc.genealogy.marketplace (for announcements of commercial services or anything for sale – commercial activity is generally frowned upon in the other genealogy newsgroups)
- soc.genealogy.medieval
- soc.genealogy.methods (for discussion of the techniques and methods of genealogy)
- soc.genealogy.misc

There are a number of groups specifically intended not for general discussion but for the posting of surname interests:

- soc.genealogy.surnames
- soc.genealogy.surnames.britain
- soc.genealogy.surnames.canada
- soc.genealogy.surnames.german
- soc.genealogy.surnames.global
- soc.genealogy.surnames.ireland
- soc.genealogy.surnames.misc
- soc.genealogy.surnames.usa

There is another range of newsgroups devoted to individual surnames. These are in the alt.family-name and alt-family-names hierarchies, for example alt.family-names.anderson, alt.family-names.lloyd. There are about 150 of these, but they are in practice of doubtful value – they are very little used and have few messages of interest to genealogists. In addition, not all news servers carry them, so their distribution is more restricted than that of other newsgroups. Only the main group alt.family-names seems to be of any use. For specific surnames, a mailing list is much more likely to be useful.

All the groups listed so far are English-language groups, but there are also non-English groups which may be of interest if you have ancestors from another European country. Obviously, the discussion is mostly in the local language, but if you post in English you may well get a response.

- de.sci.genealogie (German)
- dk.historie.genealogi (Danish, little used)
- dk.videnskab.historie.genealogi (Danish)
- fr.rec.genealogie (French)
- fr.comp.applications.genealogie (French, for genealogy software)
- no.fritid.slektsforsking.diverse (Norwegian, general genealogy)
- no.fritid.slektsforsking.etterlysing (Norwegian, searching for relatives/ancestors)
- no.fritid.slektsforsking.it (Norwegian, software)
- pl.soc.genealogia (Polish)
- se.hobby.genealogi (Swedish)
- sfnet.harrastus.sukututkimus (Finnish).

If you have ancestors from other non-English-speaking countries, you may be able to get some help by posting in an appropriate group in the soc.culture hierarchy – these groups, such as soc.culture.brazil and soc.culture.netherlands, have discussion in English on the country concerned. They may be useful for getting general information about a country from people who are familiar with it, but you should not expect to find specifically genealogical expertise.

Finally, there are two groups for heraldry, alt.heraldry.sca and rec.heraldry, and a group for adoption, alt.adoption, which may be of use in genealogical research.

Newsgroup charters

Every newsgroup has a charter which explains what topics it is intended to cover and what needs it is meant to meet. Charters for all the main genealogy newsgroups can be found at <**homepages.rootsweb.com/~socgen/**>, and this page has other useful information about these newsgroups. The charter for soc.genealogy.ireland is given on the next page as an a example – note the prohibition on things like posting photographs and political discussion.

Reading news

Once you have set up your newsreading software there are several different stages in reading news. The very first thing you need to do is get your

CHARTER: soc.genealogy.ireland

Soc.genealogy.ireland is an unmoderated group for genealogy and family history discussion among people researching ancestors, family members, or others who have a genealogical connection to any people in any part of Northern Ireland and The Republic of Ireland.

The group is open to anyone with an interest in genealogy in any of the populations in or from this area, including, but not limited to: people who live, lived, or may have lived there; emigrants; immigrants; and their descendants.

The scope of the group reflects the language, history, migrations, and the realities of researching public records and genealogical data archives, and includes questions of local customs and history, or of regional or national history which affected the lives of these people and which are difficult to research in the present. Posts may be in any language but those seeking replies from a wide spectrum of readers (or at all) would be well advised to post in English.

The focus of the group is on the genealogy of individuals, as members of ethnic groups, and as part of migration patterns. Postings on topics unrelated to genealogy, especially relating to current political or religious topics are not acceptable.

Postings concerning general surnames searches are not welcome and should be directed to the soc.genealogy.surnames.ireland newsgroup. Postings containing MIME attachments, graphics, binary or GEDCOM files, and program listings are also not acceptable.

newsreader to download the list of all the newsgroups that are available on your news server. This can take a good few minutes as there are over 50,000 groups, but it only needs to be done once. Thereafter your software will only need to download the names of any new groups each time it connects to the server. Note that at this stage no messages have been downloaded, just the names of the groups.

With a list of groups in your newsreader, you need to decide which ones to read. Newsreaders generally allow you two ways of selecting a newsgroup to read: you can either 'subscribe' to it, or you can just select it. 'Subscribing' simply means that your newsreader keeps a permanent note that you want to look at the group – it does not mean you are 'joining' the group as you are when you subscribe to a mailing list. The advantage of subscribing is that you don't need to select the group again each time you use your newsreader.

Once you have selected or subscribed to a group, the next stage is to download the message headers – this is not the contents of the messages themselves but simply the details of the messages: who they're from, their subject lines, their date of posting, their size. You have still not

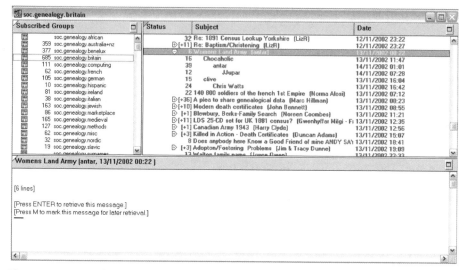

Figure 15.5 A newsreader in action. The top left pane shows the list of newsgroups, the top right pane the message headers. Clicking on the highlighted message will download it into the bottom pane.

downloaded any actual messages, and the idea of this is that you can see which messages are likely to be of interest and look at only those. This is the advantage of a newsgroup over a mailing list: you don't get a copy of every message, just the ones you decide you want to read. The first time you look at a group, or if there are a particularly large number of new messages, you will probably be offered an option to download just some of the headers rather than all of them.

Exactly how you view messages depends on your software. Netscape's built-in newsreader will automatically download and display any message your cursor rests on, while in Free Agent you have to double click on a message to display it. Another possibility is to mark all the messages you want to read and then download them in one go. If you do this, you can then disconnect from the internet and read the messages off-line, keeping down your connection time and costs. If you regularly want to download all the messages from selected newsgroups you can use your newsreading software in off-line mode, or get a dedicated 'off-line reader'. However, almost all genealogy groups are also available in mailing list format (see 'Mailing list gateways', below), and this is probably a more convenient way to ensure you get all the messages.

Posting messages

One advantage of newsgroups over mailing lists is that you don't need e-mail facilities to read the messages, nor a permanent e-mail address. Your newsreader will post your message straight to the news server and, although it may ask you to configure the software with an e-mail address, you do not need to enter an authentic working e-mail address at all. This means newsgroups are ideal for the occasional internet user and anyone who has not got their own computer and internet connection.

It also means that it is possible to send messages to newsgroups anonymously (which is not to say the computer you are using could not be traced if it were worth someone's time and trouble).

Mailing list gateways

There is another way to access some newsgroups without a news server: RootsWeb acts as a gateway that makes most of the main genealogy groups available in mailing list format. This is much more convenient if you want to make sure you don't miss any of the messages in a group. Also, because the mailing lists are available in digest form, this can be a good way of reducing the number of individual messages. Table 15.2 shows each newsgroup and its equivalent mailing list. Full details of the individual lists and how to join them can be found on RootsWeb at <www.rootsweb.com>. There is also, of course, an archive of the mailing list messages at <archiver.rootsweb.com>.

Newsgroup archives

If your ISP does not provide a news server, you can still read newsgroups and post messages to them by using one of the web sites devoted to newsgroups. If you just want to look at past messages but not to post messages yourself, Yahoo has a searchable archive at <search.yahoo.com/search/options/>. A more comprehensive site is provided by Google at <groups.google.com>.

You might think that this sort of service makes dedicated newsreading software and news servers redundant, but in fact there is a big disadvantage to Web-based news services: they are very much slower to access. Because the connection between your computer and your ISP's news server is a very short one, a newsreader will respond very quickly to your commands, whereas it will take Google, based in the US, much longer to respond to a keypress from the UK, and the entire screen will have to be redrawn every time, which slows things down even further. Unless you are only an occasional user of news, or do not have access to a news server, using a newsreader will generally be better for normal newsreading.

However, even if you use a newsreader, there are still circumstances when a news archive will be useful. The most important factor is that news servers do not keep messages for ever. Because they have limited disk space, the only way they can make room for gigabytes of new messages every day is to delete older messages which then become unavailable on the server. Exactly how quickly messages 'scroll off' a news server varies, and partly depends on how busy a particular newsgroup is, but on the whole you should not expect to find messages more than a month old on a server. For older messages, you will need to look at a newsgroup archive. For the

Table 15.2 Genealogy newsgroups and their equivalent mailing lists

Newsgroup	Gatewayed Mailing List
alt.genealogy	ALT-GENEALOGY
fr.comp.applications.genealogie	GEN-FF-LOG
fr.rec.genealogie	GEN-FF
soc.genealogy.african	GEN-AFRICAN
soc.genealogy.australia+nz	GENANZ
soc.genealogy.benelux	GEN-BENELUX & GENBNL-L
soc.genealogy.britain	GENBRIT
soc.genealogy.computing	GENCMP
soc.genealogy.french	GEN-FR
soc.genealogy.german	GEN-DE
soc.genealogy.hispanic	GEN-HISPANIC
soc.genealogy.ireland	GENIRE
soc.genealogy.italian	GEN-ITALIAN
soc.genealogy.jewish	JEWISHGEN
soc.genealogy.marketplace	GEN-MARKET
soc.genealogy.medieval	GEN-MEDIEVAL
soc.genealogy.methods	GENMTD
soc.genealogy.misc	GENMSC
soc.genealogy.nordic	GEN-NORDIC
soc.genealogy.slavic	GEN-SLAVIC
soc.genealogy.surnames.britain	SURNAMES-BRITAIN
soc.genealogy.surnames.canada	SURNAMES-CANADA
soc.genealogy.surnames.german	SURNAMES-GERMAN
soc.genealogy.surnames.global	SURNAMES
soc.genealogy.surnames.ireland	SURNAMES-IRELAND
soc.genealogy.surnames.misc	SURNAMES-MISC
soc.genealogy.surnames.usa	SURNAMES-USA
soc.genealogy.west-indies	CARIBBEAN

genealogy newsgroups the archive of the equivalent mailing list at RootsWeb can be used.

If you want to search for a particular topic across all the newsgroups, this can only be done in a news archive. Your newsreader may have facilities for searching, but these will be restricted to headers and messages you have already downloaded, and there is no way to use a newsreader to search all the messages on the server in the way that an archive's search facility can.

Finally, you may find that your local news server does not carry all the genealogy groups, in which case you will need to go to an archive.

Web forums

A third type of discussion group is the Web-based forum. There is no single term for these but they are often called 'message boards' or 'bulletin boards'. These work in very much the same way as Google's Web-based news service: a web site acts as a place where people can post messages for others to read. As with newsgroups, this does not clutter up your mailbox and does not require any long-term commitment. And, of course, it does not require you to install or configure software. However, as with Google's news service, these forums can be very slow to use, in comparison with using a newsreader to access a local news server. Also, as there is no way to select a whole group of messages for reading, you have to look separately at every single message of interest, each of which is delivered to you as a separate web page. If you want to read every message, this will be *very* tedious.

Unfortunately, there is no comprehensive list of such discussion forums, as a number of ISPs have a system for their subscribers to set up Web-based discussion groups, and there are sites like Yahoo Groups (see p. 187) or Smartgroups at <**www.smartgroups.com**>, who provide such facilities for all comers. (In fact the distinction between mailing lists and Web-based discussion groups is not absolutely clear-cut. As you can see from Figure 15.2, Yahoo Groups, for example, allows you to read messages on the Web rather than receiving them as e-mail.)

One of the major sites providing discussion forum facilities for genealogy is GenForum at <**genforum.genealogy.com**>. There are forums for over 100 countries, including all parts of the British Isles. On the page for each country there is also a link to 'Regions for this Country', which leads to forums for individual counties or major towns, though not every county has its own forum. (Figure 15.6 shows some of the messages on the Glamorgan forum.) There is a forum for each US state, and around 80 devoted to general topics (e.g. emigration, Jewish genealogy, marriage records), including 20 or so devoted to computers and genealogy software. There are thousands of forums relating to individual surnames.

Another site that provides a large number of genealogy forums is Ancestry, which offers over 120,000 genealogy 'message boards' at <**boards.ancestry.com**>. There are boards for all parts of the UK and Ireland. There is at least one message board for each county, as well as boards for: most other countries; many of the individual counties in each US state; and thousands of individual surnames. A wide range of general topics have dedicated message boards:

- Adoptions
- Ancestry Daily News
- Ancestry.com
- Cemeteries & Tombstones

Home: Regional: Glamorgan, Wales Genealogy Forum

Glamorgan, Wales Genealogy Forum

Search this forum:

| Go |

Find all of the words ▾

311 Messages Posted

Jump to # | Go |

| Post New Message | Latest Messages | Today's Messages | Last Seven Days |

Next Page | Page Listings | All Messages

- Margaret Lewis - Glamorganshire @1864 - **Stephanie** *11/13/02*
- CLIFT and SMITH in Ystradyfodwg, LLOYD in Merthyr Tydfil - **Andrew Simmons** *11/04/02*
    - Re: CLIFT and SMITH in Ystradyfodwg, LLOYD in Merthyr Tydfil - **Welsh Jen** *11/06/02*
        - Re: CLIFT and SMITH in Ystradyfodwg, LLOYD in Merthyr Tydfil - **Andrew Simmons** *11/06/02*
            - Re: CLIFT and SMITH in Ystradyfodwg, LLOYD in Merthyr Tydfil - **Welsh Jen** *11/06/02*
- 1841 Census Help, Swansea Glamorganshire~ HAWES - **Welsh Jen** *10/31/02*
- Glamorgan Record Office Lookups - **Peter Niblett** *10/28/02*
- Ystradyfodwg-NORTHEY, MORGAN, MIDDLETON - **Karen Krich** *10/16/02*
- Ystradyfodwg-SMITH, NORTHEY, HABBERFIELD, WILLIS - **Karen Krich** *10/16/02*
    - Re: Ystradyfodwg-SMITH, NORTHEY, HABBERFIELD, WILLIS - **Andrew Simmons** *11/04/02*
        - Re: Ystradyfodwg-SMITH, NORTHEY, HABBERFIELD, WILLIS - **Karen Krich** *11/04/02*
            - Re: Ystradyfodwg-SMITH, NORTHEY, HABBERFIELD, WILLIS - **Andrew Simmons** *11/04/02*
- Ruth Davies(Davis) - **Jennifer Flood (Hughes)** *10/15/02*
    - Re: Ruth Davies(Davis) - **Sian Morris** *10/21/02*
        - Re: Ruth Davies(Davis) - **Jennifer Flood (Hughes)** *10/21/02*
            - Re: Ruth Davies(Davis) - **Sian Morris** *10/25/02*
- Mary John born about 1803 in Coity, - **Sian Morris** *10/12/02*
- Edney family in Cardiff - **Philippa Schrader** *9/28/02*
    - Re: Edney family in Cardiff - **Peter Niblett** *10/13/02*

Figure 15.6 Genforum's Glamorgan Genealogy Forum at <genforum.genealogy.com/wales/glamorgan/>

- Census
- Crime
- Disasters
- Ethnic / Race
- Folklore, Legends & Family Stories
- Genealogy Software
- Government
- Immigration and Emigration
- Major Events
- Medical
- Medieval History
- Methods
- Migration
- Military
- Newspaper Research
- Occupations
- Organisations and Societies
- Orphans and orphanages
- Pioneer Programs

- Projects
- Religions and Religious
- Research Groups
- Research Resources
- Reunion Announcements
- RootsWeb
- Royalty and Nobility

To assist in finding messages on particular topics and relevant message boards, there is a global search facility.

Forums on other providers can be found by using a search engine, and a link to any forum relating specifically to UK genealogy should be found on the relevant county page on Genuki.

Frequently Asked Questions (FAQ)

Once you have been on a mailing list or looking at a newsgroup for some time, you will realise that certain questions come up again and again. Needless to say, regular members of a list don't relish the thought of repeatedly taking the time to answer these basic questions, so most newsgroups and general-interest mailing lists (i.e. those not dedicated to particular surnames) have what is called an FAQ, a file of frequently asked questions. The FAQ for a newsgroup is normally posted to the group once a month, but practice varies in mailing lists. Many newsgroup FAQs are also archived on the Web – those for the genealogy newsgroups can be found at <**www.woodgate.org/FAQs/**>.

If you are thinking of asking a question in a particular newsgroup for the first time, and especially if you are just starting to research your family tree, it's a good idea to consult the FAQ for the group. This will give you a guide as to what are considered appropriate or inappropriate issues to discuss and above all provide answers to some of the most obvious questions asked by beginners.

By way of example, here is the list of topics covered in the FAQ for the soc.genealogy.britain newsgroup, taken from <**www.woodgate.org/FAQs/socgbrit.html**>, which also has the answers:

- Is there such a thing as an Email Virus?
- What is a 'cockney'?
- What is Britain, and how is it sub-divided?
- What is an IRC? Snail mail to and from the UK.
- Is there a list of old Occupations online that can tell me what a French Polisher does? A Cordwainer? A Whitesmith, etc?
- What county is (...) in? Is there a Gazetteer of UK placenames online?
- What is the IGI? Is it going online? Can I buy it on CD-ROM?
- What are the actual dates the UK Census was taken?

- Is the UK census online?
- What do full-age/fa/ofa/bofa/minor/mi/do/DO mean in Public Records, etc?
- Is there a list of Causes of Death online? My gggf died of 'Asthenia'.
- What is Jno short for?
- What naming conventions are there?
- Is there a coat of arms for SMITH family (or other surname?)
- Why are parent details missing from the certificate?
- Where does the term Black Irish originate?
- Are 'World Books of (Your Surname)' worth buying?
- Posting Guidelines
- Where do I find other FAQs?
- What is the charter of this group?

The last three questions are to do with the customs of the particular newsgroup, and the remainder concern basic information for those new to British genealogy, including topics commonly raised by people living outside the UK.

Particularly if you are going to post information about your surname interests to one of the soc.genealogy.surnames groups, you should make sure you read the relevant FAQ, because there are fairly strict guidelines about appropriate formats for postings to these groups, which, unlike most groups, are not intended for general discussion.

The FAQs for all the main newsgroups can be found at <**www.faqs. org**>.

Netiquette

Mailing lists and newsgroups are essentially social institutions and, like face-to-face social institutions, they have a set of largely unwritten rules about what counts as acceptable or unacceptable behaviour. While individual newsgroups and mailing lists may spell some of these out in an FAQ or charter, most of these rules are common to all on-line discussion groups and are often referred to collectively as 'netiquette'.

Of course, no one can stop you making inappropriate postings to a newsgroup, but breaking the rules will not make you popular: those who repeatedly breach them are likely to be on the receiving end of rebukes, and some people may configure their newsreading software to ignore messages from such miscreants. A mailing list is very likely to make some of these rules explicit conditions for its use, and list owners usually exclude those who persistently ignore them. Even though people are pretty tolerant of mistakes from beginners, it is worth reading the FAQ for a newsgroup or mailing list, and the welcome message from a mailing list.

The culture of newsgroups is rather different from that of mailing lists. The main reason for this is that whereas every mailing list has an owner, no one is in charge of a newsgroup. In fact, newsgroups are one of the few social institutions that are genuinely anarchic. (The only control is that the operator of each news server decides which groups to take and which to ignore.) This means that if people 'misbehave' in a newsgroup, there is no one to appeal to.

Some mailing lists and a very small number of newsgroups are 'moderated'. This can mean that the messages pass through some sort of editorial control before being posted publicly; or it can mean that those who post inappropriate messages will be reprimanded and possibly, in the case of a list, forcibly unsubscribed.

Advice on 'Basic newsgroup and mailing list Netiquette' will be found at <**www.woodgate.org/FAQs/netiquette.html**>. The complete text of Virginia Shea's book *Netiquette* is on-line at <**www.albion.com/netiquette/book/**>. Malcolm Austen has some useful 'Notes on List Etiquette' at <**www.mno.org.uk/listiquette**>.

Good manners

Manners can be a problem in on-line discussion forums. The absence of the normal cues we expect in face-to-face interaction seems to make people less restrained (i.e. less polite), and such groups can contain a very diverse mix of individuals, both socially and geographically. This means you cannot rely on instincts developed in the off-line world to guide your behaviour. The following are generally accepted rules for electronic discussion forums:

- Make sure that any messages you send are relevant to the topic of the list or group. Some will tolerate the occasional 'off-topic' message, some will not. If the list owner or others in a newsgroup ask you to discontinue a topic, you should do so.
- Be very wary of using humour and irony, particularly if you are new to a group or list. Even those who share your language may not share your cultural norms. You can use a smiley ;-) to signal a joke.
- Don't be rude to others, no matter how ignorant or rude they may seem (an abusive message is called a 'flame'). An apparently stupid question about, say, English counties may be perfectly reasonable if it comes from someone who has limited familiarity with the history and geography of the British Isles.
- Never send an angry message as an immediate response to another message. Allow yourself time to cool down, because once you have sent the message you cannot cancel it when you have second thoughts.
- Avoid politics and religion, except where strictly relevant to a genealogical issue.
- Messages which are all in upper case are very difficult to read. If you post a message all in upper case, people will tell you 'DON'T SHOUT!'. Reserve upper case for highlighting surnames.

- If you are going to criticise, try and be positive and constructive. Much of what is on the internet for genealogists is the result of volunteer projects and individuals giving up their free time. While it is, of course, legitimate to subject any genealogical material or project to criticism, criticising individuals in the public forum of a newsgroup because they have not done something the way you would have done it is not going to improve the genealogical world. Criticising commercial services is another matter but, even so, there is no need to be rude. In any case, a defamatory message in an on-line discussion group could lay you open to a libel prosecution.

- Messages which advertise goods or services are out of place in most mailing lists and all genealogy newsgroups except <soc.genealogy. marketplace>. They can actually be counter-productive, as people tend to take a dim view of self-promoting commercial postings. However, it is perfectly legitimate to make recommendations about books or software, as long as you are not the author or retailer. Advertising a personal, non-commercial web site or any sort of free service is OK as long as it is not done too frequently.

- If you are using one of the twinned newsgroup/mailing lists described above, bear in mind that mailing list messages will reach all members very shortly after the original mailing, but news messages may take some time to make their way around the world. This means that newsgroup users sometimes appear slightly out of touch with the discussion, but that is an artefact of the technology, not a personal failing.

- Don't pass on a virus warning to a list, as almost all virus warnings are hoaxes. If you think it is not a hoax (check at sites like Vmyths <www.Vmyths.com>), mail it to the list owner, and he or she can then post it to the list if it seems to be genuine, i.e. it comes from an authoritative computer security source.

- Don't post messages containing other people's data or data from CD-ROMs. This is more than bad manners, it's copyright infringement.

- Don't forward to a list a message sent to you personally unless you have the original sender's permission or it is obvious from the content that it is meant for wider dissemination.

These last two points are discussed in more detail in Chapter 19 under 'Copyright' and 'Privacy' (p. 276f.).

Appropriate replies

One of the basic rules of on-line discussion is that any reply to a previous message should be 'appropriate'. What this means in practice is:

- Don't post a reply to the list or group if your answer is going to be of interest only to the sender of the original message – e-mail that person directly. So if someone asks how to locate particular records, any reply is likely to be of interest to all; an offer to lend a microfiche reader is only of interest to the person who posted a message asking for one.

• Don't quote the entirety of a previous message in a reply, particularly if your reply comes right at the bottom – just quote the relevant part.[11]

• As mentioned above, if you receive a mailing list as a digest, not only are you going to need to edit out most of the original text in your reply, you will also need to change the subject to something more appropriate. If you don't, people will not know what your message relates to and most will not even look at it.

Asking questions

While discussion groups contain much discussion, they also provide places for people to post queries and receive help and advice. One of the reasons that the internet is so useful for family historians is that it provides a huge pool of experience and expertise. In fact much of the discussion in genealogy groups arises out of particular queries. If you are asking a mailing list or newsgroup for help or advice, there are a number of things to bear in mind to ensure you get the help you want.

1. **Post your query in the right place**
   There is little point in posting a Scottish query to a Channel Islands mailing list, or asking about a surname in <**soc.genealogy.computing**>. For very general queries, newsgroups and their equivalent mailing lists are probably the best places to ask: *any* question relating to British genealogy is within the scope of soc.genealogy.britain, for example. To be sure, check the group's charter (see p. 200). Do not post the same query to a lot of groups or mailing lists – this is called 'cross posting' and is generally frowned upon. It asks several groups of people to help you and the duplication of effort in replying wastes everyone's time and trouble. (However, cross-posting of announcements is acceptable, as long the message is relevant to each discussion group.)

2. **Give an explicit subject line**
   One of the most important things in any message asking for assistance is making sure people who could assist you notice the message. This applies particularly in a newsgroup or a busy mailing list with many messages a day.
   • Make sure your subject line is explicit and helpful. If you use subject lines like 'genealogy' or 'problem' in a genealogy newsgroup or mailing list, few people will even bother to look at your message.

---

[11] One of the great religious schisms on the internet is between the 'top-posters' and the 'bottom-posters', who have different views on where in the message one should add one's own remarks when replying.

- Put any surnames you are enquiring about in upper case in your subject line. This makes it easy for people who are scanning a list of message headers to notice the surname. Ideally, do this in the body of your message, too.

3. **Don't have unreasonable expectations**

   Some of the more experienced and active members of discussion groups devote considerable time to answering queries from relative beginners, but it is important not to abuse this willingness by having unreasonable expectations of what people will do for you.

   - Don't ask a question that is covered in the FAQ if there is one.
   - Don't expect people to give you factual information that you can easily look up in a standard reference book or find on-line for yourself. If you ask, 'Is the Family Records Centre open on Saturdays?' it means you cannot be bothered to use a search engine to find its web site (and were not paying attention in Chapter 9!), and are expecting other people to take the time to provide you with the information. If you are a genealogist living in Britain, you really ought to have a good atlas of the country, so questions like 'Where is Newport Pagnell?' should only come from non-UK residents. On the other hand, questions requiring detailed local knowledge ('Is such and such a building still there?') are entirely reasonable on the county mailing lists.
   - Don't expect other list members to teach you the basics of genealogical research. You really need to have a good book on the subject, and should look at the tutorial material discussed in the Introduction (p. 6).
   - If you are looking for help with computer software problems (whether specifically genealogical or not), consider looking at the web site or discussion forum of the software supplier before asking on a non-technical mailing list or newsgroup.

On the other hand, any request for recommendations and advice is fair enough – the pooling of expertise in a discussion group makes it one of the most sensible places to raise such questions.

Starting your own discussion group

There are many sites that allow you to start your own discussion group. As mentioned above, you may find that your own ISP provides facilities to set one up on their web site. Alternatively, you could look at using Yahoo Groups at <groups.yahoo.com> or Smartgroups at <www.smartgroups.com>. The advantage of using well-known services like these is that people will be much more likely to come across your group.

RootsWeb hosts an enormous number of genealogical mailing lists and is a good place to create a new one. Details of how to request a new mailing list will be found at <resources.rootsweb.com/adopt/>. There is detailed coverage of mailing list administration at <**helpdesk.rootsweb. com/listadmins/**>.

Bear in mind that maintaining a mailing list or discussion group could end up requiring a significant amount of your time if it becomes popular. Unless a list is small, it is certainly much better for it to be maintained by more than one person so that responsibilities can be shared. On the other hand, a mailing list for a particular surname is not likely to generate nearly as much mail as one on a general topic. RootsWeb provides detailed information about the responsibilities of list owners on their system, and other sites that provide discussion forums will do the same.

Starting a new newsgroup is another matter entirely. Generally, a newsgroup can only be set up after the publication of a Request For Discussion (RFD) which outlines the group's proposed purpose (and why existing groups do not meet the same needs), which is then followed by a discussion period. Ultimately a Call For Votes (CFV) is published and all interested can vote for or against the creation of the new group. Clearly, this is not something you could do, as an individual, on the spur of the moment. However, you can set up a newsgroup under the alt. hierarchy without the formal procedure for other groups, though this is not something for the technologically faint-hearted. Given the ease of setting up a mailing list or a Web-based discussion forum, it is difficult to see a good reason for setting up a new genealogy newsgroup except by the accepted consensual method.

Which discussion group?

Which mailing lists or newsgroups you read will, of course, depend on your genealogical interests. The main general group for British genealogy is soc.genealogy.britain and its associated mailing list, GENBRIT. If you are not already familiar with mailing lists, you may not want it to be the first one you join – you could be a bit overwhelmed with the 50-plus messages per day arriving in your mailbox, and may prefer to look at the newsgroup rather than the mailing list. Also, it can be a rather boisterous group.

If you know where your ancestors came from, it may be more useful to join the appropriate county mailing lists (see <**www.genuki.org.uk/ indexes/MailingLists.html**>). There are fewer messages, and more of the postings are likely to be relevant. You will certainly have a better chance of encountering people with whom you share surname interests, not to mention common ancestors. Other useful lists are those for special interests, such as coalminers or the Boer War.

You might think that the best thing to do is join the lists for your surnames of interest, and there are thousands of lists and web-based forums devoted to individual surnames. However, they differ widely in their level of usefulness. Some have very few subscribers and very few messages, while, particularly in the case of reasonably common English surnames, you may well find lists dominated by US subscribers with mainly post-colonial interests. But with a reasonably rare surname in your family tree, particularly if it is also geographically limited, it is very likely that some other subscribers on a surname list will share your interests. Whereas the relevant county mailing list is certain to be useful, with surname lists it's more a matter of luck.

The simplest way to see whether any discussion forum is going to be worth joining is to look at the archives for the list to see the kind of topics that are discussed. This also has the advantage that you can get a rough idea of how many messages a month you would be letting yourself in for. You could also simply join a group and 'lurk', i.e. receive and read the messages without contributing yourself.

16 Search Engines

One of the most obvious features of the internet that makes it good for genealogical, or indeed any research, is that it is very large, and the amount of material available is rapidly increasing. It is impossible to get an accurate idea of the size of the Web, but it would be reasonable to assume at the very least 6,000 million pages, and that does not include any data held in on-line databases.[12] But the usefulness, or at least accessibility of this material is mitigated by the difficulty of locating specific pages. Of course, it is not difficult to find the web sites of major institutions, but much of the genealogical material on the Web is published by individuals and small organisations and this can be harder to find. Also, since there is no foolproof way to locate material, a failed search does not even imply material is not on-line.

The standard tool for locating information on the web is a search engine. This is a web site that combines an index to the Web and a facility to search the index. Although many people do not recognise any difference between directories, gateways and portals on the one hand, and search engines on the other, they are in fact very different beasts (which is why they are treated separately in this book) and have quite different strengths and weaknesses, summarised in Table 16.1.

These differences mean that directories, and particularly gateways and portals, are likely to be good for finding the sites of organisations, but much less well suited to discovering sub-pages with information on individual topics. Even genealogy directories with substantial links to personal web sites and surname resources probably don't include more than a fraction of those discoverable via a search engine.

---

[12] This is only a very rough estimate, based on (a) the fact that in July 2003, Google, the most comprehensive search engine, claimed to cover just over 3,000 million web pages, and (b) the assumption that no search engine indexes more than half the web. A study conducted by Steve Lawrence and C. Lee Giles, 'Accessibility of information on the web' in *Nature*, 8 July 1999, pp. 107–9 (summary at **<wwwmetrics.com>**) found 800 million publicly accessible web pages in early 1999, and observed that no search engine covered more than 25% of the Web. Although this study is several years old, there has not been any major breakthrough in search engine technology which might invalidate the general trend of the results.

Table 16.1 Comparison of directories, etc., with search engines

Directories, Gateways and Portals	Search Engines
Directories and gateways list web *sites* according to general subject matter.	Search engines list individual web *pages* according to the words on the page.
Directories are constructed and maintained by intelligent humans. In the case of genealogy gateways you can assume they actually have some expertise in genealogy.	Search engines rely on indexes created automatically by 'robots', software programs which roam the internet looking for new or changed web pages.
Directories and particularly specialist gateways for genealogy categorise genealogy web sites intelligently.	While some search engines know about related terms, they work at the level of individual words.
Directories are selective (even a comprehensive gateway like Genuki only links to sites it regards as useful).	Search engines index everything they come across.
Directories, offering a ready-made selection, require no skill on the part of the user.	The number of results returned by a search engine can easily run into six or seven figures, and success is highly dependent on the searcher's ability to formulate the search in appropriate terms.
Gateways often annotate links to give some idea of the scope or importance of a site.	A search engine may be able to rank search results in order of relevance to the search terms, but will generally attach no more importance to the web site of a major institution than to that of an individual genealogist.

Sometimes it is essential to search for words contained in a page; sometimes it is actually unhelpful. If you were trying to find the opening times of the Family Records Centre, it would be very irritating to retrieve thousands of web pages which mention the Family Records Centre, let alone all those that include the words *family* or *records* or *centre* – for finding a site like this a gateway is ideal. But if you are looking for pages which mention the name of one of your ancestors, there is little point in using a directory or gateway. You have to use a search engine.

Using a search engine

There are many different search engines. Table 16.2 lists the main ones (i.e. the largest and most popular) and others mentioned in this chapter.

Table 16.2 The main search engines

AltaVista	<www.altavista.com> also: <av.com>
AskJeeves	<www.ask.com>
FAST Search (All the web)	<www.alltheweb.com>
Google	<www.google.com>
Hotbot	<www.hotbot.lycos.com>
Lycos	<www.lycos.com>
Teoma	<www.teoma.com>

There are UK versions of AltaVista at <uk.altavista.com> and of Lycos at <www.lycos.co.uk>. The UK version of Hotbot at <www.hotbot.lycos. co.uk> is actually more useful than the general site, which simply offers access to other search engines. For a comprehensive set of links to search engines, see Yahoo's listing for Search Engines & Directories at <dir.yahoo.com/Computers_and_internet/internet/World_Wide_Web/ Searching_the_Web/Search_Engines_and_Directories/>.

In spite of the more or less subtle differences between them, all search engines work in basically the same way. They offer you a box to type in the 'search terms' or 'keywords' you want to search for, and a button to click on to start the search. The example from Fast Search shown in Figure 16.1 is typical. Once you've clicked on the Search button, the search engine will come back with a page containing a list of matching web pages (see Figure 16.2), each with a brief description culled from the page itself, and you can click on any of the items listed to go to the relevant web page. Search engines differ in exactly how they expect you to formulate your search, how they rank the results, how much you can customise display of the results, and so on, but these basics are common to all.

Most search engines will report the total number of matching web pages found, called 'hits', and if there is more than a pageful (typically 10 or 20),

all the web, all the time

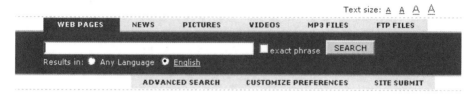

Figure 16.1 The Fast Search home page at <www.alltheweb.com>

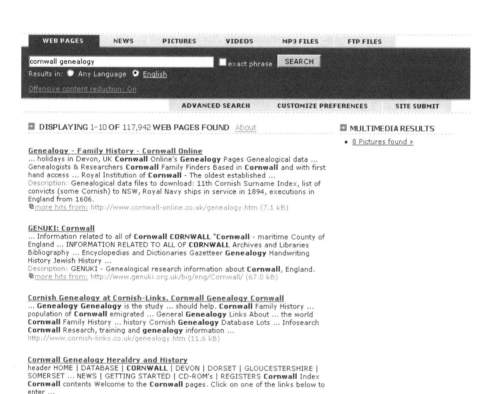

Figure 16.2 Results of a search on Fast Search

it will provide links to subsequent pages of hits. (In Figure 16.2, you can see this information juts above the first search result.) Usually the words you have searched on will be highlighted in some way.

Formulating your search

Your success in searching depends in part on your choice of search engine (see p. 229), but is also greatly dependent on your skill in choosing appropriate search terms and formulating your search.

In this chapter I have put search terms between square brackets. To run the search in a search engine type in the text between the brackets *exactly*, but don't include the square brackets themselves. Note that the figures given for the number of hits have indicative status only – they were correct when I tried out these searches, but the indexes used by search engines grow daily, so you will not get identical results. However, the differences between the various *types* of search and formulation should be of the same order.

Basic searching

There are actually several different types of search offered by search engines. In the basic search – the one you get if you don't select any options and just type in words to be searched for – the results will include all web pages found that contain *all* the words you have typed in the search field. This means that the more words you type in, the fewer results you will get. If you type in any surname or place name on its own, unless it's a fairly unusual one you will get thousands of hits. So it's always better to narrow down your search by entering more words if possible. This type of search is called an AND search.

Looking for alternatives

One thing to avoid in a basic search is entering a set of alternatives, because then you will miss some, perhaps many relevant pages. Supposing you have ancestors who were Grimsby trawlermen, it might seem like a good idea to enter both [trawlerman] and [trawlermen], possibly adding [trawler] for good measure. But each extra word reduces the number of matching pages found. On Google, a search for [Grimsby trawlermen] produces 154 hits, [Grimsby trawlerman] 88 hits, while the combination [Grimsby trawlerman trawlermen] gives only 19. The same will happen if you give alternative surname spellings: for example Google gives around 10,000 hits for [Waymark] and 5,000 for [Wymark], but [Waymark Wymark] produces less than 20, a tiny number of pages which have both variants.

The AND search is not suitable for looking for alternatives, unless you really do require pages that have both on them. What you need instead is an OR search, which will retrieve all pages containing at least one of the search words.

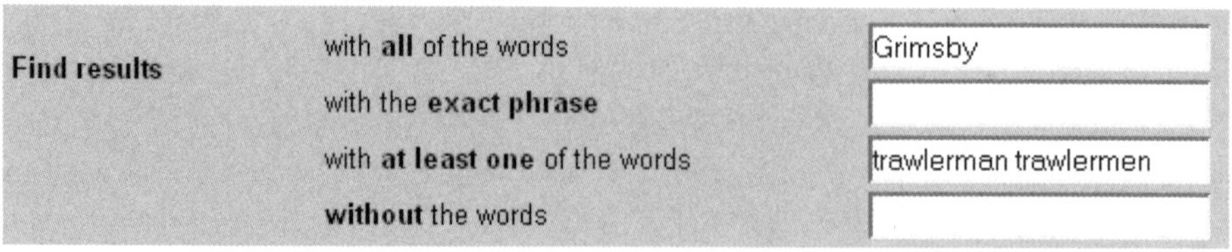

Find results	with **all** of the words	Grimsby
	with the **exact phrase**	
	with **at least one** of the words	trawlerman trawlermen
	without the words	

Figure 16.3 An OR search on Google's Advanced Search page

All the main search engines offer the option of doing an OR search, though there may be limitations on how it can be combined with an AND search. Figure 16.3 shows how to find your trawlerman ancestors on Google's Advanced Search page at <www.google.com/advanced_search>. As you'd expect, this gives you more results than any of the individual AND searches.

Some search engines allow you to specify an OR search by typing the word OR in the basic search field. If so you will need to bracket the terms together, include an AND between your alternative and any other search terms, as in the following search with which you can carry the search shown in Figure 16.3 on Altavista:

[Grimsby AND (trawlerman OR trawlermen)]

Boolean searches

AND and OR are just the most commonly used parts of a general technique for formulating searches called Boolean logic.[13] Some search engines allow you to enter much more complex Boolean expressions. For example, if you were looking for pages containing genealogical information on the surname Robinson in either Devon or Cornwall, you would be unable to formulate it just by entering keywords, since it combines two different types of search. Instead you need to formulate a fully fledged Boolean expression which captures the exact relation between the items you want to retrieve, something like:

[Robinson AND (genealogy OR "family history") AND (Devon OR Cornwall) AND (cobbler OR cordwainer)]

AltaVista and Fast Search allow you to do this in the basic search. Search engines that don't, often have a Boolean option in an advanced search page. Google's Boolean option is not entirely authentic – it doesn't require ANDs or parentheses, automatically recognising words either side of an

---

[13] This topic can be handled only briefly here. For more information on using Boolean expressions for searching, look at the help pages of the search engines or the BrightPlanet tutorial at <www.brightplanet.com/deepcontent/tutorials/search/part4.asp>.

OR as alternatives – but it works in the same way:

[Robinson genealogy OR "family history" Devon OR Cornwall cobbler OR cordwainer]

Lycos takes the opposite approach, and terms within parentheses are automatically treated as parts of an OR expression:

[Robinson (genealogy "family history") (Devon Cornwall) (cobbler cordwainer)]

Other Boolean operators include AND NOT, NEAR, BEFORE and AFTER, though not all of these are available in the main search engines – it is a good idea to check any help pages to see exactly which Boolean operators can be used on a particular search engine. Lycos has an extensive series of operators, which allow you to specify, for example, exactly how close together two words need to be.

If you want to do more advanced searches of this sort, it is essential to look at the help pages of the search engine in question to find exactly how it expects queries to be formulated.

The reason for putting the Boolean operators AND/OR in upper case, incidentally, is that these are small words which search engines normally ignore, so-called 'stop words': [Waymark OR Wymark] finds 3339 hits on AltaVista, [Waymark or Wymark] finds only 9 – the 'or' has been ignored and the alternative spellings treated as an AND search.

Exclusion

Often you will find yourself searching on a word that has several meanings or distinct uses, in which case it can be useful to find a way of excluding some pages. The way to do this is to choose a word which occurs only on pages you don't want, and mark it for exclusion, which most search engines do by prefixing with a hyphen. For example [Bath −wash] would be a way to ensure that your enquiry about a town in Somerset was not diluted by material on cleanliness.[14]

There is one very common problem when searching for geographical information which this technique can help to alleviate: names of cities and counties are used as names for ships, regiments, families and the like; also, when British emigrants settled in the colonies they frequently reused British place names. This means that many searches which include place names will retrieve a good number of irrelevant pages.

If you do a search on [Gloucester], for example, you will soon discover

---

[14] This hyphen to be regarded as a substitute for the typographically correct minus sign, which your browser would almost certainly ignore and therefore not submit as part of your search.

that there is a Gloucester County in Virginia and in New Brunswick, a town of Gloucester in New South Wales and Massachusetts (not far from the town of Essex), and you probably do not want all of these included in your results if you are looking for ancestors who lived along the Severn. Then there is HMS Gloucester, the Duke of Gloucester, pubs called the Gloucester Arms and so on. Likewise, if you're searching on [York], you do not really want to retrieve all the pages that mention New York.

Obviously it would be rather tedious to do this for every possibility, but you could easily exclude those which an initial search shows are the most common, e.g. [Gloucester −Virginia] or [York −"New York"].

Another case where this technique would be useful is if you are searching for a surname which also happens to be that of a well-known person: [Gallagher −Oasis] or [Blair −Tony −Orwell] will reduce the number of unwanted results you will get if you are searching for the surnames Gallagher or Blair, and do not want to be overwhelmed with hundreds if not thousands of hits relating to one or two high-profile bearers of the name. In the first example, [Gallagher] gives over a million hits on Google, while [Gallagher −Oasis] cuts this down to about 700,000. Unfortunately, if you are searching for a surname which is also a place name, e.g. Kent or York, there is no simple way to exclude web pages with the place name, though on p. 231 I suggest a technique for restricting your hits to personal genealogy web sites.

The counterpart of the − sign for exclusion is the + sign, indicating that the term *must* be in the pages retrieved. Given that all the main search engines do this by default for all terms you type in, the only real use is to include stop words. For searching on names, places and occupations, this is not likely to be very useful, unless you have ancestors from Oregon (abbreviation "OR") or an Orr family who sometime dropped the second r.

In Boolean terms, − is the equivalent of AND NOT, and + the equivalent of AND.

Phrases and names

Another important issue when using a search engine is how to group words together into a phrase. If you just type in a forename and surname, or a two-part place name, search engines will treat this as an AND search on the two components.

This *may* not matter, especially if you are looking for something very specific, as search engines tend to put near the top of their listings those hits which include all search terms in the title. For example, a Google search on [Historical Manuscripts Commission] produces over 70,000 hits, but the HMC's official site is at the top of the list (see Figure 16.4). As the third item in the screenshot shows, however, Google has *not* looked for this as a complete phrase. A search for ["Historical Manuscripts Commission"] produces around half that number and will not include

Historical Manuscripts Commissic   Google Search

Web | Images | Groups | Directory | News

Searched the web for **Historical Manuscripts Commission**.   Results **1 - 10** of about **77,600**.   Search took **0.11** seconds.

Historical Manuscripts Commission
... Register | Advice | Publications | Archives in Focus **Historical Manuscripts Commission**
Tel: +44 (0) 20 7242 1198 Fax: +44 (0) 20 7831 3550 Email: nra@hmc.gov ...
Description: The UK's central advisory body on archives and **manuscripts**. It maintains the National Register of...
Category: Reference > Archives > Government > United Kingdom
www.hmc.gov.uk/ - 14k - Cached - Similar pages

> **Historical Manuscripts Commission** | ARCHON
> ... for record repositories in the United Kingdom and also for institutions elsewhere
> in the world which have substantial collections of **manuscripts** noted under ...
> Description: Portal to an electronic directory of repositories holding manuscript sources for British history
> and...
> Category: Reference > Archives
> www.hmc.gov.uk/archon/archon.htm - 14k - Cached - Similar pages
> [More results from www.hmc.gov.uk]

The Irish **Manuscripts Commission** - **Historical Manuscripts**
The Irish **Manuscripts Commission** was established to report on **manuscripts**
of **historical** interest relating to Ireland. <--larchives ...
Description: Publisher of sources for Irish history.
Category: Regional > Europe > Ireland > Society and Culture > History

Figure 16.4 A search for [Historical Manuscripts Commission] on Google

pages for Ireland's similarly but not identically named body.

The standard way of indicating that your words form a phrase is to surround them with inverted commas, e.g. ["North Shields"] or ["Thomas Walker"]. Some search engines will in fact recognise well-known two-part place names and easily recognisable forename+surname combinations without requiring inverted commas. You can easily see if this is the case by trying a search for phrases like [High Wycombe] or [Queen Victoria] and seeing if you get fewer hits than when doing an AND search on the two words.

However, although it is obviously preferable to get the 177,000 hits that AltaVista gives for ["John Smith"] rather than the millions for [John Smith], the phrase search will miss pages with "Smith, John" and "John Richard Smith", so it is not an unmixed blessing. Both of these, however, could be found with [John NEAR Smith] on those search engines, such as AltaVista and Lycos, which support the NEAR operator.

Some search engines let you search for phrases by selecting this option from a menu, whether as an alternative to using inverted commas, or as the only way of selecting a phrase (for example in Fast Search, as you can see from Figure 16.1). However, this option is of little use unless *all* your search words combine to form a single phrase.

Case

It can also be important to use initial capital letters on names. If you enter a lower case letter in your keyword, all search engines will include instances where that letter is upper case. On the other hand, if you make a letter upper case, some search engines will ignore examples of the word where that letter is lower case. So AltaVista finds the same 2,667 results for [trubshaw], [TRUBSHAW] and even [TRuBSHaW], but putting inverted commas round these spellings tells it you want exact spellings and this produces 109 for ["TRUBSHAW"], and none at all for ["TRuBSHaW"].

You will need to check the help pages to see whether and how a search engine caters for case-sensitive searching. Google, for example, does not have this facility, which can cause problems when searching for surnames which are also ordinary words – the Walker family from Reading will be much harder to find on a search engine that is not case-sensitive.

Truncation and wild cards

The use of an OR search has already been mentioned as a technique for dealing with surname variants. But there may be an easier way in some search engines. AltaVista, for example, permits the use of truncated word forms, with an asterisk indicating additional groups of letters. For example, [Burrow*] would find Burrow, Burrowes and Burrows. You can use the * anywhere within a word after the first three letters, so [Glo*ster] would find both Gloster and Gloucester. The UK version of Hotbot has a similar 'stemming' feature, which, however, seems to work only on dictionary words.

Natural language searching

Some search engines claim to offer natural language searching, i.e. you type in your query not as a terse series of keywords, but as a question formulated in a full sentence. This might make you feel marginally less intimidated by the technology, but in fact it will do nothing to improve your search results. All the search engine does is strip out the small, common words and search on the remainder. On AskJeeves, for example, at <www.ask.com> the query [where can I find wills for London?] appears to produce exactly the same list of results as [wills London].

Refining your search

If you're looking for something very specific, you may find it immediately, as with the search in Figure 16.4. Otherwise, however, you shouldn't assume that your initial search will find what you want and produce a manageable list of results. If, for example, you are looking for individuals or families, or trying to find information on a particular genealogical topic, it is likely that you will have to look at quite a lot of the hits a search engine retrieves before finding what you are looking for. This makes it important to refine your search as much as possible.

The previous pages offer some advice on formulating your search as well as possible, but however well you formulate it for the first run, you will often be able to refine it once you have looked at the initial results. Search engines provide a search box with your search terms at the top of each page of hits, so it is very straightforward to edit this and re-run the search. Some search engines, such as Google, allow you to run a new search within the results you have already retrieved. In Google, clicking on the 'Search within results' link at the bottom of a results page takes you to another search page where you can specify a narrower search with additional words. AltaVista offers related key words which can be used to refine your search (see Figure 16.5).

Search tips

Apart from taking care to formulate your query, there are a number of other things to bear in mind if your searching is going to be successful and not too time consuming.

First, the better you know the particular search engine you are using, the better results you will get. Look at the options it offers, and look at the Help or Tips pages. Although I have highlighted the main features of search engines, each has its idiosyncrasies. And while it is quite easy to find what a search engine will do, sometimes the only way to find out what it *will not* do is to see what is missing from the Help pages. It is also worth trying out some different types of query, just so you get a feel for how many results to expect and how they are sorted.

If you carry out searches on your particular surnames on a regular basis, it can be worth adding the URL of the results pages to your bookmarks (Netscape) or favorites (Internet Explorer), making it easy to run the same query repeatedly.

This works because in most search engines the browser submits the search terms as an appendage to the URL, so, for example, when you search Google for [Robinson AND Exeter], the browser sends the URL <www.google.com/search?q=Robinson+Exeter&btnG=Google+Search>, which is then shown as the address of the first page of results.

Figure 16.5 Refining a search in AltaVista

Bookmarking this page will allow you to retrieve the entire URL and then re-run the search.

There is one simple browser technique which will save you time when searching. Once you have got a list of search results that you want to look at, open each link you follow in a new window or tab so that the original list of search results remains open. (On Windows browsers a right mouse click over the link will bring up a menu with this option; on the Macintosh shift+click). Otherwise, each time you want to go back to your results the search engine will run the search all over again. Another useful trick for a long page of results is to save it to your hard disk so that you can explore the hits at your leisure later.

Searching for files

Increasingly, search engines can be used for finding other types of material on-line in addition to web pages. This material falls into two broad categories, which are generally dealt with in distinct ways.

First, there are files with textual material but which are in a proprietary document format rather than the HTML format used for web pages. Traditionally, search engines do not index such material, but there are a number of such formats which are now often indexed by search engines, notably Adobe Acrobat (PDF) files, described in more detail on page 253, and to a lesser extent Microsoft Word files. The content of such files is usually included automatically in the search engine's index, so you do not need to specify a particular file type when searching (though Google allows this on its advanced search page). AltaVista offers only PDF files, while Google's index also includes Excel, PowerPoint, PostScript and RTF files, though these are probably not used much for genealogical information. You'll need to refer to the help pages to see what each search engine offers.

Multimedia files are generally handled differently, and the tendency is to have a separate search facility for each format. As you can see in Figure 16.2, FastSearch has separate tabs for pictures, videos and MP3 (audio) files, while AltaVista offers the same option on its Image, MP3/Audio, and Video tabs above the search box on the home page. Google has a separate image search facility at <**images.google.com**> (or click on the Images tab on the Google home page).

Searching for photographs
Of the various multimedia file types, those of most interest to genealogists will be the graphics files of scanned or digital photographs. An overview of the sorts of photographs you can expect to find on-line is given in Chapter 14.

When searching for images, you can't simply use the standard facilities of the search engines, since these look for text. Although any search results *will* include pages with images on them, particularly where there are relevant captions, this will not be obvious from the list of search engine results. This might be a way to find sites or pages that are devoted to photographs or postcards, but it will be a time-consuming way to find individual photographs.

Google has an excellent image search facility at **<images.google.com>**, which claims to have over 425 million images indexed (see **<images.google. com/help/faq_images.html>**. The search results pages show thumbnail versions of the images which match your search criteria – clicking on an image takes you to a two-panel page with the image at the top and the page it comes from below.

Mostly you will just get a normal search box, but if there is an advanced image search this should allow you to be more precise about the sorts of image you want, such as that from Google shown in Figure 16.6.

For a list of other image search engines, look at the BIG Search Engine Index, which has a list of about 20 image search engines and databases at **<www.search-engine-index.co.uk/Images_Search/>**, with brief descriptions.

The Boston Universities Library site has a brief guide to finding images on the Web at **<www.bu.edu/library/training/webimages.htm>**, which includes information on using standard search engines to find images. The Open University also has a good page on finding images at **<library. open.ac.uk/wh/resources/images.htm>**.

Limitations

It is important to bear in mind some of the limitations of search engines. First, no search engine indexes the whole of the Web. The study by Lawrence and Giles mentioned at the start of this chapter (p. 215, footnote 12) found that even the best search engines did not index more than 25% of the estimated totality of the Web, and not even their combined coverage captured half the Web.

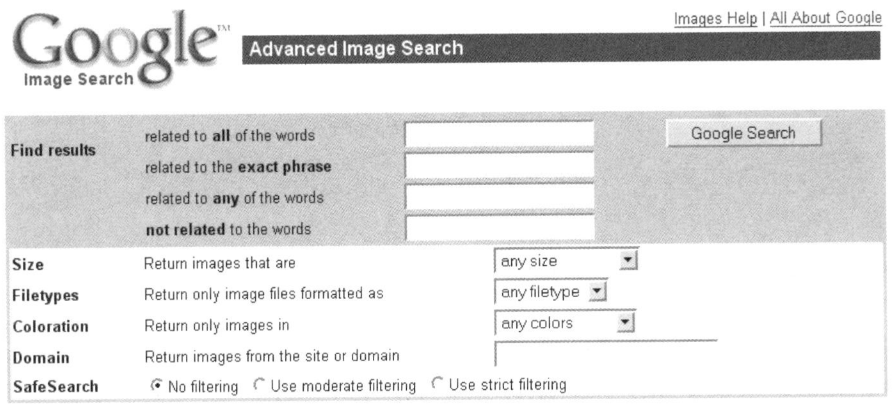

Figure 16.6 Google's Advanced Image Search

For this reason, when you cannot find a resource when using a search engine, it does not mean it is not there – a search engine is not a library catalogue.

Second, do not expect all results to be relevant. Even a fairly precisely formulated query may get some irrelevant results, and web pages which have long lists of names and places will inevitably produce some unwanted matches. For example, a surname interest list which contains a Robinson from Lancashire and some other surname from Devon would appear among the results for a search on [Robinson Devon]. Particularly if you do not include terms like [genealogy] or ["family history"], or something that occurs more frequently on genealogy sites than elsewhere – ["monumental inscriptions"] or ["parish register"], for example – you will get many irrelevant results. And, of course, searching for a fairly common surname may retrieve numerous genealogical pages that are nothing to do with your own line.

There are ways to cut down on irrelevant results if you are looking for a particular family. The more precise your geographical information the better: if you know your Robinsons came from Exeter, search not for [Robinson Devon] but for [Robinson Exeter Devon]. (Keep Devon in – you do not want Exeter College, HMS Exeter, Exeter in New Hampshire, etc.) If you search on both surnames of a married couple, even if they are individually quite common, you are much more likely to get relevant results, for example [Robinson Armstrong Exeter Devon genealogy]. If you use full names, all the better – even ["John Smith" "Ann Williams"] only finds 250 odd pages on AltaVista; if you add [Yorkshire], it comes down to 15!

You will still tend to retrieve a few surname listing pages, but there is little that can be done about that, unless you use a search engine such as Lycos or AltaVista which has a special NEAR operator which will find two search terms within 25 words of each other.

Another important problem in finding surname material on the internet is that much of it is simply available not in permanent web pages, but in databases. The only way to find the information is to go to the site with the database and carry out a search. This material *cannot* be retrieved by search engines, and the individual items of data have no place in directories either. This means that the material discussed in Chapters 4 to 8 will not show up in search engine results. The same is true for much of the material covered in Chapter 10.

Finally, the Web is full of spelling errors. For example, Google finds 225 pages which mention a supposed county of "Yorskhire", which may elude you in your search for [Yorkshire].

Choosing a search engine

Which is the best search engine depends on a number of factors. The over-riding factor is what you are looking for. There are several different aims you might have when using search engines. You might be trying to locate a particular site that you know must exist – you only need one result and you will recognise it when you see it. This is usually a search for a particular organisation's web site, or some particular resource that you've heard of but can't remember the location of.

Alternatively, you may be trying to find any site which might have information on a particular surname, or even a particular ancestor. The difference between this and the previous search is that there is no way of telling in advance what your search will turn up, and probably the search results will include a certain number, perhaps even a lot, of irrelevant sites. Another difference is that in the first case, you almost certainly have some idea of what the site might be called.

With this in mind, there are three main criteria to consider when deciding which search engine to use:

- the size of the index
- the way in which results are ranked
- the range of search options available.

Size

The first of these is the most fundamental. Other things being equal, the search engine with the larger index is more likely to have what you are looking for. However, while this will be very important in looking for pedigree-related information, it will be largely irrelevant if you are looking for something like the Family Records Centre web site, which you would expect *all* search engines to have in their indexes.

Since search engines are constantly striving to improve their performance and coverage, there can be no guarantee that what is the most comprehensive search engine at the time of writing will still hold that position when you are reading this. However, Google has consistently had the largest index over the last few years, and is not likely to lose that position overnight.

It's hard to be sure exactly how large search engine indexes are. To give you some idea, Table 16.3 quotes the claimed figures for a number of search engines at the end of 2002, along with an estimate made by Greg Notess of Search Engine Showdown. For comparison, Table 16.4 shows the number of hits for [genealogy] on some of the larger search engines at the start of 2003. All the figures should be treated with some caution as there is no way to verify their accuracy – certainly differences of 10% or less are unlikely to be genuinely significant for real-life searching.

Table 16.3 Estimated sizes of search engine indexes (December 2002) from Search Engine Showdown at <www.searchengineshowdown.com/stats/sizeest.shtml>

Search Engine	Showdown Estimate (millions)	Claim (millions)
Google	3,033	3,083
AlltheWeb	2,106	2,112
AltaVista	1,689	1,000
WiseNut	1,453	1,500
Hotbot	1,147	3,000
MSN Search	1,018	3,000
Teoma	1,015	500
NLResearch	733	125
Gigablast	275	150

Table 16.4 Hits for [genealogy] on a range of search engines

Google	10.6m
Lycos (uses Fast)	7.3m
Fast	7.0m
Teoma	4.7m
WiseNut	3.8m
AltaVista	3.5m
NLResearch	0.7m

Ranking

Unless you get only a handful of results, one of the issues which will determine the usefulness of search results will be whether the most relevant ones are listed first. In fact poor ranking effectively invalidates the virtues of a large index – a page which is ranked 5,000 out of 700,000 might as well not be included in the results at all because you're never going to look at it.

It's difficult to be specific about how search engines rank their results but they seem to have a measure of relevance based on:

- the frequency of your search terms in the pages retrieved
- the presence of these words in high-profile positions such as the page title, headings, etc.

Google explicitly uses a popularity rating, giving higher priority to pages which many others are linked to, though probably other search engines do this, too. This is good if what you want are recommendations – which is the best site on military genealogy, say. But if you are searching for surnames and pedigrees, which are probably on personal web sites, it may be positively unhelpful, as these will automatically rank lower than well-connected commercial sites which happen to have the same surname on them. Almost any surname search will tend to list the major genealogy sites high up, especially those with pages for individual surnames or surname message boards. A useful option on AltaVista's advanced search page is that when you use a Boolean expression you can specify which of your search terms should be prioritised in the listing.

It is not straightforward to invert this priority. FastSearch has an option (in advanced search) to search only in personal home pages. It does this by looking for the ~ character which is often found in the URLs of personal pages, but this is hardly reliable (my own personal pages are at <homepages.gold.ac.uk/peter/>, for example). For personal genealogy pages, the only way I have found of doing this is to include the phrase ["surname list"] in the search terms. The basis for this is that many of the software packages used to create a web site from a genealogy database (see Chapter 17) will create a page with this as a title or heading. The results will also include, of course, some non-personal sites such as the county surname lists mentioned on page 111, but the phrase does not seem to be common on non-genealogy sites, and is less likely to be encountered on commercial genealogy sites.

Features

The most important features offered by search engines have been discussed in some detail earlier in this chapter. The implications for choice of search engine are that if you can't get the number of hits down to a manageable figure, and the search engine's ranking system doesn't put what you want near the top, your only option is to formulate a more sophisticated search, even if this means using a search engine with a smaller index.

While Google may have the largest index of any of these search engines, which makes it justifiably popular, its lack of facilities to execute some of the searches I have used as examples in this chapter makes it less valuable for more complex searches: case sensitivity, truncation and full Boolean searches are all missing.

Evaluation

There are useful comparative tables of some of the main search engine features on Ian Winship's 'Web search service features' page at <**www.unn.ac.uk/central/isd/features.htm**> and in Infopeople's 'Search tools Chart' at <**www.infopeople.org/search/chart.html**>. For evaluation of the different search engines, see the links on the 'Evaluation Of Internet Searching And Search Engines' page at <**www.umanitoba.ca/libraries/units/engineering/evaluate.html**>. Search Engine Watch at <**www.searchenginewatch.com**> and Search Engine Showdown at <**www.searchengineshowdown.com**> are good sites devoted entirely to information about search engines and have information on search engine size and ranking.

Meta-search engines

One technique for overcoming the fact that no search engine indexes the whole of the Web is to carry out the same search on several different search engines. To do this by hand would, of course, be immensely time-consuming, not to mention tedious, but there are two ways of making the task easier.

One is to use an 'all-in-one' search page, which allows you to submit a search to many different search engines. An example of this is Proteus Internet Search at <**www.thrall.org/proteus.html**>, where you type your search terms in the Find box and then select which search engine to submit them to (see Figure 16.7). Proteus keeps a record of your searches in any

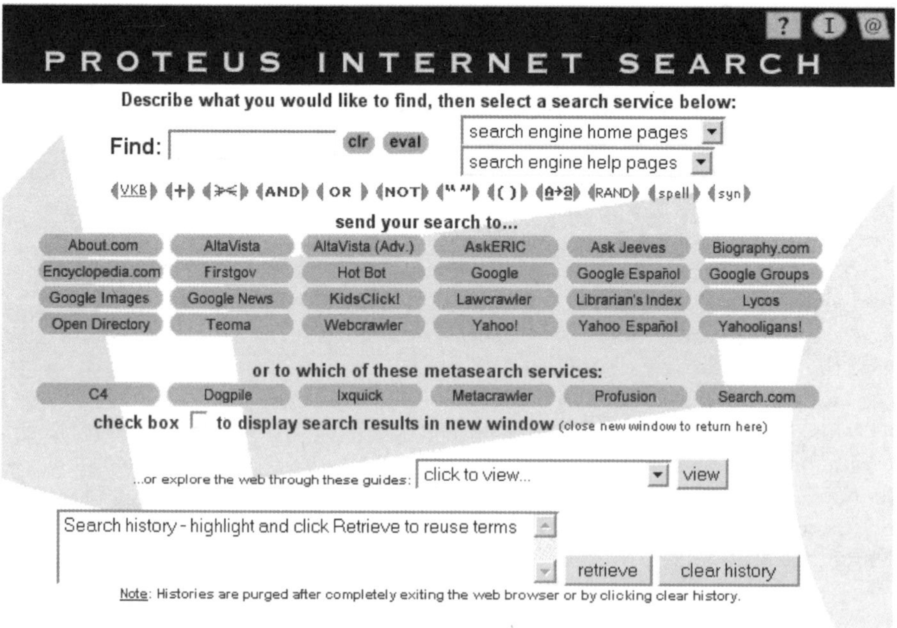

Figure 16.7 Proteus Internet Search, an 'all-in-one' search page

one session, so you can easily rerun them. You can also choose to have the search results displayed in a new window so that you do not keep having to click on the Back button. Cyndi's List has a small all-in-one search facility on its Search Engines page at <www.cyndislist.com/search. htm#Forms>. Here you have to enter your search terms in a different box for each search engine, but you can easily do that by cutting and pasting. Yahoo has a list of All-in-One Search sites. Its URL is 140-odd characters long, so it is best located by going to <www.yahoo.com> and running a search for ["All-in-One Search"].

Even more labour-saving are meta-search engines. In these you enter your search only once and it is then automatically submitted to a range of search engines. One of the most popular is DogPile <www.dogpile.com>, which automatically submits a query to a number of search engines and directories (listed on the Custom Search page at <www.dogpile.com/t/tools/custom>). You can tell DogPile which to use out of AltaVista, Direct Hit, DogPile Open Directory, FindWhat, Google, GoTo, Infoseek, Kanoodle, LookSmart, Lycos, RealNames, Sprinks from About, Web Catalog, and Yahoo. It submits your query to each search engine in turn, pausing when it has given you a page of 10 results. You can in fact customise the order in which it goes to the search engines. However, you have no control on how your keywords are submitted to the individual engines.

Another well-known meta-search engine is MetaCrawler at <www.metacrawler.com>. This has more sophisticated input options (you can specify AND, OR or phrase search). Since it does all the searches before giving you the results, it can also allow you to choose the order in which they are presented (sorted by relevance, by site or by search engine). Figure 16.8 shows the entry of a search for Boyd's Marriage Index in MetaCrawler and Figure 16.9 shows the first few results.

It might seem that these types of search facility make visiting the individual search engines redundant, and they might well do so for certain types of search. But there are important limitations. First, if you look at the list of search engines used by DogPile, for example, the absence of some of the largest (AltaVista and Teoma) is disconcerting. Second, while you can do an AND search or a phrase search by this method, anything more complex is going to fall down because of the different facilities offered by the different engines. Third, it is important to recognise that meta-search engines give *fewer* results for many searches than the individual search engines do – for example, ["Boyd's Marriage Index"] on Google gives over 2,000 hits, most of which MetaCrawler has ignored. This is because meta-search engines select the first few results from each search engine, typically the first ten. Also, a meta-search engine may retrieve no results at all from a search engine which is slow to respond and is timed out. However, MetaCrawler is good in that it gives you control over these facilities on its 'custom search' page at <www.metacrawler.com/customize/>.

For these reasons, meta-search engines are not appropriate for all types

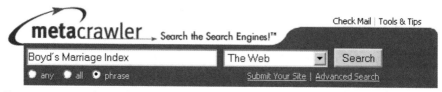

Figure 16.8 MetaCrawler search

Figure 16.9 Results of the search in Figure 16.8

of search. They are best when you are looking for a particular site, or want to find the most popular sites devoted to a particular subject – in this example, the site with Boyd's is near the top of the list. But they are ill-suited to locating pages devoted to particular pedigrees or surnames.

Search software

A similar tool for searching is a 'searchbot', sometimes also called an 'intelligent agent'. Rather than a web site which you must go to in order to carry out a search, a searchbot is a piece of software that runs on your own computer, allowing you to formulate searches off-line and then go on-line to do the search. Searchbots work like meta-search engines – they submit a query to many different search engines – and have the same strengths and weaknesses. The advantage of a searchbot, though, is that the full results are then stored to your hard disk, and you can examine them at your leisure. It will also store the details of each search, making it easy to repeat. There are dozens of searchbots, available as shareware or freeware from software archives such as Tucows (see **<tucows.mirror.ac.uk/searchbot95. html>** for Windows searchbots).

Both Internet Explorer and Netscape have built-in search facilities. Netscape allows you to choose one of a number of search engines, including Google and Lycos, to submit your searches to. Internet Explorer has a search facility which uses the less comprehensive MSN Search.

Genealogy search tools

The search tools discussed so far have been general-purpose tools, but there are also many special-purpose tools. Some of these are discussed elsewhere in the text: there is a whole range of search engines dedicated to locating living people, by geographical location or e-mail address (see p. 124), and image search tools are discussed earlier in this chapter. Other useful dedicated tools are gazetteers, which allow you to locate places (see p. 156). Chapter 9 covers on-line catalogues to material which is itself not on-line. All of these are likely to be better for their particular purpose than the general search engines. However, there are also some search tools devoted solely to genealogy. Two of these are described in the following sections, and others will be found on the 'Search Engines' page at <www.cyndislist.com/search.htm#Genealogy>.

Genuki search

Probably the most useful search engine devoted to 'official' web sites with material on UK genealogy is the Genuki Search at <**www.genuki.org.uk/ search/**>, because it provides an index not only to Genuki itself, but also to the web sites of the National Archives, the Society of Genealogists, the Federation of Family History Societies and the Guild of One-Name Studies. Also indexed are the contents of all the family history society web sites and county surname interest lists to which Genuki provides links. Currently, it allows AND, OR and Boolean searches, though phrase searching is promised for the future.

Origin Search & Irish Origins

Origins has two dedicated genealogy search engines. Origin Search at <www.originssearch.com> is a subscription service (currently $15 for 14 days, or $5 for 24 hours) which has an index of over 400 million names on genealogy pages, while Irish Origins at <www.irishorigins.com> is a free service which includes only the Irish material from Origin Search (see Figure 16.10).

Unlike normal search engines, these are designed to list only genealogy pages in their results, and have some sophisticated name matching techniques which general-purpose search engines don't have. For example, it can recognise a range of variants for both surnames and forenames, and you can specify how exactly names should be matched. These sites also allow you to search by category of document, so you can restrict your search to military or immigration pages.

Tutorials

Because of the importance of searching to serious use of the internet there are many sites with guides to search techniques and tutorials on searching.

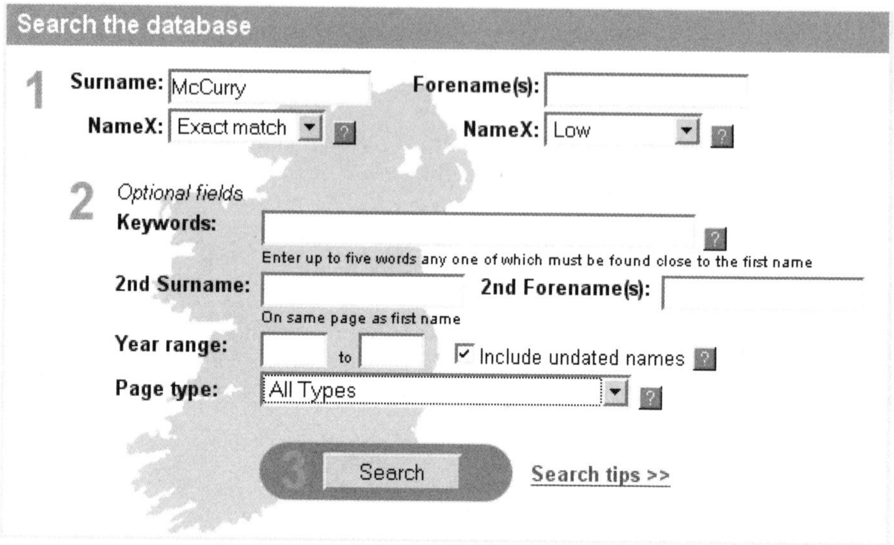

Figure 16.10 The Search box on Irish Origins

In addition to the sites listed under 'Choosing a search engine' on p. 229ff., the University of California at Berkeley has an on-line tutorial 'Finding Information on the Internet' at <www.lib.berkeley.edu/TeachingLib/ Guides/Internet/FindInfo.html>, while Bright Planet has a 'Guide to Effective Searching of the Internet' at <www.brightplanet.com/ deepcontent/tutorials/Search/index.asp>. Rice University has a useful and concise guide to 'Internet Searching Strategies' at <www.rice.edu/fondren/ tmp/netguides/strategies.html>. There is a guide to searching specifically for genealogy sites and pages in 'Finding your ancestors on the Internet' at <genealogy.about.com/library/weekly/aa041700a.htm>. You will find the full text of my book *Finding Genealogy on the Internet* on-line at <www.spub.co.uk/fgi/> with links to many relevant sites. The 'Search Engines' page on Cyndi's List at <www.cyndislist.com/search.htm> has many links to resources related to search techniques.

17 Publishing Your Family History On-line

So far we have been concentrating on retrieving information and contacting others who share your interests. But you can also take a more active role in publicisng your own interests and publishing the results of your research for others to find.

Some of the ways of doing this have already been touched upon. You can post a message with details of your surname interests to a suitable mailing list or to one of the surnames newsgroups (see Chapter 15). Although your message may be read by only a relatively small number of readers (compared to the total number of people on-line, that is), it will be archived, providing a permanent record. You can submit your surname interests to the surname lists for the counties your ancestors lived in (Chapter 10). This will be easier for others to find than material in mailing list archives, since anyone with ancestors from a county is likely to check that list. Both of these methods are quick and easy, but they have the limitation that they offer quite basic information, which may not be enough for someone else to spot a link with your family, particularly with more common surnames. The alternative is to publish your family history on the Web.

Publishing options

There are two ways of putting your family history on-line: you can submit your family tree to a pedigree database such as those discussed in Chapter 10, or you can create your own web site. In fact, these are not mutually exclusive, and there are good reasons for doing both, as each approach has its own merits.

Pedigree databases
There are obvious advantages in submitting your family tree to one of the pedigree databases:

- It is a very quick way of getting your tree on-line.
- The fact that these sites have many visitors and are obvious places to search for contacts means that you are getting your material to a large audience.

But there are a couple of disadvantages to note:

- The material is held in a database, which means it can only be found by going to the site and using the built-in search facilities. It will not be found by anyone using a general Web search engine such as those discussed in Chapter 16.
- You can only submit material held in your genealogy database, and you will not be able to include any other documentary or graphical material relating to your family history.

Neither of these are reasons *not* to submit your pedigree to a database. They simply mean that you might want to consider having your own web site as well.

A *personal web site*

Creating your own web site may sound like much more work, but there are a number of reasons why it can be better than simply uploading your family tree to a database:

- You can put a family tree on your own site almost as easily as you can submit it to a database.
- You can include any other textual material you have collected which may be of interest: transcriptions of original documents, extracts from parish registers or General Register Office indexes for your chosen names.
- You can include images, whether they are scanned from old photographs in your collection or pictures you have taken of places where your ancestors lived.
- If you submit the address of your site to search engines, all the individuals in your tree and all the other information on your site will be indexed by them, so they can be found by the techniques discussed in Chapter 16.

The great thing about a personal web site is that it is not like publishing a book: you do not have to do all these things at once. You can start with a small amount of material – a family tree, or just a list of your surname interests, perhaps – and add to it as and when you like.

But there are a couple of drawbacks to be aware of if you are going to create your own site:

- If you set it up in free web space provided by your ISP you will probably have to move the whole site if you subsequently switch to another provider. Search engines and everyone who has linked to your site will have to be informed.
- If your site is going to provide more than a basic family tree, you will need to learn how to create web pages.

Both of these issues are tackled later in this chapter.

It is worth pointing out that apart from the major on-line databases, much of the genealogical material on the Web is the result of the efforts of individuals making it available on personal sites. If you have any genealogical information that may be of interest to others, in addition to your personal pedigree, you should consider making it available on-line.

Whichever of these options you choose, you should avoid publishing information about living people, a topic that is discussed in more detail on p. 277.

Family trees for the Web

Probably the most important thing to put on the Web is your family tree. This will make it possible for other genealogists to discover shared interests and ancestors, and get in touch with you.

Whether you are going to submit your family tree to a pedigree database or create your own site, you will need to extract the data from your genealogy database software in a format ready for the Web. (If you are not yet using a genealogy database to keep a record of your ancestors and what you have discovered about them, look at 'Software' in Chapter 18, p. 266.) The alternative would be to type up the data from scratch, which would be both time-consuming and prone to error.

GEDCOM

GEDCOM, which stands for **GE**nealogical **D**ata **COM**munication, is a standard file format for exchanging family trees between one computer and another, or one computer program and another. It was developed in the 1980s by the LDS Church as a format for users of Personal Ancestral File (see p. 267) to make submissions to Ancestral File (see p. 117). It has subsequently been adopted and supported by all major genealogy software producers to enable users to transfer data into or out of their programs. It can also be used to download records from the various LDS databases in a format that allows them to be imported into a genealogy program. Although designed by the LDS Church for its own use, it has become the de facto standard for exchanging genealogical data electronically.

The reason you need to know about GEDCOM is that all the pedigree databases expect you to submit your family tree in the form of a GEDCOM file. Also, provided your genealogy software can save your pedigree information in GEDCOM format, there are many programs which can automatically create a set of web pages from that file. On the PC, GEDCOM files have the file extension .ged.

You do not need to know the technical details of GEDCOM in order to publish your family tree on the Web, but Cyndi's List has a page devoted to GEDCOM resources at <**www.cyndislist.com/gedcom.htm**>, with links to explanatory material and technical specifications. Dick Eastman has a straightforward explanation of what GEDCOM is at <www.eogn.com/archives/news0219.htm>, while David Hawgood's *GEDCOM Data Transfer, moving your family tree* is a useful printed guide showing you how to use it to transfer data between genealogy programs (details at <www.hawgood.co.uk/gedcom.htm>). For the technically inclined, the GEDCOM specification is at <www.gendex.com/gedcom55/55gctoc.htm>.

Whatever genealogy software you are using for your family tree, you should be able to find an option to export data to a GEDCOM file. Typically, this option will be found under **Export** on the **File** menu but if not, the manual or the on-line help for your program should contain information on GEDCOM export.

GEDCOM converters

When you submit your tree to an on-line pedigree database they will only need the GEDCOM file, and they will have software for indexing it and converting into the right format for the site.

However, if you are using a GEDCOM file because your genealogy software has not got any built-in facilities for creating web pages, you will need to use a special converter program to turn the file into an on-line pedigree. A large number of such programs are available. All are freeware or shareware and can be downloaded from the Web. For those that are shareware, you generally need to pay the registration fee (typically £10 to £20) if you continue to use the program after a trial period of 30 days. There are considerable differences in how these programs create web pages and what the results look like. In addition, there are important differences in the options available. There is not space here to list or discuss all the programs available, but there is a listing on the web site for my book *Web Publishing for Genealogy* at <www.spub.co.uk/software.html> and on Cyndi's List at <www.cyndislist.com/construc.htm#plan>.

Until recently, these converters were essential tools for genealogical web publishing. But now that recent versions of all the main genealogy database programs have got built-in facilities for creating a web pedigree they are less significant. Indeed, even if you are using an older piece of software without web publishing features there is a very easy way to create a web pedigree without using a converter: just download Personal Ancestral File, Legacy 3.0 or Ancestry Family Tree (all free of charge, see Chapter 18, p. 267). These programs can import a GEDCOM file and turn it into a set of web pages.

Even so, it is well worth having a look at examples of the pages created by the converters, as you may find you prefer their appearance to the output of your genealogy database program. Mark Knight's web site at <help.surnameweb.org/knight/> shows sample output for most current converters, and the Surname Web has reviews of several GEDCOM converters at <surnameweb.org/help/conversion.htm>.

Web trees

All recent versions of the main genealogy database programs have facilities to create a set of web pages, including the following:

- Ancestral Quest
- Family Matters
- Family Origins
- Generations
- Kinship Archivist
- Legacy
- The Master Genealogist
- Personal Ancestral File
- Relatively Yours
- Reunion (Macintosh)
- Ultimate Family Tree
- Win-Family.

If you have one of these programs, it will be the most straightforward tool to use for turning your pedigree on-line into a set of web pages.[15]

The programs vary in what they actually produce for a web site, but at the very least all will give you:

- a surname index
- an index of individuals
- a series of linked pages with either family groups or details of individuals.

You should have a choice between an ancestor tree, a descendant tree, or a full pedigree, and there are many options about which individuals, and what information about them, to include.

By way of example, Figure 17.1 shows a page created by Legacy 4.0. This is a web version of a standard descendancy report. Whereas in a printed pedigree you have to turn manually to other pages, here the highlighted names are links which will take you straight to the entries for children. The small superscript numbers link to descriptions of the sources.

Web publishing basics

If you are just going to upload a GEDCOM file to a pedigree database, you do not need to know anything else about web publishing. But if you are

---

[15] I have excluded Family Tree Maker from this listing. Although it can create web pages, these can only be uploaded to the manufacturer's web site, and doing so you give them an unlimited right to distribute or sell your data. See <familytreemaker. genealogy.com/ftm_uhp_home.html>.

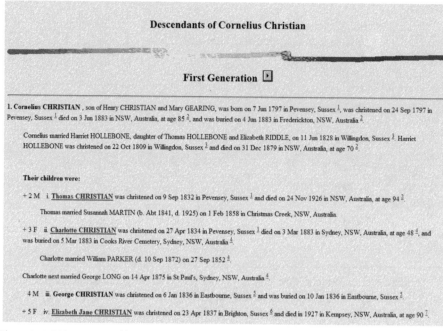

Figure 17.1 Web page created by Legacy

going to create your own web site you will need to familiarise yourself with what is involved in the process. While it is increasingly possible to create a web site without in-depth technical knowledge, it is still essential to have some understanding of what is involved. There is not space here to deal with the topic in detail, but this and the following sections cover the basics and there are suggested sources of further information at the end of this chapter.

What is a web site?

A web site is simply a collection of individual files stored on a web server, which is a computer with (usually) a permanent connection to the Web and the capacity to deal with lots of requests for web pages from all over the internet. While larger companies have their own dedicated computers to act as web servers, smaller organisations and home users simply get a portion of the file space on the server belonging to their Internet Service Provider (this is called web hosting).

When you create a web site, you first create all the pages on your own computer, then you upload the files to your space on the web server.

Assuming you already have internet access, what you need in order to create a web site is:

- web space
- software for creating web pages
- software for uploading the pages to your web space.

If you are going to have photographs or scanned images of documents on your site, you will also need graphics editing software.

One important aspect of web publishing is that it can be done with any computer and a wide range of software. You do not need a specially powerful computer, and you almost certainly have web publishing software on your computer already without knowing it (see p. 247). You will probably be able to use your browser for uploading pages, though there is dedicated freeware and shareware software which will make the process easier.

The other thing you need for a web site is time. Even though basic web publishing is not difficult, you will need to learn how it works and you will want to experiment before unleashing your site on the public. You will also need to give some thought to exactly what material you are going to publish, and how best to organise it so that your visitors can find the information they are looking for – just as you would for a book, in fact.

Web space

In order to have a web site you need to have space on a web server for the files which make up your web site. If you are paying your Internet Service Provider for your dial-up connection to the internet, you will almost certainly find that your subscription includes this facility at no extra cost. It is usual for ISPs to give their customers at least 10Mb of space, and 20Mb or more is not uncommon. Unless you are intending to include many high-quality graphics or a *very* large amount of primary data on-line this should be more than enough space for a personal genealogy site. It is even quite a respectable amount for a family history society.

While the free ISPs do not always give subscribers free web space, quite a number of them do. If yours does not, there are a number of companies that offer web space entirely free of charge regardless of who your ISP is. FortuneCity <**www.fortunecity.co.uk**>, for example, offers 25Mb with more available on application, while Tripod <**www.tripod.lycos.co.uk**> offers 50Mb. A good place for genealogy sites is RootsWeb <**www.rootsweb.com**> with its 'Freepages', free unlimited web space. Details will be found at <**accounts.rootsweb.com**>. (Other companies can be found by searching Yahoo for the phrase 'free web space'.) The disadvantage of such services is that they will include advertising on your pages, either as a banner ad at the top of a page or as adverts in a separate pop-up window. There may also be some restrictions on what you can put on your site, though this is unlikely to be of concern to genealogists creating personal sites.

The web address of your site will depend on who is providing your web space and what sort of account you have with them. There are a number of standard formats for URLs of personal web sites. The address of my personal genealogy page is <homepages.gold.ac.uk/peter/>, which is the name of the server the site is on, followed by my username on that system. Some providers actually combine the username with the server name directly, which gives you what appears to be your own web server. For example, free web-space provider Tripod gives user sites a name of the format <user-id.tripod.com>.

If you are planning a substantial web site with material of general interest rather than simply your own pedigree, or if you are going to set up a site for an organisation or genealogy project, it is useful to have a permanent address rather than one that is dependent on your current ISP or web space provider. The three ways of doing this are:

- Register your own domain name (see the Nominet site at <www.nic.uk> for information).
- Use a 'redirection service' such as V3 <www.v3.com> to be allocated a permanent free web address of the format <go.to/user-id/>, which redirects people to your actual web space, wherever it is.
- Get another organisation to host your material. RootsWeb <www.rootsweb.com>, for example, provides domain names and web space for genealogy projects such as the Immigrant Ships Transcribers Guild <istg.rootsweb.com> and FreeBMD <freebmd.rootsweb.com>.

Having your own domain name is the ideal solution, but the registration and hosting will require some modest annual expenditure. There is a straightforward guide to setting up your own domain in Dick Eastman's newsletters for 23rd and 30th September 2002, archived at <www.eogn.com/archives/news0238.htm> and <www.eogn.com/archives/news0239.htm>.

What is a web page?

When viewed on a web browser, web pages look like a form of desktop publishing and you might think that you need very complex and expensive software to produce a web site. In fact the opposite is true. Web pages are in principle very simple – each page is simply a text file with the text that is to appear on the page along with instructions to the browser on how to display the text. The pictures that appear on a page are not strictly part of it, they are separate files. The page contains instructions telling the browser where to download them from. (This is why you can often see the individual images being downloaded after the text of a page has already appeared in the browser window.) In a similar way, all the links on a web page are created by including instructions to the browser on what page to load when the user clicks on the links. (You can easily get a general idea of how this all works if you load a web page, ideally a fairly simple one, into your browser and use the **View Source** option in Netscape or Internet

Explorer, on the **View** menu in both browsers.)

This means that a web page is not a completed and fixed design like the final output of a desktop publishing program on the printed page. It is a set of instructions which the browser carries out. And the reader has a certain amount of control over how the browser does this, telling it not to load images, what font or colour scheme to use, what size the text should be and, most obviously, controlling the size and shape of the browser window it all has to fit into. The reason for this flexibility is that those who view a web page will be using a wide variety of different computer equipment, with a range of screen sizes and resolutions and no guarantee that particular fonts will be available, or even that the reader has a full colour display. Also, readers will be using a range of different web browsers. The web page designer has to create a page that will look good, or at least be readable for all these users.

Figure 17.2 shows the text for a very simple web page. Figure 17.3 shows what this page looks like when displayed in a browser.

The angled brackets mark the 'tags' which act as instructions to the browser, so the tag <IMG...> tells the browser to insert an image at this point. The tags are collectively referred to as 'markup', because they instruct the browser what to do with the text in the same way that an editor marks up a manuscript for typesetting. All the text that is not inside angled brackets appears on the page, but the tags themselves do not. Many of the tags work in pairs, for example the tags <EM>...</EM> tell the browser to find a way to emphasise the enclosed text, which is usually done with italics. Links to other web sites and other pages on your own site are created by putting the tag <A HREF="site-or-file-name">...</A>

```
<HTML>
<HEAD>
<TITLE>This appears at the top of the browser window</TITLE>
</HEAD>
<BODY>
<H1>Here's the main heading</H1>
<P>Here's a very brief paragraph
of text with <STRONG>bold</STRONG> and <EM>italics</EM>.</P>
<P><IMG SRC="tree.gif">Here's another paragraph with an image at
the start of it.
</P>
<P>Here's a link to the
<A HREF="http://www.nationarchives.gov.uk/">National Archives</A>
web site.</P>
</BODY>
</HTML>
```

Figure 17.2 The text file for a simple web page

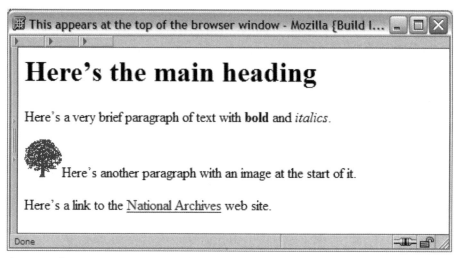

Figure 17.3 The page in Figure 17.2 viewed in a browser

round the hotspot, i.e. the text you want the reader to click on, with the web address or file name between the inverted commas ('A' stands for 'Anchor').

You can get a good idea of how this works by saving a copy of the page shown in Figure 17.3 from <**www.spub.co.uk/tgi2/dummypage.html**> and then editing it in Notepad to see what happens if you move or delete tags. (Do not try it with a word processor!)

The set of tags that can be used to create web pages is specified in a standard called Hypertext Markup Language (HTML). The standard is controlled by the World Wide Web Consortium (W3C) <**www.w3.org**> on the basis of extensive consultation with those who have an interest in the technology of the Web. HTML has been through several versions since its inception in 1991, and the latest is version 4, which came into use at the beginning of 1998. You may be accustomed to the fact that documents created by more recent programs often cannot be read by previous versions. With web pages, however, an older browser, released before HTML 4.0, will simply ignore tags it does not understand, which is unlikely to cause any problems for web pages consisting mainly of text. There will not be another version of HTML, since the next development on the web is XML (eXtensible Markup Language), but HTML pages will remain readable and will not become obsolete.

Software

In order to create your web site you will need suitable software, and there is quite a range of possibilities. Which is best depends on what software you have already got, what your web site is to contain and how serious you are about your site. One thing to remember is that no matter what software you use, the output is always a plain text file. It is not a file in a proprietary format belonging to a single manufacturer, which is what makes exchanging files between different word processors so problematic. This means you can use a variety of software programs to edit a single page.

Another important point is that you almost certainly do not need to buy additional software – you may well already have some web publishing tools installed on your computer, and if not there are free programs which will provide all the facilities you need.

There are three basic approaches to creating web pages:

- You can create them 'by hand', i.e. by typing in the tags yourself using a text editor.
- You can use a program which works like a word processor but automatically converts the page layout into the appropriate text and tags.
- You can use a program which automatically generates pages from a set of data.

The following sections look at the sorts of software that can be used to create web pages.

Editors

In the early days of the Web there was no special-purpose software designed for creating sites, and commercial software had no facilities for turning material into web pages. The only way to create a site was with a text editor, typing in both the text of a page and the HTML tags. The surprising thing is that, in spite of the many pieces of software that are now able to create web pages, text editors are still in use among professional web authors. The reason is that these give you complete control and do not make decisions for you. The disadvantage, of course, is that you will need to know what the relevant tags are and how to use them. But even if you mainly use another program to create your web pages, a text editor can still be useful. This is particularly the case where you have been using a program that is not designed specifically for web authoring, but has the facility to save files in HTML format as an add-on. All such programs have *some* failings in their web page output. If you need to correct these, it is easiest to use a text editor.

Although you can use a very basic text editor like the Windows Notepad, you will find it is hard work to create web pages with something so primitive, and it is better to use a more sophisticated editor. Some, like TextPad or NoteTab (downloadable from <**www.textpad.com**> and <**www. notetab.com**> respectively), even though designed as general-purpose text editors, offer a number of features to make web authoring easier. TextPad, for example, allows you to have many documents open at once, and has a comprehensive search and replace function covering all open documents. It has a 'clip library' of the main HTML tags – just clicking on an entry in the library adds the tags to your page (see Figure 17.4).

Word processors

Assuming you have got a reasonably recent version of one of the main word processors, you will be able to use that to create web pages – see if there is a web or HTML option on the **File** menu. This way of creating pages is particularly useful if you already have material typed up, because you will be able to turn it into web pages very easily. But note that this will not create a web page for each *page* of your word-processed document, it will turn each *document* into a single web page. Once you have saved a page (and thereby given it a file name) you will able to make links to it from other pages.

You might think that with this sort of facility there is no real need for other web authoring software but, unfortunately, word processors are not particularly good at producing web pages that will read well on the wide variety of set-ups internet users have. In particular, they often try to reproduce precisely every nuance of the word-processed document, which, since the layout facilities of HTML are strictly limited, can lead to very cumbersome web pages that may download slowly. However, for text-only pages with a straightforward layout, this is a very quick way to get material on to the Web.

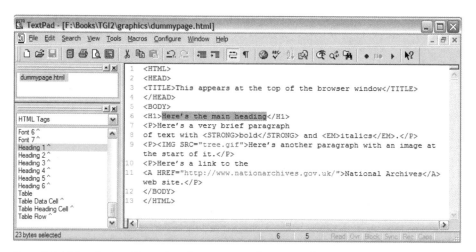

Figure 17.4 Web authoring with an editor: the <H1> tags in the main window were inserted *around* the text simply by selecting the text and then clicking on Heading 1 in the left-hand panel.

Desktop publishing

If you have desktop publishing software such as QuarkXPress or Microsoft Publisher, you might think these would be useful for creating web sites, since they offer much more sophisticated page layout. Unfortunately, web pages created by these programs are often poor for readers, since they try to reproduce *exactly* what would appear on a printed page. This is quite misguided: on the Web, the page designer has no control over the size and shape of the browser window, the absolute sizes of fonts, etc. Pages created by programs like these can be full of problems for readers that a novice web author is unlikely to be able to deal with, even if the hassle were worthwhile.

Dedicated web authoring software

A better all-round option is a piece of dedicated web authoring software. This will provide *only* the layout facilities that are available in HTML. Many such packages offer both a design/layout mode, which looks like a word processor, and a text editing mode which allows you to work directly with tags. Currently, the most highly regarded commercial program is Macromedia Dreamweaver (see Figure 17.5). Unfortunately, the cost of this program would be difficult to justify for a small personal web site,

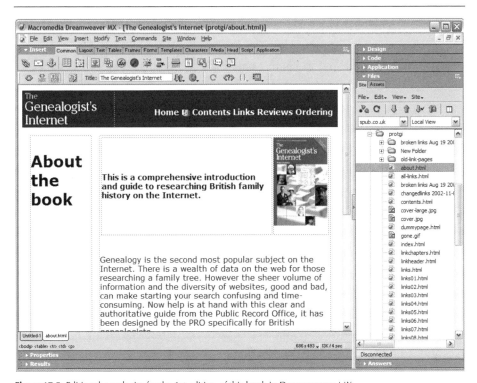

Figure 17.5 Editing the web site for the 1st edition of this book in Dreamweaver MX

though a trial version can be downloaded from the Macromedia web site at <www.macromedia.com>, and there are substantial discounts for educational users.

If you are only going to create a fairly simple site, you do not need to pay for a commercial web authoring package, as there are a number of free options.

Netscape Composer

is a built-in web editor that comes with Netscape Navigator (to be found on the 'Communicator' menu). This does not have anything like the facilities of Dreamweaver, but it has all you need for doing straightforward pages. It works as a WYSIWYG ('what you see is what you get') editor, with all the main HTML functions available from toolbars and menus. You can view the HTML code but you cannot edit at the text level within Composer, though there is nothing to stop you loading the text into NotePad and viewing both on the screen at once. Netscape can be downloaded free of charge from <www.netscape.com> and is often found on computer magazine CD-ROMs.

EvrSoft's FirstPage

can be downloaded free from <www.evrsoft.com>. It is particularly good for those new to web authoring, as long as you don't mind working with tags, as it has Easy, Normal, Expert and Hardcore modes, with more and more complex features available as you progress. Although there is no WYSIWYG editing, there is a preview window which can show you immediately the effect of adding to the page (see Figure 17.6).

FrontPage Express

is a cut-down version of Microsoft's web authoring package FrontPage, included with versions 4 and 5 of Internet Explorer. This was considerably simpler to use than the full commercial version, but rather more flexible than Composer. Unfortunately, since version 5.5 it is no longer included in Explorer or available free from the Microsoft web site, but you may still be able to locate a copy on-line – go to the FrontPage Express Resources Center at <www.accessfp.net/fpexpress.htm> or do a web search for ["FrontPage Express" download]. Some ISPs still have older versions of Internet Explorer in their file download areas, but you should be very wary of installing these on a computer with a later version.

Trial versions of web authoring packages are frequently to be found on the cover CD-ROMs of computer magazines such as *PC-Pro* and *Internet Magazine*, and many other shareware packages are available for free downloading. The best place to look is Tucows, which has a wide selection of web authoring software under 'Web Building Tools' at <tucows. mirror.ac.uk/internet.html>.

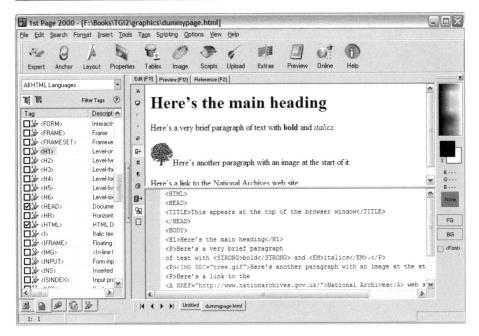

Figure 17.6 Editing with FirstPage. In some ways this is quite similar to an editor like TextPad, but note the preview panel which shows what the page looks like as well as the actual HTML below, and the colour palette at the right.

On-line software

Some free web space providers have on-line tools for creating web sites directly on the site without having to upload it from your own computer. Obviously, this will not help you convert your family tree for on-line viewing, but it is a quick way to get a web site up and running. Some of the providers offering this facility are:

- Freeservers <www.freeservers.com>
- Homestead <www.homestead.co.uk>
- Tripod <www.tripod.lycos.co.uk>
- Yahoo! GeoCities <geocities.yahoo.com>.

Databases and spreadsheets

If you store some of your genealogical information in a spreadsheet or database, there are several ways of putting the data on a web site.

First, most recent database software can create web pages directly (probably via a **File | Export** menu or a **File | Save As** menu option). By way of example, Figure 17.7 shows data from my Microsoft Access database of Sussex births for the surname Christian extracted from the GRO indexes. This was created with the 'autoformatting' option in Access, which gives labels for each column, and in the same font as the original data. Of course, since this page has been created in HTML format, it can be opened in any web authoring package for further editing.

A second option, which may be useful if you have an older database with no HTML facilities, is to use your word processor's mailmerge function to create a document that extracts data from the database. You can then use your word processor's HTML output function.

Finally, if neither of these options are available, there is a last resort: plain text. Your database or spreadsheet will undoubtedly have a **Save as text** function, and all browsers can display plain text files. This will not look as good as the examples above, but if someone finds an ancestor in your list, that will be the last thing they will be worried about. Figure 17.8 shows how this looks in a browser.

You can even take this text file and embed it in a proper web page. There is a special pair of tags, `<PRE>...</PRE>` (for *pre*formatted) which, when put round formatted text like this, will preserve all the line breaks and the multiple spaces, thus maintaining the original format.

In an ideal world, all of this would be unnecessary. You would simply upload the database file to your web site and people could use their browser to search it, just as you do on your desktop. There are in fact ways of doing this, but it's not something that can easily be set up without some database and programming skills. Also, it requires special software on the web server, which you will not often find with free web space providers or with non-corporate ISP accounts, though these facilities are becoming more widely available.

GRO - Sussex Births

Event	District	Year	Quarter	Forename	Surname	Volume	Page	Notes
B	Battle	1839	3	John	CHRISTIAN	7	154	
B	Hastings	1839	3	Mary Ann	CHRISTIAN	7	210	
B	Hastings	1840	4	female	CHRISTIAN	7	255	
B	Brighton	1841	1	Sarah	CHRISTIAN	7	198	
B	Battle	1847	3	Thomas	CHRISTIAN	7	183	
B	Hastings	1850	1	Mary Ann	CHRISTIAN	7	303	
B	Hastings	1850	2	Mary Jane	CHRISTIAN	7	242	
B	Battle	1851	1	Philly	CHRISTIAN	7	203	
B	Hastings	1851	1	William	CHRISTIAN	7	295	
B	Battle	1852	2	Elizabeth Emma	CHRISTIAN	2b	30	
B	Hastings	1852	4	Emily	CHRISTIAN	2b	0	page no unclear
B	Brighton	1854	2	Emma Augusta	CHRISTIAN	2b	187	
B	Battle	1854	3	Matilda	CHRISTIAN	2b	34	

Figure 17.7 A web page exported from Microsoft Access with 'autoformatting'.

```
B1839   3   John              CHRISTIAN        Battle
B1839   3   Mary Ann          CHRISTIAN        Hastings
B1840   4   female            CHRISTIAN        Hastings
B1841   1   Sarah             CHRISTIAN        Brighton
B1847   3   Thomas            CHRISTIAN        Battle
B1850   1   Mary Ann          CHRISTIAN        Hastings
B1850   2   Mary Jane         CHRISTIAN        Hastings
B1851   1   Philly            CHRISTIAN        Battle
B1851   1   William           CHRISTIAN        Hastings
B1852   2   Elizabeth Emma    CHRISTIAN        Battle
B1852   4   Emily             CHRISTIAN        Hastings
B1854   2   Emma Augusta      CHRISTIAN        Brighton
B1854   3   Matilda           CHRISTIAN        Battle
```

Figure 17.8 Plain text from a database

Adobe Acrobat

All the software mentioned so far creates pages in HTML. But in fact browsers can cope with files in other formats, either by starting up the relevant application or by using a 'plug-in', an add-on component to display a particular file type.

Adobe Acrobat is a program that can turn any page designed for printing into a document for the Web. It does this not by creating a page in HTML, but using a proprietary file format ('PDF', which stands for 'portable document format') for which a free reader is available. This can be used as a plug-in by any browser, allowing PDF files to displayed in the browser window when they are encountered. (If you have not already got it installed, the Adobe Acrobat reader can be downloaded free of charge from <**www.adobe.com**>.)

This is not a complete answer to creating a genealogy web site – a site consisting solely of PDF files would be very cumbersome, since the files are much larger than plain HTML files and would download slowly. But it is a good way to make existing material that you already have in word-processor files quickly available. It is particularly good for longish documents which people will want to save to disk or print out rather than read on screen. (Web pages do not always print well.) For example, if you want to put on-line one of the longer reports that your genealogy database can create, turning this into a PDF file would be a good way to do it. Figure 17.9 shows an Ahnentafel report from Personal Ancestral File turned into a PDF file – you can view the whole file at <**www.spub.co.uk/tgi2/fwm.pdf**>. This can also be a good solution for putting trees on-line.

Adobe's own software for creating PDF files is a commercial product costing over £200, an expense it would be hard to justify for a personal web site. But there are a number of shareware and freeware programs available which can be used to create PDF files. Though they lack the more

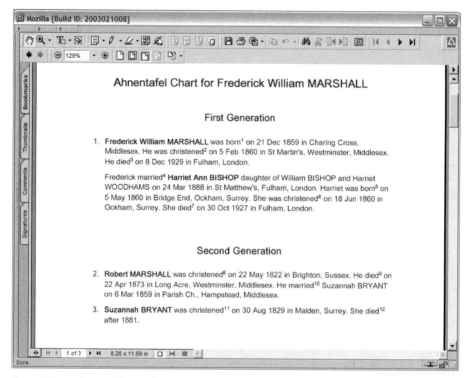

Figure 17.9 An Ahnenetafel report from Personal Ancestral File in PDF format

sophisticated document management features of Adobe Acrobat itself, they will be perfectly adequate for turning word-processor documents into web pages. You can find a list and downloads at <**tucows.mirror.ac.uk/ mmedia/pdf95_default.html**>. Dick Eastman's newsletters of 25th February and 7th October 2002 have articles on creating PDF files, which explain the process and look at two of the converters – see <**www.eogn.com/archives/ news0208.htm**> and <**www.eogn.com/archives/news0240.htm**>.

Web site design

Although there is a great deal of material, both in print and on-line, about web site design, for someone publishing family history on the Web a few basic principles should suffice. What is important is to work out what the overall structure of your site will be (which other pages is each page going to link to?), and to do so *before* you start creating actual pages. There are also a few technical matters, such as file-naming conventions and file formats for graphics (see below).

There is no single right way to design a web site. It depends on what it contains and who it is aimed at. For a personal genealogy site, your main visitors will be other genealogists looking for information on individuals and surnames that might be part of their own ancestry. If you have expertise in a particular area of genealogy, or have collected useful material on a particular topic, people may come looking for general background information. Your main job, then, is to make sure visitors to your site can see whether you have anything useful to them and can access it easily. While it is better, of course, if your site looks good, you should not be worrying about state-of-the-art graphic design, special effects, animation, background music, hit counters or any of the other things that amateur web authors seem to find irresistible, but which irritate or distract readers and make pages slower to download.

Filenames

It is usual to give files for web pages names ending in .html. If you call a file *index.html* or *index.htm* it will be loaded by default, i.e. if the URL you have entered in your browser does not specify a particular file. For example, when you go to Genuki's home page at <**www.genuki.org.uk**> you get exactly the same page as when you enter <**www.genuki.org.uk/index.html**> – in the first instance, the server delivers *index.html* because you have not asked for any specific file. (The filenames *default.html* or *default.htm* are used instead on some servers, such as the National Archives' – try <**www.nationalarchives.gov.uk/default.htm**>). This means your home page should always be called *index.html* and be placed in the main folder in your web space.

On almost all web servers filenames are case sensitive: *index.html*, *Index.html* and *INDEX.HTML* are different files. To save confusion stick to lower case.

Graphics

Web browsers can display graphics in three of the many graphics formats: GIF, JPEG and PNG, of which the last is not widely used. For colour photographs you need to use JPEG as it allows graphics with up to 16.7 million colours and is therefore capable of displaying subtle variations in tone. (JPEG files have the file extension .jpg on the PC). The GIF format, which allows a maximum of 256 colours, is poor for colour photographs but good for black and white photographs, as well as for navigation buttons, logos, maps and the like, which have simple colour schemes. You can compare the strengths and weaknesses of these two formats by looking at the examples at <**www.spub.co.uk/wpg/figures/figure10.html**>.

If you are going to use graphics extensively, you will need a basic graphics editing program such as Photoshop Elements or PaintShop Pro. If you just need to crop images and convert them to GIF or JPEG format, there are freeware or inexpensive shareware tools that will do the job – look under 'Image Tools' at Tucows <**www.tucows.com/mmedia.html**> or try the cover CDs of computer magazines.

Each graphic is kept as an individual file on the web server, and any page which uses it has a tag which contains the file name. If you have downloaded *dummypage.html* to your own computer, it will not display the tree unless you also download the file *tree.gif* into the same folder, so that when the browser attempts to interpret the tag `<IMG SRC="tree.gif">` it can find the file.

You can use the same graphic on many different pages, so if you have a graphic such as a logo which appears on every page on your site, you only need to put one copy of the file on the server.

Adding your family tree

If you are designing your own site you will need to know how to include the pages showing the family tree you have created from your genealogy database software. Whatever software you use for your genealogy, it will almost certainly create a new folder on your hard disk and put all the created files in it, perhaps in a number of sub-folders.

You need to upload this new folder and all the files it contains on to your web site (see 'Uploading your web site', below), retaining the filenames and folder structure. If you change filenames or move files you will find that some parts of the tree do not link correctly.

From your home page you will need a link to the index file in the family tree folder. So suppose you have called the folder *johnson* because it contains your Johnson family tree, you would have a link

```
<A HREF="johnson">Johnson family tree</A>
```

on your home page. If you find this does not work, you may need to specify the exact filename of the index file (this should be fairly obvious if you look at the filenames in the family tree folder), for example:

```
<A HREF="johnson/default.htm">Johnson family tree</A>
```

When you are creating a web tree with your genealogy software, it is always worth checking for an option to make filenames lower case. There are other reasons for giving the exact filename, discussed on p. 260.

Design tips

The Web is a good source of advice about the design of web pages. Here are the most important points:

- Have a home page which tells visitors what they will find on the site, and provide links to the main areas of your site.
- Give each page a helpful title and heading, so that if someone bookmarks it, or comes to it directly via a link from another site (perhaps a search engine), they can immediately see what the page is about.

- Conversely, make sure that every page has a link back to the home page or some other higher level page, so that if someone comes to your site from a search engine they can get to other pages.
- Don't make your pages too long, and don't include large or unnecessary graphics, as this will only increase the time it takes your pages to download, and potential visitors will be put off.
- Don't use unusual colour schemes. They are unusual for a good reason – they make text unreadable.
- Don't put light text on a dark background – this can make it impossible to print out from some browsers.
- Put your e-mail address on the site so that people can contact you.

For further advice, look at Webmonkey <hotwired.lycos.com/webmonkey/design/> or the 'Design Tips' area of Usable Web at <usableweb.com>.

Uploading your web site

Once you have created a set of pages on your own computer, you need to go on-line and upload them to your web space. The standard way of doing this is to use a program called an FTP client. FTP stands for File Transfer Protocol, which is a long-established method for transferring files on the internet. There are many free and shareware FTP programs available from software archives like Tucows at <**tucows.mirror.ac.uk**>. CuteFTP and WS-FTP are among the most popular.

1. Before you connect to the internet to upload, you will want to set up an entry for your web site in your FTP client's list of sites. You need to enter:
   - The address of the site. If you are not certain what it is, your ISP/web space provider will be able to tell you, and their help pages will probably provide detailed instructions for uploading files.
   - Your username and password for that site.
   - You should be able to enter the location of the folder containing your web site, though you will also be able to select a particular folder once you are connected.
2. Next connect to the internet. Once you are logged in, you should see something like Figure 17.10, where I am preparing to upload a family tree to the genealogy folder on my personal web site.
3. To upload your files, simply drag the icons for the files to be uploaded across to the right-hand panel. If you drag a folder icon, all the files in that folder will be included in the upload.
4. Finally, start your browser and type in the URL of your site to check it. You can see the results of the upload in Figure 17.10 at <homepages.gold.ac.uk/peter/genealogy/sealey/>.

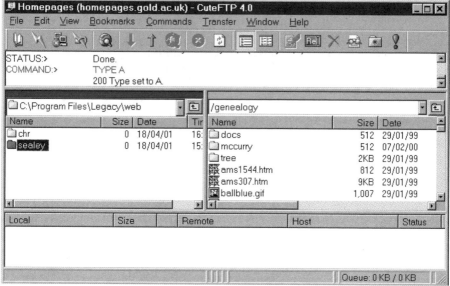

Figure 17.10 Using FTP to upload files to a web site

Web browsers can also be used to transfer files – see the on-line help in your browser for details of how to do this.

Publicity

Once you have created and uploaded your web pages, you will need to publicise the existence of your site. One simple way to do this is to put its URL in the signature attached to your e-mail messages. Apart from that, there are three main ways of approaching this:

- submitting the site to search engines
- notifying people via mailing lists and newsgroups
- asking others to provide links to your site.

Search engines

Making sure your site is known to the main search engines is probably the most effective way to publicise your web site. Since search engines index pages automatically, they have no way of knowing what the most important aspects of your site and your individual pages are unless you help them by organising the material on each page. Among the things search engines look for when estimating the relevance of a page to a search done by a user are:

- words appearing in the page title and between heading tags
- the initial section of text
- words which appear frequently in the page.

In addition, there are special tags you can add to a page to provide a brief description of the page and the site. These are <META> tags, which are placed in the <HEAD> section of the page. They will not be visible to someone reading your page, but they are used by search engines.

```
<META NAME="description" CONTENT="The last will and
testament of Zebediah Poot, died 1687, Wombourn,
Staffordshire, England">
```

When a search engine lists this page in the results of a search, it will normally list its title (i.e. the text between the <TITLE> tags) and your description. If there is no description, it will take the first couple of lines of text from the <BODY> of the page.

You may see reference to a "keywords" <META> tag, but this is of limited usefulness as it seems that search engines do not now make use of it in indexing.

Mailing lists and newsgroups

A good way to draw attention to a new site is to post a message to appropriate mailing lists and newsgroups. You might think it is a good idea to post to every one you possibly can, to get maximum publicity, but there is little point in posting details of a Yorkshire web site to a Cornish list. Choose the county lists relevant to the material you are putting on the Web, and any special interest lists. It will be worth notifying the soc.genealogy.britain newsgroup (the GENBRIT mailing list). There is also a special mailing list, NEW-GEN-URL, for publicising new web sites. If there is a mailing list relating to some social group your ancestors belonged to it will be worth notifying that list, so if you have information on coalmining ancestors on your site, for example, it would be worth posting to the COALMINERS list (see Chapter 15).

Requesting links

You can request other people to link to your pages, but you need to be realistic about expecting links from other personal sites. People will generally only do this if there is some connection in subject matter between your site and theirs, and if you are prepared to create a link to their site in return. Do not expect major institutions like the National Archives or the SoG to link to a site with purely personal material, just because you have made a link to theirs.

If your site has material relating to a particular subject, it will be well worth contacting the maintainers of specialist web sites relating to that subject, such as those discussed in Chapters 11–13.

If you have transcriptions of original source material of broader interest than extracts for individual surnames you should contact Genuki, who attempt to provide links to all UK source material on-line.

News

A number of genealogy newsletters will give a mention to personal web sites if you mail the editor (see Chapter 18, p. 264). If you have a web site which contains material of sufficiently general interest, i.e. not just your personal pedigree, you may also be able to get a mention in the 'Computer Intelligence' section of *Family Tree Magazine*.

Preserving your family history

While the Web is seen as a way of publishing your family history, in one important respect it is not like publishing it in print. A printed family history donated to a genealogy library will be preserved for ever, while your account with your web space provider is doomed to expire when you do, unless you can persuade your heirs otherwise.

But since a web site is just a collection of files, there is no reason why all the information cannot be preserved, even if not on-line. If you copy all the files that constitute your site onto writeable CDs, these can be sent to relatives and deposited in archives just like printed material. The advantage of distributing your material in this way is that people do not need special software – a particular word processor or the same genealogy database as you – in order to view the files, and everyone with a computer has access to a web browser. HTML is a universal, non-proprietary standard which uses plain-text files, and is therefore much more future-proof than the file formats used by most current software.

If you are intending to do this you should make sure that every link gives a specific filename, as mentioned in 'Filenames' on p. 255. A web server knows to deliver a file called *index.html* if a link doesn't specify a filename; a stand-alone computer doesn't.

Further information

Obviously, this chapter has not been able to cover all you need to know about web authoring, but there is plenty of information available in books and on the Web.

A search on <www.amazon.co.uk> for 'HTML' or 'web publishing' will list the hundreds of general books on the subject, though it's probably best to browse in a physical bookshop to make sure you choose a book at the right technical level. I know of only two books devoted specifically to publishing genealogical information on the Web:

- Peter Christian, *Web Publishing for Genealogy*, 2nd edn (David Hawgood, 1999). There is also a US edition published by the Genealogical Publishing Co. (2000). The web site for the book, at <**www.spub.co.uk/wpg/**>, has links to the web pages for web authoring software, genealogy software companies and GEDCOM converters, and to tutorial materials on the Web.
- Richard S. Wilson, *Publishing Your Family History on the Internet* (Writers Digest Books, 1999) <**www.compuology.com/book2.htm**>.

An excellent overview of genealogical web publishing with links to relevant software and tutorial materials is Cyndi's 'Genealogy Home Page Construction Kit' at <**www.cyndislist.com/construc.htm**> and Cyndi Howells has a book on this subject, *Planting Your Family Tree Online: How to Create Your Own Family History Website*, due for publication in November 2003. The archive of Dick Eastman's newsletter (see p. 264) has a number of articles about creating a web site for your genealogy.

Computers in Genealogy and *Genealogical Computing* are specialist genealogy magazines which regularly carry articles on web publishing. In the case of *CiG* some of the articles are available on-line at <**www.sog.org.uk/cig/**>.

For links to some of the many on-line resources relating to web design in general, see <**www.spub.co.uk/wpg/reference.html**>.

18 The World of Family History

Previous chapters have looked at ways of using the internet in direct connection with your own pedigree. This chapter looks at the 'non-virtual' world of family history which exists off-line, and how you can use the internet to find out about it.

Societies and organisations

National bodies

There are a number of national genealogical bodies, all of which have web sites:

- The Society of Genealogists (SoG) <www.sog.org.uk>
- The Institute of Heraldic and Genealogical Studies (IHGS) <www.ihgs.ac.uk>
- Federation of Family History Societies (FFHS) <www.ffhs.org.uk>
- The Guild of One-Name Studies (GOONS) <www.one-name.org>
- Scottish Genealogy Society <www.scotsgenealogy.com>
- Scottish Association of Family History Societies (SAFHS) <www.safhs.org.uk>
- Association of Family History Societies of Wales <www.rootsweb.com/~wlsafhs/>.

Family history societies

There are around 200 local family history societies in the UK and Ireland, the overwhelming majority of which have web sites. Most of these societies are members of one or more of the three national federations/associations listed above (which are themselves umbrella organisations, not family history societies in their own right). The FFHS includes many member societies from Wales and Ireland, and most English societies are Federation members.

The definitive starting point for finding FHS web sites is Genuki's 'Family History and Genealogy Societies' page at <www.genuki.org.uk/Societies/>. This lists the national societies and has links to separate pages for the constituent nations of the British Isles, where details of local societies are to be found.

The individual FHS web sites vary greatly in what they offer, but all will have contact details and usually a list of publications. Most do not have their own on-line shops, but about 60 of them have an on-line 'stand' at Family History Books, the FFHS on-line shop at <**www.ffhs.co.uk**>.

For genealogical data from family history societies, look at the FamilyHistoryOnline site at <**www.familyhistoryonline.net**> described in detail on p. 37.

Events

There is a wide range of genealogical meetings, lectures, conferences and fairs in the UK, from the individual meetings of family history societies to major national events such as the SoG's annual Family History Fair. One of the easiest ways to find out about such events is via the Web.

The major source for the whole of the UK is the Geneva page (the Genuki calendar of GENealogical EVents and Activities) at <**users.ox.ac. uk/~malcolm/genuki/geneva/**>, run by Malcolm Austen on behalf of Genuki and the FFHS. This lists events from the SoG's programme, any family history society events submitted and the regional family history fairs regularly held around the country. The 'Genuki UK Family History News' newsletter (see pp. 264–5) also regularly lists forthcoming events. The National Archives' programme of events, many of which are of interest to genealogists, can be found on-line at <**www.pro.gov.uk/events/**>.

Quite a few societies have computer groups which organise lectures on internet-related topics, details of which can be found on their web sites. The SoG offers a substantial programme of IT-related events, many of which cover the use of the internet for genealogy. It organises an annual one-day genealogical computing conference in association with a local family history society, and holds two one-day events each year devoted to internet genealogy. Details of all these will be found on the Society's web site at <**www.sog.org.uk/events/calendar.html**>.

Print magazines and journals

Many genealogical publications have a related web site, with at least a list of contents for the current issue and in some cases material from back issues.

The web site of *Family Tree Magazine* can be found at <**www.family-tree.co.uk**>, while its sister publication, *Practical Family History*, has a page on the same site at <**www.family-tree.co.uk/sister.htm**>. Each lists the contents of the current issue. There is an on-line list of contents for the IHGS's journal, *Family History,* at <**www.family-history.org**>. *Family History Monthly* does not have a web site at the time of writing.

The National Archives' *Ancestors* magazine has a web site at <**www.ancestorsmagazine.co.uk**>, which includes extracts from the articles in each issue. There is a regular internet news section and articles about on-line genealogy. The *Ancestors* web site includes a subject index to all issues, and there is a list of the internet topics covered in each issue at <www.spub.co.uk/ancestors.html>.

The SoG's web site has a subject and name index to the *Genealogists' Magazine* at <www.sog.org.uk/genmag/>. The Society's computer magazine, *Computers in Genealogy*, has a web site at <www.sog.org.uk/cig/> with lists of contents and synopses of articles. A number of the articles are also available on the site.

While *Computers in Genealogy* is the only UK computer genealogy journal, a number of others which cover on-line genealogy are published in English-speaking countries. Foremost among these is *Genealogical Computing*, a US journal published quarterly by Ancestry.com, which covers 'how to use your computer, the Net, and other tools like scanners, printers, digital cameras, palm pilots' in genealogy. It also carries reviews of software, data collections and new computer hardware of interest to the family historian. Details can be found in the Ancestry.com on-line bookshop at <shops.ancestry.com>. Copies are available at the SoG and other major genealogical libraries.

The bimonthly magazine *Local History* has a web site at <www.local-history.co.uk>, with an index to the contents of past issues at <www.local-history.co.uk/Issues/>, as well as the usual listing for the latest issue. The site also provides links to other local history resources on the Web.

The most comprehensive on-line listing is the 'Magazines, Journals, Columns & Newsletters' page on Cyndi's List at <www.cyndislist.com/magazine.htm>. Subtitled 'Print & Electronic Publications for Genealogy', this page provides links to web sites for many print magazines, though many of course will be of interest only to those with North American ancestry.

PERSI, the Periodical Source Index, at <www.ancestry.com/search/rectype/periodicals/persi/main.htm> is a subscription database at Ancestry.com containing 'a comprehensive subject index to genealogy and local history periodicals written in English and French (Canada) since 1800'.

For sites relating to non-genealogical publications, see 'Newspapers' on p. 86.

On-line publications

As well as print publications there are, of course, on-line columns and newsletters for genealogists. Links to these will be found on Cyndi's List at <www.cyndislist.com/magazine.htm>. The majority of these are US-based, so are not of relevance to UK genealogists where they deal with genealogical records, but many have useful material on general genealogical topics, including using the internet.

For the UK, there is the 'Genuki UK Family History News' e-mail newsletter, edited by Rob Thompson and published three or four times a month. This carries details of new genealogy books and CD-ROMs, forthcoming events and new material on Genuki. It is the only on-line publication in the UK to carry regular web site reviews, and that alone makes it worth subscribing to. To subscribe send a message containing only the word subscribe to UK-FAMILYHISTORYNEWS-L-request@ Rootsweb.com. Full details and links to past issues will be found at <www.genuki.org.uk/news/>.

It is impossible here to give an overview of all the US publications, but a good place to start is Ancestry.com, which hosts a number of weekly columns, all accessible from <www.ancestry.com/learn/library/ columnists/main.htm>. Of these, Drew Smith's 'Digital genealogy' and Elizabeth Kelley Kerstens' 'GC extra' are particularly recommended for material on the use of computers and the internet in genealogy.

Probably the best known of these columns to UK genealogists is Dick Eastman's weekly Online Genealogy Newsletter, which originated on the Genealogy Forum in CompuServe, long before CompuServe was part of the internet. It carries details of new genealogy software and CD-ROMs, genealogical developments on the internet, new web sites and more. Although the main focus is on genealogy and IT, it is not exclusively so. Dick has many contacts in the UK, and regularly includes items of genealogy news from Britain.

There are two versions of the newsletter. The Standard Edition is available free of charge and you can read the articles on-line at <**www.eogn. com**>. The Plus Edition is only available by paying a subscription of $3 for three months or $10 for a year. It contains all the articles in the Standard Edition with the addition of one or two extra items each week – the titles of these articles are included in the Standard Edition so you can see what else is being covered. For the Standard Edition you can sign up to receive an e-mail when it is published; the Plus Edition is e-mailed to you. There is also a discussion board where you can discuss individual articles and general IT topics with Dick and other readers. You can subscribe to the e-mail version of the newsletter from <**www.eogn.com/plus/**>. All issues back to the very first in January 1996 can be searched by keyword from <www.eogn.com/search/>, while there is also a browsable archive of newsletters up to October 2002 at <**www.ancestry.com/library/view/ columns/eastman/eastman.asp**>.

There are a few specialist mailing lists which are used to disseminate news. As mentioned on p. 187, John Fuller's NEW-GENLIST mailing list will keep you up to date with new genealogy mailing lists, while NEW-GEN-URL allows people to publicise new genealogy web sites. Subscription details for all these lists will be found at <**www.rootsweb.com/~jfuller/ gen_mail_computing.html**>. The CyndisList mailing list announces additions to Cyndi's List (see <**www.cyndislist.com/maillist.htm**>).

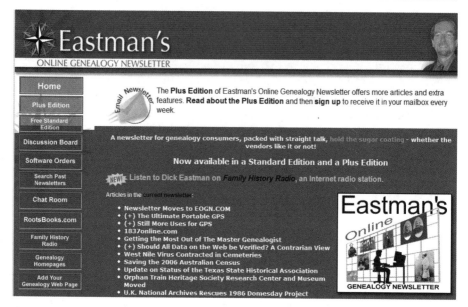

Figure 18.1 Dick Eastman's Online Genealogy Newsletter

History in Focus is an on-line history magazine at <ihr.sas.ac.uk/ihr/ Focus/> (note the upper-case *F*) published by the Institute of Historical Research in London. It takes a thematic approach to history, with each issue designed to 'provide an introduction to the chosen topic and to help stimulate interest and debate – the series will concentrate on highlighting books, reviews, web sites and conferences that relate to the theme'. Although the material derives from recent academic research, and genealogists are not the target readership, many issues contain items relating to social history that are likely to interest the family historians.

Many of the major organisations and data services mentioned in this book have electronic newsletters designed to keep you informed of developments – the National Archives, the FFHS, Scotlandspeople and Origins, to name just a few. There will normally be a link to information about such newsletters on the home page of a site.

Software

The Web is an excellent source of information about genealogical software, since all the major software companies, and many individual software authors, have web sites providing details of their products. Genealogy shareware can be downloaded from the sites, and even for normal commercial products there will often be a trial or demo version available for download.

It is not possible here to provide a guide to genealogy software, but there are a number of useful resources on the Web to point you in the right direction.

A very comprehensive listing is the one on Cyndi's List at <www.cyndislist.com/software.htm>. George Archer has a 'Guide to Online Searching for Genealogical Software' at <wdn.com/~garcher/gsguide.txt> and a listing of 'All Known Genealogy Software Programs in the World' downloadable from <wdn.com/~garcher/allgen.zip>.

With so many software packages available, deciding which to buy can be very difficult. There is a useful comparative guide by Bill Mumford at <www.mumford.ca/reportcard/> which scores all the main Windows genealogy programs on a dozen criteria, including data recording, reports, source documentation, multimedia and internet features, etc. The Genealogy Software Springboard at <www.gensoftsb.com> has comprehensive coverage of genealogy software, with a page devoted to each package outlining the main features and links to the producer's web site.

If you are just starting to use a computer for genealogy, it is probably worth downloading one of the three major freeware genealogy database programs for Windows:

- **Personal Ancestral File** (currently at version 5.2) is a program developed by the LDS Church for its own members and made available for free download. It can be downloaded from the FamilySearch site at <www.familysearch.org> – click on **Order/Download Products** on the opening screen. A manual can also be downloaded.
- **Legacy** (currently version 4.0) has been made available as freeware by The Millennia Corporation, and this can be downloaded from <www.legacyfamilytree.com>. This is the Standard Edition, which can be upgraded to the Deluxe Edition for $19.95.
- **Ancestry Family Tree** is a freeware program from Ancestry.com, downloadable from <aft.ancestry.com>. Note that currently you can only download the program with Internet Explorer and not with other browsers.

You need to be aware that these are very substantial downloads (between 5Mb and 13Mb) and could be lengthy if you have a modem rather than broadband connection.

Software retailers are included in the on-line shops discussed below.

On-line shops

There are an increasing number of on-line shops for genealogy books, data and software. Almost all use secure on-line ordering, though some are just on-line lists and orders must be sent by e-mail or post.

The FFHS's on-line shop is at <www.ffhs.co.uk> and sells not only the Federation's own publications, both books and data, but also books from many other publishers. In order to make an on-line purchase your browser needs to download the shopping software, but you can browse the site without doing this. As mentioned on p. 262, the site also includes many 'stands' where the publications of local family history societies can be bought. (These used to be part of GenFair, which merged with the FFHS shop in Spring 2003.)

The IHGS has an on-line shop at <www.ihgs.ac.uk/shop/>. In addition to buying books and software on-line, you can also use the site to book places on the Institute's courses.

The National Archives has an on-line bookshop at <www.pro.gov.uk/bookshop/>, though it deals only with the National Archives' own publications.

The Internet Genealogical Bookshop run by Stuart Raymond has a web site at <www.samjraymond.btinternet.co.uk/igb.htm>. Books must be ordered by e-mail and paid for on receipt of invoice.

Many other bookshops are listed on Cyndi's List at <www.cyndislist.com/books.htm>. For a list of genealogy bookshops in the UK, North America and Australasia, consult Margaret Olson's 'Links to Genealogy Booksellers' at <homepages.rootsweb.com/~socgen/Bookmjo.html>.

If you are searching for second-hand books you will find many book-sellers on-line. Yahoo UK has a substantial list at <uk.dir.yahoo.com/Regional/Countries/United_Kingdom/Business_and_Economy/Shopping_and_Services/Books/Bookstores/Antique__Rare__and_Used/> (note the double underscores around *Rare*). There are also sites, such as UKBookworld at <ukbookworld.com> or Abebooks at <www.abebooks.co.uk>, that will search the catalogues of many individual booksellers. On-line auction sites such as eBay <www.ebay.co.uk> are also very likely to have second-hand books and CD-ROMs of interest to genealogists.

If you are looking for software, then the IHGS bookshop has a selection, while specialist suppliers have a wider range and can offer more detailed advice. The main suppliers of genealogy software in the UK are:

- Back to Roots <www.backtoroots.co.uk>
- S&N Genealogy <www.genealogy.demon.co.uk>
- TWR Computing <www.twrcomputing.co.uk>.

Most genealogical software companies also have on-line ordering facilities.

Finally, the newsgroup soc.genealogy.marketplace carries postings by those selling genealogical products or individuals trying to find a taker for second-hand material.

Secure purchasing

Concern is often expressed about the security of on-line payments, but the reservations are out of all proportion to the actual risks. In fact, on-line transactions are much more secure than handing your credit card to a waiter in a restaurant or ordering over the phone. As long as your browser is using a secure connection, which means that anything you type in is encrypted before being sent across the internet to the supplier, your card details will be infinitely more secure than most of the ways you already use your card.

The clearest indication that the security risks on the internet are low is that the credit card companies themselves are not unduly concerned. Their on-line leaflet 'Card Fraud the Facts 2001' at <**www.apacs.org.uk/downloads/ Card%20Fraud%20the%20Facts%202001.pdf**> says, 'Whether making a transaction at the point-of-sale, through the phone, mail order or internet, card security partly relies upon cardholder vigilance. If cardholders follow some simple guidelines when making internet transactions, it is no different from paying for purchases by phone or mail order. Most internet fraud involves using card details fraudulently obtained in the real world to make card-not-present transactions in the virtual world.'

Official guidance from the Department of Trade and Industry about secure on-line shopping can be found on The Consumer Gateway, which has an 'e-shopping' section on its web site at <**www.consumer.gov.uk/ consumer_web/e-shopping.htm**>.

The only real dangers are that a supplier will subsequently store your credit card details unencrypted on a computer which is then stolen or hacked into (which is just as likely to happen with telephone orders), or that you have bought something from a bogus company. As long as you are dealing with an established supplier, such as those mentioned here, there is no reason to be suspicious of on-line transactions.

Although individual credit card purchases are the most common way of paying for goods and services over the internet, there is an alternative method you may come across. Web-based payment systems like PayPal (<**www.paypal.com**>) and WorldPay (<**www.worldpay.co.uk**> for the UK site) work by giving you an account from which you can then make on-line payments. All your financial transactions are with the payment system itself, which pays other sites on your behalf, so you are only giving your financial details to a single site. This sort of system is particularly good for traders who may not qualify to accept credit card payments, and is much used by on-line auction systems such as eBay, where the participants are private individuals rather than businesses and would not be permitted to accept credit card payments

Service On-line

In fact a more significant problem with on-line suppliers is getting hold of them to deal with problems relating to your order or the product you have bought, particularly if the web site gives no phone number or postal

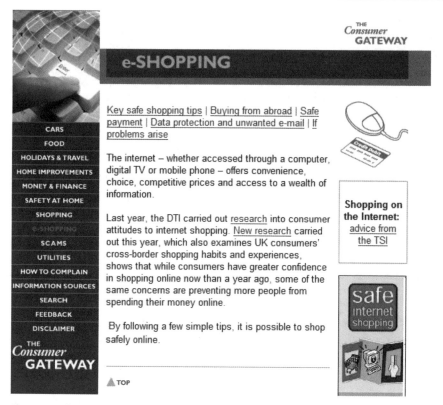

Figure 18.2 The Consumer Gateway's e-shopping page

address. However, on-line traders based in the UK are bound by the same consumer protection legislation as any other trader, and there is a non-profit organisation called TrustUK **<www.trustuk.org.uk>**, endorsed by the Government, which has been set up to promote good practice in on-line trading. The TrustUK web site has a page devoted to 'What to look out for when buying on-line', which offers advice on how to make trouble-free purchases on-line.

TrustUK also approves other schemes for guaranteeing good practice and levels of service in on-line shopping. Any business trading on-line under a TrustUK-approved scheme undertakes to:

- protect your privacy
- ensure that your payments are secure
- help you to make an informed buying decision
- let you know what you have agreed to, and how to cancel orders should you need to
- deliver the goods or services ordered within the agreed time period

- protect children
- sort out any complaints, wherever you live.

Before the advent of the internet, purchasing anything abroad from the comfort of the UK was far from straightforward. On-line shopping has made this much easier and, of course, those who live outside the UK can now easily order materials from British genealogy suppliers. Some practical difficulties remain: returning wrong or faulty products is not made easier by the internet, though of course it is no more difficult than with traditional catalogue-based home shopping.

Also, you are less likely to be familiar with the reputations of overseas traders, which could be a source of concern in areas where UK consumer legislation does not apply – an impressive web site does not guarantee quality of service, let alone financial viability. However, one of the strengths of the internet is that it is a good word-of-mouth medium, and it is very unlikely that there could be an unreliable company whose misdeeds have escaped being reported in the genealogy newsgroups or mailing lists. These are therefore good places to look for reports from other customers on their experiences with companies, or to place a query yourself. For software, the soc.genealogy.computing newsgroup is full of comments, positive and negative, on software products and the companies that supply them. For UK genealogy companies, look at the archives of the soc.genealogy.britain newsgroup for past comments on genealogy suppliers, or post a query yourself.

Professional researchers

There are many reasons, even with the internet, why you might want to employ a professional genealogist to undertake research for you: if you cannot get to the repository where original records are held, whether for reasons of time or distance; or if the records themselves are difficult for the non-specialist to use or interpret.

The SoG has a leaflet 'Employing a professional researcher: a practical guide' on its web site at <**www.sog.org.uk/leaflets/researcher.html**>, while Cyndi's List has a page on 'Professional Researchers, Volunteers & Other Research Services' at <**www.cyndislist.com/profess.htm**>.

The Association of Genealogists and Researchers in Archives (AGRA) is the professional body for genealogical researchers, with a web site at <**www.agra.org.uk**>. This provides a list of members, and an index to this by specialism, whether geographical or subject-based. Many but not all of the Association's members can be contacted by e-mail. The Association's code of practice is also available on the site. Note, however, that this site is very poorly designed – most of the information is presented in large graphic images – and you may find difficulty navigating.

The National Archives' web site also has a database of Independent

Researchers who are prepared to undertake commissions for research in records at the National Archives. The database is accessible from <www.pro.gov.uk/research/irlist/> and can be searched only by subject matter.

For Scotland, the Association of Scottish Genealogists and Record Agents (ASGRA) is the professional association for researchers, and its site at <www.asgra.co.uk> has details of members and their specialisms.

If you have Irish ancestry, the Irish Family History Foundation's network of genealogy centres may be of use. There is a centre for each county, both in the Republic of Ireland and in Northern Ireland, and these hold copies of local material from many of the main sources for Irish genealogy (census, tithe applotments, etc.) as well as transcripts of many parish registers. The centres provide research services using these records. The Foundation's web site at <www.irishroots.net> has links to all the local centres as well as details of services available.

Individual researchers for Ireland can be found on the National Archives of Ireland web site at <www.nationalarchives.ie/gen_researchers.html> and the Association of Professional Genealogists in Ireland at <indigo.ie/~apgi/>.

Lookup services

If all you need is someone to check a particular reference for you, employing a professional researcher will be overkill. The internet makes it easy to find someone with access to particular printed publications, or records on CD-ROM, who will do a simple lookup for you. So-called 'lookup exchanges' give a list of publications and the e-mail address of someone prepared to do searches in each. Most are county-based and there are links to the relevant exchanges from the individual Genuki county pages. The County Lookup Exchange Central at <www.lookupcentral.f9.co.uk/volunteers.html> provides an overall listing.

Since these services are provided entirely on a voluntary basis, requests should be as specific as possible, and you may need to use a specific subject line in your message – see the details at the top of each page before sending a request. And, of course, be reasonable in what you expect someone to do for you in their own time.

19 Issues for On-line Genealogists

While on-line genealogy is essentially about finding and making use of information, it is important to be aware of some general issues involved in using internet resources and in using the Web as a publishing medium. Also important are the limitations in what is and is not likely to be on the internet. The aim of this chapter is to discuss some of these issues.

Good practice

Needless to say, technophobes, Luddites and other folk of a backward-looking disposition are happy to accuse the internet of dumbing down the noble art of genealogy – anything so easy surely cannot be sound research. Loath as I am to agree with technophobes, there is actually some truth in this. Though the medium itself can hardly be blamed for its misuse, the internet does give scope to a sort of 'trainspotting' attitude to genealogy, where it is just a matter of filling out your family tree with plausible and preferably interesting ancestors, with little regard for accuracy or traditional standards of proof. Because more can (apparently) be done without consulting original records, it becomes easy to overlook the fact that a family tree constructed solely from on-line sources, unchecked against *any* original records, is sure to contain many inaccuracies even if it is not entirely unsound. This is far from new, of course; today's is hardly the first generation in which some people have been more concerned for their family tree to be impressive rather than accurate. The internet just makes it easier both to construct and to disseminate pedigrees of doubtful accuracy.

But genealogy is a form of historical research, and you cannot really do it successfully without developing some understanding of the records from which a family history is constructed, and the principles for drawing reliable conclusions from them.

Some of the tutorial materials mentioned in Chapter 2 address these issues, but the most coherent set of principles and standards available on-line are those developed by the US National Genealogical Society, which can be found at **<www.ngsgenealogy.org/comstandards.htm>**:

- Standards for Sound Genealogical Research
- Standards for Using Records, Repositories, and Libraries

- Standards for Use of Technology in Genealogical Research
- Standards for Sharing Information with Others
- Guidelines for Publishing Web Pages on the internet.

The first of these is essential reading for anyone new to genealogy. The third is important enough in the context of this book to bear reproducing in full:

Standards For Use Of Technology In Genealogical Research
Recommended by the National Genealogical Society
  Mindful that computers are tools, genealogists take full responsibility for their work, and therefore they –

- learn the capabilities and limits of their equipment and software, and use them only when they are the most appropriate tools for a purpose.
- refuse to let computer software automatically embellish their work.
- treat compiled information from on-line sources or digital databases like that from other published sources, useful primarily as a guide to locating original records, but not as evidence for a conclusion or assertion.
- accept digital images or enhancements of an original record as a satisfactory substitute for the original only when there is reasonable assurance that the image accurately reproduces the unaltered original.
- cite sources for data obtained on-line or from digital media with the same care that is appropriate for sources on paper and other traditional media, and enter data into a digital database only when its source can remain associated with it.
- always cite the sources for information or data posted on-line or sent to others, naming the author of a digital file as its immediate source, while crediting original sources cited within the file.
- preserve the integrity of their own databases by evaluating the reliability of downloaded data before incorporating it into their own files.
- provide, whenever they alter data received in digital form, a description of the change that will accompany the altered data whenever it is shared with others.
- actively oppose the proliferation of error, rumor and fraud by personally verifying or correcting information, or noting it as unverified, before passing it on to others.
- treat people on-line as courteously and civilly as they would treat them face-to-face, not separated by networks and anonymity.
- accept that technology has not changed the principles of genealogical research, only some of the procedures.

Using on-line information

The nature of the primary data on-line has an important implication for how you use information found on the internet: you need to be very cautious about inferences drawn from it. For a start, *all* transcriptions of any size contain errors – the only question is how many. Where information comes from parish registers, for example, you need to be cautious about identifying an individual ancestor from a single record in an on-line database. The fact that you have found a baptism with the right name, at about the right date and in about the right place, does not mean you have found an ancestor. How do you know this child did not die two weeks later; how do you know there is not a very similar baptism in a neighbouring parish whose records are not on-line; how do you know there is not an error in the transcription? As more records are put on-line with images accompanying transcriptions or indexes, the last question may become less important, but no future internet development will allow you to ignore the other questions.

Unfortunately, the very ease of the internet can sometimes make beginners think that constructing a pedigree is easier than it is. It is not enough to find a plausible-looking baptism on-line. You have to be able to demonstrate that this must be (not just 'could be') the same individual who marries 20 years later or who is the parent of a particular child. The internet does not do this for you. It can only provide *some* of the material you need for that proof, and even then you will have to be more careful with on-line material than you would be with original records.

In particular, negative inferences (for example so and so wasn't born later than such and such a date) can be very important in constructing a family tree, but the original material on the internet will rarely allow you to make such inferences. Not even where a particular set of records has been put on-line in its entirety could you start to be confident in drawing a negative inference. For example, there is no simple conclusion to be drawn if you fail to find an ancestor in the 1901 census. He or she could have no longer been alive, or was living abroad, or is in the census but has been mistranscribed in the index, or was in the census until the relevant enumeration book went missing. Of course, such problems relate to all indexes, not just those on-line, but you can never be *more* confident about on-line records.

Also, you need to be very cautious about drawing conclusions based not on primary sources but on compiled pedigrees put on-line by other genealogists. Some of these represent careful genealogical work and come with detailed documentation of sources, others may just have a name and possible birth year, perhaps supplied from memory by an ageing relative – insufficient detail to be of great value, and with no guarantee of accuracy. You should regard such materials as helpful pointers to someone who might have useful information, or to sources you have not yet examined yourself. It would be very unwise simply to incorporate the information in your own pedigree simply because it appears to refer to an individual you have already identified as an ancestor.

Copyright

The internet makes it very easy to disseminate information, but just because you *can* disseminate material it does not mean that you *should*. Both web sites and e-mail messages are treated by the law as publications. If you include material you did not create, you may be infringing someone's copyright by doing so. Of course, genealogical facts themselves are not subject to copyright, but the particular formulation in an original record may be, and a compilation of facts in a database is also protected, though for more limited duration.

This means you should not put on your own web site, upload to a database, or post to a mailing list:

- material you have extracted from on-line or CD-ROM databases
- material scanned from books that are still in copyright
- genealogical data you have received from others (unless they give their permission of course).

There is a exemption of 'fair use' which allows some copying, but this is only for purposes of criticism or private study, not for republishing. Extracting a single record from a CD-ROM and e-mailing it to an individual is probably OK, but posting the same information to a mailing list, which means it will be permanently archived, is not. Note that some companies include licence conditions with CD-ROMs stating that you must not supply the information to third parties. Whether or not such a strict condition would stand up in court – a similar ban on look-ups in a reference book would seem to be ridiculous – the supply of genealogy data on CD-ROM would be threatened by significant levels of copyright infringement.

A number of people have been shocked to find their own genealogical databases submitted to an on-line pedigree database without their knowledge. Mark Howells covers these issues very thoroughly in 'Share and Beware – Sharing Genealogy in the Information Age' at <www.oz.net/~markhow/writing/share.htm>. Rhonda McClure tackles the same issues in 'He Stole My Ancestors – Ethics in Copyright' at <www.ngsgenealogy.org/newsart-stole.htm>. Barbara A. Brown discusses the dissemination of 'dishonest research' in 'Restoring Ethics to Genealogy' at <www.iigs.org/newsletter/9904news/ethics.htm.en>.

The recently revised Crown Copyright rules, however, mean that you *can* include extracts from unpublished material held by the National Archives as long as the source is acknowledged (see 'Crown Copyright in the Information Age' at <**www.hmso.gov.uk/archives/copyright/information_age.htm**>). In general, you should have no qualms about the textual content of other historical material over 150 years old if you are transcribing it yourself. But a transcription of a manuscript document is probably to be regarded as an original work, and recently made images of documents are certainly copyright, regardless of the status of the original document. If in doubt, consult the repository concerned.

David Hawgood's 'Copyright for Family Historians' at <**www.genuki. org.uk/org/Copyright.html**> offers some guidance tailored for genealogists, while for more general information, there is the official government-sponsored web site on copyright at <**www.intellectual- property.gov.uk**>.

There is a mailing list, LEGAL-ENGWLS, for the discussion of 'legal aspects of genealogical research in England and Wales including copyright, database rights, data protection, and privacy' – details at <**lists.rootsweb. com/index/intl/UK/LEGAL-ENGWLS.html**>.

Privacy

Another thing to avoid is publishing material about living people without their permission. It is probably not an infringement of the UK Data Protection Act if the information is drawn from public sources such as birth certificates, but many people still regard it as an invasion of privacy. Most genealogy database programs have facilities for filtering out sensitive information from a web family tree (if in doubt just exclude everyone born less than 100 years ago). Sometimes this means that the individual's entire entry is removed, or it may be that their place in the pedigree is retained, but name and personal details are deleted. There are also a number of privacy programs which will remove living individuals from GEDCOM so that you can submit it to an on-line pedigree database or convert it to a personal web site. Cyndi's List has links to these at <**www.cyndislist.com/ gedcom.htm#Privacy**>. The on-line pedigree databases either remove living individuals automatically or insist that you do so before submitting – this is discussed in more detail on p. 123.

Myra Vanderpool Gormley discusses these issues in 'Exposing Our Families To The Internet' at <**www.ancestry.com/columns/myra/ Shaking_Family_Tree06-19-97.htm**>.

Digitisation

Quite apart from the obvious facts that more and more genealogists are getting on-line and more of the people who are on-line are getting interested in genealogy, a large number of major, well-funded projects are under way to put British records on the Web. As little as five years ago almost none of the material discussed in Chapters 4 to 8 was available on the internet. There is now the prospect that within a few years all civil registration indexes and census records over 100 years old will be on-line. What is more difficult to assess is whether, and when, other material will be put on-line. It is easy to see that there is a market for census records; and to appreciate the rationale for Lottery funding for projects like Access to Archives <**www.a2a.pro.gov.uk**> to make catalogues available on-line. But it is more difficult to see how county record offices, say, might be able to fund the digitisation of material with a more limited appeal. The limitation on digitisation is not technical; it is the amount of manpower required to transcribe handwritten documents. Barring a dramatic breakthrough in handwriting recognition, it would be optimistic to expect the technical situation to change, so it will be a matter of funding and potential income.

But you can get some idea of what might be coming from the ARCHON Portal's list of current archival digitisation projects at <**www.hmc.gov.uk/ archon/searches/KeywordList.asp?ARP=Digitisation**>. Insight into other possible future developments is provided by the National Archives' 'Opportunities for Digitisation' page at <**www.pro.gov.uk/corporate/ licensed/recommendations.htm**>. This lists the classes of record the National Archives' users have expressed most demand for in digital form. Genealogists make up a sizeable and growing constituency, and there is no reason why substantial Lottery grants should not be forthcoming to fund digitisation projects if archives and genealogical organisations can draft the required proposals, and genealogists put pressure on them to do so.

Data services

There has been one significant problem associated with the digitisation of public records which is likely to remain an issue. Where government agencies run pay-per-view services in commercial partnerships, the choice of partner is decided by public tender, as one would expect. However, the two largest such contracts for genealogical sources suggest a fundamental contradiction in this process.

Both the old PRO's contract with Qinetiq for the 1901 census and the GROS's contract with Scotland On-line for Scotlandspeople went to companies with no experience in digitisation or data services on the scale of these projects. It was therefore no surprise that users found much to criticise when these services were initially launched, and that both companies involved had much to do to regain the confidence of genealogical users. It was perhaps worse in the case of Scotlandspeople, where the new site replaced one which seems to have been highly regarded by those who used it.

On the one hand, it's quite right that contracts aren't renewed automatically or only given to established providers – that would just lead to the field being dominated by the first few companies to specialise in such services. And of course, it is also in the interest of family historians for more companies to start offering data services. On the other hand, awarding contracts to companies new to the field, based on assurances from bidders that they have the relevant skills and facilities rather than a proven track record, will always be a gamble.

This conflict between the legal requirements of the tendering process and the need for guaranteed levels of performance is not the fault of any one party to this process, it is built into the system. There is a potential dilemma for public bodies in choosing between the best bid financially and the best bid technically. This is, of course, part of a larger issue in the relation between commercial contractors and public services, and is not something that the genealogical world alone is subject to.

At best, genealogists can only put pressure on government agencies to be rigorous in their assessment of the technical ability of bidders and to regard acceptable levels of service as a high priority in awarding contacts. Genealogists cannot expect to be in on the contract awarding process, but advisory panels, such as both the National Archives and Scotlandspeople have, allow both family history organisations and individuals some influence in how priorities are set in such projects.

'Shy' data

There is an awful lot of genealogical data material which has already been digitised and *could* be on-line – data held on a computer for lookups to be done or sold commercially on CD-ROM.

But there are good reasons why data-owners should be reluctant to publish this material on-line. For a dataset to be secure, it can't simply be published on open web pages where anyone can download the whole lot – it needs to be stored in an on-line database which will deliver individual records or groups of records in response to a search. This is not quite as straightforward as the basic web publishing process described in Chapter 17, though it is getting easier. Free software such as PHP and MySQL, which together can be used to run an on-line database, is increasingly available on the web space provided by ISPs, though some programming skills are still required.

The other problem is that it is not easy for individuals and small organisations, charitable or commercial, who depend on such data for all or part of their income, to set up their own pay-per-view on the internet. Systems like WorldPay (see p. 269) are good for one-off payments and subscription systems and are not difficult to make use of. But setting up the account management required in pay-per-view systems such as those described in Chapter 4 is not a job for the amateur and, of course, it requires continued attention and maintenance. On the other hand, CD-ROM publication is now so cheap and straightforward that it is understandable if holders of electronic data feel on-line publication is not worth exploring.

At present, the best way forward is for individual holders of data to license it to one of the major commercial data providers. The FamilyHistoryOnline site has allowed family history societies to start doing this, and it seems likely that we will soon start to see this spread beyond this group to individuals who have compiled their own indexes. The benefits of drawing income from genealogists who might not be willing to buy a CD-ROM in the hope of finding one or two relevant records, but who would pay an on-line charge to retrieve them when located by a free index, should not be underestimated.

Finding material

While every increase in the amount of genealogical material on the internet must be welcomed, information is not much use if you cannot find it. Search engines are already able to capture only a fraction of the material on the Web. Of course, it is impossible to foresee technological advances, but there is no sign at the moment that the coverage of search engines will improve significantly. Web sites of individual genealogists, in particular, will probably become harder to find. In addition, the increasing amount of data held in on-line databases is not discoverable by search engines, and it becomes more important than ever for gateways and directories (or even books!) to direct people to the sources of on-line data.

The quality of indexing provided by search engines is limited by the poor facilities currently available for marking up text in HTML with semantic information. Search engines cannot tell that Kent is a surname in 'Clark Kent' but a place name in 'Maidstone, Kent'. This is because web authors have no way of indicating this in HTML markup. As so many British surnames are the names of places or occupations, this is a significant problem for UK genealogists.

The situation could improve when XML starts to be used widely on the Web, since this would allow the development of a special markup language for genealogical information. Such a development (and its retrospective application to material already published on the Web) is some way off and will require considerable work, though the LDS Church has made a start by proposing an XML successor to GEDCOM (see the GEDCOM FAQ at <www.familysearch.org/Eng/Home/FAQ/faq_gedcom.asp>.)

Another problem is the increasing number of sites with surname resources, making it impossible to check *everywhere* for others who share your interests. Mercifully, the number of pedigree databases (see Chapter 10) remains manageable for the present, but the number of sites with surname-related material makes exhaustive searching impossible.

Looking ahead

Nothing that happens on the internet over the next decades is going to affect what genealogists need to do: consult records and share information.

The internet is not going to 'automate' family history or modify its principles and methods. There is in fact nothing wrong with the traditional methods of genealogy. What the internet has revolutionised is not the process of genealogy, but the ease with which some aspects of it can be carried out.

The key aspects of this are:

- the number of people with shared interests who have internet access
- the increasing amounts of data available on-line.

Although microfilm and microfiche are not going to disappear in the immediate future, any more than books are, the internet is now the publishing medium of choice for all large genealogical data projects, whether official, commercial or volunteer-run. The only real competitor is CD-ROM and, eventually, DVD.

It is difficult to know what proportion of UK genealogists are on-line, but it must surely be over 50%.[16] The fact is that both the number of internet users and the amount of data available have now reached a critical mass, so that the genealogist without internet access is going to be in a minority and disadvantaged in access to data and contact with other genealogists. The fact that new census releases are going to be available mainly via the internet is already a pointer in that direction. Indeed, for anyone with Scots ancestry the internet is already an essential tool, with England and Wales starting to catch up.

Of course you can still research your family tree without using the internet, but why would you choose to?

---

[16] According to Oftel, in August 2002 42% of UK households had internet access (see <www.oftel.gov.uk/publications/research/2002/trenr1002.htm>). National statistics report that during September 2002, 53% of the adult population accessed the internet (see <www.nationalstatistics.gov.uk/pdfdir/inta1202.pdf>) and this report shows an annual rise of 6% in households with internet access. A survey conducted by the SoG early in 2003 (published in the September 2003 *Genealogists' Magazine*) shows 78% of the Society's UK members with home internet access.

Internet Glossary

Adobe Acrobat	A file format, popular for documents which need to be made available on-line with fixed formatting. Files have the extension .pdf, and so the term 'PDF file' is often used. See p. 253.
charter	The description of the aims and coverage of a newsgroup.
client	A piece of software on a user's computer which connects to a *server* to retrieve or submit data, e.g. your e-mail software is an 'e-mail client' which connects to your provider's e-mail server; your browser is a 'web client' which gets data from a web server.
database	1) A collection of individual items of information ('records') which can be retrieved selectively via a search facility. 2) A software program for managing data records (short for 'database management system').
directory	1) A collection of links to internet resources, arranged in a hierarchy of subject headings. 2) On some operating systems, a hierarchical folder containing individual computer files.
domain name	The part of an internet address which is formally registered and owned and which forms the latter parts of a server or host name, e.g. *bbc.co.uk* is the domain name, while <news.bbc.co.uk> and <www.bbc.co.uk> are individual servers within that domain.
download	To transfer a file from another computer to your own computer.
FAQ	Frequently Asked Questions, a document listing common questions in a particular area, along with their answers.
flame	A rude or abusive message.
freeware	Software which can be downloaded and used free of charge (cf. *shareware*).
FTP	File Transfer Protocol, a method of transferring files across the internet (see p. 257).

gateway	1) A subject-specific *directory*. 2) A link which allows messages to pass between two different systems, e.g. newsgroups and mailing lists.
GIF	A graphics file format, mainly used on the web for graphic design elements, less suitable for colour photographs.
hit	A matching item retrieved in response to a search.
host	A computer connected to the internet which allows other internet users access to material stored on its hard disk.
hosting	Providing space on a *host* for someone's web pages.
HTML	HyperText Markup Language, in which web pages are written.
ISP	Internet Service Provider.
JPEG	A graphics file format, mainly used for photographs.
mailing list	A discussion forum which uses e-mail.
meta-search engine	A site which automatically submits a search to a number of different *search engines*.
mirror	A duplicate of a web site in a different location, used to improve the availability and response time for a popular resource.
netiquette	The informal, consensual rules of on-line communication.
newsgroup	Open discussion forums held on an internet-wide network of 'news servers'.
plug-in	A piece of software used by a web browser to display files it cannot handle on its own.
portal	A collection of internet resources for a particular audience – see the discussion on p. 13.
robot	A piece of software which trawls the internet looking for new resources, used by search engines to create their indexes.
search engine	Commonly, a web site which has a searchable index of web pages, though more accurately *any* piece of software which searches an index.
searchbot	A piece of software which searches the web for you (a contraction of 'search robot').
server	A computer, usually with a permanent internet connection, which responds to requests from a *client* for data. There are different types of server according to the service offered, e.g. mail server, web server, list server.

shareware | Software which can be downloaded free of charge, but requires payment for registration after a trial period (cf. *freeware*).
spam | Unsolicited messages sent to multiple recipients.
subscribe | To join a mailing list.
URL | Uniform Resource Locator, a standard way of referring to internet resources so that each resource has a unique name. In the case of a web page, the URL is the same as the web address.
World Wide Web | A collection of linked pages of information retrievable via the internet.
XML | eXtensible Markup Language, a more sophisticated and flexible markup language than *HTML*, likely to be increasingly used for web sites.

There are many internet glossaries on-line:

- The Internet Language Dictionary at <**www.netlingo.com/inframes. cfm**>
- Foldoc (the Free On-Line Dictionary of Computing) <**foldoc.doc.ic. ac.uk/foldoc/**>
- Google Groups Usenet Glossary <**groups.google.com/googlegroups/ glossary.html**>
- Living Internet <**livinginternet.com**>.

For glossaries of genealogy terms see page 11.

Bibliography

Amanda Bevan, *Tracing Your Ancestors in the Public Record Office*, 6th edn (Public Record Office, 2002)

Peter Christian, *Web Publishing for Genealogy*, 2nd edn (David Hawgood, 1999)

Peter Christian, *Finding Genealogy on the Internet*, 2nd edn (David Hawgood, 2002). Full text on-line at <**www.spub.co.uk/fgi/**>

Jean Cole & John Titford, *Tracing your Family Tree*, 4th edn (Countryside Books, 2002)

David Hawgood, *FamilySearch on the Internet* (David Hawgood, 1998)

David Hawgood, *Genuki* (Federation of Family History Societies, 2000) Full text on-line at <**www.hawgood.co.uk/genuki/**>

Mark Herber, *Ancestral Trails* (Sutton, 2000)

David Hey, *Journeys in Family History: The National Archives Guide to Finding Your Ancestors and Exploring Their Times* (The National Archives, forthcoming 2004)

Cyndi Howells, *Cyndi's List*, 2nd edn (Genealogical Publishing Company, 2001)

Cyndi Howells, *Planting Your Family Tree Online: How to Create Your Own Family History Website* (Rutledge Hill Press, forthcoming 2003)

Reader's Digest, *Explore Your Family's Past* (Reader's Digest, 2002)

Virginia Shea, *Netiquette* (Albion Books, 1996). Full text on-line at <**www.albion.com/netiquette/book/**>

Richard S. Wilson, *Publishing Your Family History on the Internet* (Betterway Books, 1999)

Index